"Ike Miller is one of the brightest youn[g] [...] [...] [...] [...] [...]ng *by the Light* reveals. Miller draws up[o]n [...] [...] and Barth, in conversation with Johannine literature, to construct a trinitarian view of illumination that accounts for the affectional, intellectual, and ethical dimensions of life. The result is a methodologically sophisticated, multidisciplinary volume that makes a significant contribution to current debates about illumination, participation in Christ, interpretation of Johannine literature, and theological method. An extraordinary volume. Highly recommended."

Bruce Riley Ashford, author of *The Gospel of Our King* and professor of theology and culture at Southeastern Baptist Theological Seminary

"A wonderful achievement—an enlightening study about divine illumination. In a time and world where we have too often turned Scripture into a dead text, Ike Miller's remarkable book sheds light on how we are called to live faithfully before God through our dynamic engagement with Scripture. A beautiful book."

L. Gregory Jones, dean and Williams Distinguished Professor of Theology and Christian Ministry, Duke Divinity School

"One way to summarize the story of the Bible is to say, with Jesus (quoting Isaiah 9:2), 'The people who walked in darkness have seen a great light.' Today there is conflict not only between the kingdoms of light and darkness but also over rival sources of light. Moderns, who previously celebrated the light of reason, are now groping for ways to cope with post-Enlightenment, postmodern blues. Ike Miller has written a tract for the times that sets forth a Christian theological account of how the God who is light distributes his light to the world in Jesus Christ via the Spirit-illumined readings of the biblical texts that testify to him. This is a dogmatic account of the triune economy of illumination that, in shedding light on Augustine and Barth and other readers of Scripture, participates in the very phenomenon it describes. Take up and see!"

Kevin J. Vanhoozer, research professor of systematic theology at Trinity Evangelical Divinity School

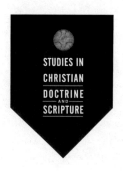

STUDIES IN
CHRISTIAN
DOCTRINE
—AND—
SCRIPTURE

SEEING BY THE LIGHT

Illumination in Augustine's and Barth's
Readings of John

◆◆◆◆◆◆◆◆◆◆◆◆◆◆◆◆◆◆◆◆◆◆◆

Ike Miller

Academic
An imprint of InterVarsity Press
Downers Grove, Illinois

InterVarsity Press
P.O. Box 1400, Downers Grove, IL 60515-1426
ivpress.com
email@ivpress.com

InterVarsity Press® is the book-publishing division of InterVarsity Christian Fellowship/USA®, a movement of students and faculty active on campus at hundreds of universities, colleges, and schools of nursing in the United States of America, and a member movement of the International Fellowship of Evangelical Students. For information about local and regional activities, visit intervarsity.org.

Cover design: Cindy Kiple
Interior design: Beth McGill
Images: Saint Augustine/Wikimedia Commons/United States Public Domain

ISBN 978-0-8308-4885-0 (print)
ISBN 978-0-8308-5392-2 (digital)

Printed in the United States of America ∞

InterVarsity Press is committed to ecological stewardship and to the conservation of natural resources in all our operations. This book was printed using sustainably sourced paper.

Library of Congress Cataloging-in-Publication Data
A catalog record for this book is available from the Library of Congress.

P	23	22	21	20	19	18	17	16	15	14	13	12	11	10	9	8	7	6	5	4	3	2	1
Y	39	38	37	36	35	34	33	32	31	30	29	28	27	26	25	24	23	22	21	20

To two of the brightest lights in my life: my mother, Ellen Miller,
who was most instrumental in leading me to see the light
of Christ, and my brilliant and radiant wife, Sharon,
who inspires me to walk more faithfully
in that light everyday

God, source of all light, by your Word you give light to the soul.
Pour out upon us the spirit of wisdom and understanding
that, being taught by you in Holy Scripture,
our hearts and minds may be opened to know
the things that pertain to life and holiness;
through Jesus Christ our Lord. Amen.

PRAYER FOR ILLUMINATION,
PRESBYTERIAN *BOOK OF COMMON WORSHIP*

Contents

Acknowledgments

T HE GRATITUDE THAT I FEEL toward all who have been a part of making this book possible far exceeds my capacity to express it. Looking across the span of time in which this journey has taken place, so many people have stepped into our lives not only to make this journey possible but to make it a fulfilling and enrichening experience for my entire family. We have been fortunate enough to have found truly life-giving community in three different churches at various stages in this process. Serving in ministry alongside Andrew and Melissa Brownback at Willow Creek North Shore not only proved to be an important pastoral balance to life in academia but also afforded us a friendship with an extraordinary couple that will truly be lifelong.

Not long after the birth of our first son, Isaac, we connected with an incredible community of people at Alpine Chapel. Dave Mudd and Alex and Caryn Hartmann opened their church, their life, and their friendship to us in ways that rarely happen more than once in a lifetime. In the small group we led there we found what may be one of the warmest communities of friends we will ever know. Moving away from this community of friends will long be one of the more heartbreaking decisions we have had to make.

And now, as we have journeyed over the last year of answering the call to plant Bright City Church in Durham, North Carolina, we have developed such an incredible community of people, dedicated to this mission and gifted for this task of church planting in ways only God could have foreknown. Bright City is a light that shines the glory of God on earth and is a foretaste of that coming kingdom, which needs no sun because God himself gives it light. Thank you to an incredible team of people who have made Bright City a reality. You are surely the embodiment of the light of divine life on earth.

Two people without whom this work would have been categorically impossible are my father-in-law and mother-in-law, Rich and Deborah Hodde. As Sharon and I worked simultaneously to complete PhD programs, write books, have children, and plant a church, there is simply no way it could have all been done without the endless time and energy that they have so generously and abundantly given to us. On top of that, they have offered tremendous affirmation and emotional support at times when we have needed it most. Thank you!

My mother, Ellen Miller, has likewise offered me tireless support. This support has come not least in the form of weekly trips to our home to help with our little ones so that Sharon did not carry the weight of this work herself. She has offered incredible encouragement at every turn, and in an intangible way, there are few greater joys in the world than to see your parents playing with your children. She has loved me so well, but not simply by loving me, but by loving well the other most important people in my life.

Early in my doctoral program, Thomas McCall not only challenged me to think with a relentless pursuit of clarity in academic matters but proved an important and even reassuring voice as I worked to find my place in the Trinity Evangelical Divinity School community. Richard Averbeck was nothing short of a pastor to our community of PhD students and the model of an individual who truly approaches his academic work as his ministry. Finally, I want to express the inexpressible, my unspeakable gratitude to Kevin Vanhoozer, who directed the project that serves as the backbone and basis of the present study. His dedication to me as a student, to this project, to the advancement of theology, and above all to my spiritual and theological formation have been evident at every point in this journey. His remarkable capacity to both encourage and instruct with an incredible humility made him a pleasure to work under, even as he would accept nothing less than excellence in this project's execution. Above all else, his attentiveness has not ceased to amaze me. He has cared not only for the project but for me as the person behind the project, and for that I am eternally grateful.

The gratitude I owe the very most of all, however, is to my wife. I could write a book simply on all the reasons I am thankful for you, Sharon. At the very heart of it all is your steadfastness. You have been my anchor. Regardless of the challenges of being in doctoral programs together while having children, working full-time, serving in ministry, and writing—and now colaboring as we plant Bright City Church—you are what makes the beauty of "us" happen. You are both my inspiration and my place of peace, my motivation and my escape. You and our children—Isaac, Coen, and Sadie—make my world go around, and life with you four is full of unspeakable joy. I love you.

Series Introduction

Studies in Christian Doctrine and Scripture (SCDS)

Daniel J. Treier and Kevin J. Vanhoozer

T HE STUDIES IN CHRISTIAN DOCTRINE and Scripture (SCDS) series attempts to reconcile two disciplines that should never have been divided: the study of Christian Scripture and the study of Christian doctrine. Old walls of disciplinary hostility are beginning to come down, a development that we hope will better serve the church. To that end, books in this series affirm the supreme authority of Scripture, seeking to read it faithfully and creatively as they develop fresh articulations of Christian doctrine. This agenda can be spelled out further in five claims.

1. We aim to publish constructive **contributions to systematic theology** rather than merely descriptive rehearsals of biblical theology, historical retrievals of classic or contemporary theologians, or hermeneutical reflections on theological method—volumes that are plentifully and expertly published elsewhere.

The initial impetus for the SCDS series came from supervising evangelical graduate students and seeking to encourage their pursuit of constructive theological projects shaped by the supremacy of Scripture. Existing publication venues demonstrate how rarely biblical scholars and systematic theologians trespass into each other's fields. Synthetic treatments of biblical theology garner publication in monograph series for biblical studies or evangelical biblical theology. A notable example is a companion series from IVP Academic, New Studies in Biblical Theology. Many of its volumes have theological significance, yet most are written by biblical scholars. Meanwhile, historical retrievals of theological figures garner publication in monograph series for historical and systematic theology. For instance, there have been entire series devoted to figures such as Karl Barth or the patristic era, and even series named for systematic theology tend to contain figure-oriented monographs.

The reason for providing an alternative publication venue is not to denigrate these valuable enterprises. Instead, the rationale for encouraging constructively evangelical projects is twofold and practical: The church needs such projects, and they form the theologians undertaking them. The church needs such projects, both addressing new challenges for her life in the world (such as contemporary political theology) and retrieving neglected concepts (such as the classic doctrine of God) in fresh ways. The church also needs her theologians not merely to develop detailed intellectual skills but also ultimately to wrestle with the whole counsel of God in the Scriptures.

2. We aim to promote **evangelical** contributions, neither retreating from broader dialogue into a narrow version of this identity on the one hand, nor running away from the biblical preoccupation of our heritage on the other hand.

In our initial volume, *Theology and the Mirror of Scripture*, we articulate this pursuit of evangelical renewal. We take up the well-known metaphor of mere Christianity as a hallway, with particular church traditions as the rooms in a house. Many people believe that the evangelical hallway is crumbling, an impression that current events only exacerbate. Our inspection highlights a few fragmenting factors such as more robust academic engagement, increased awareness of the Great Christian Tradition and the variety of evangelical subtraditions, interest in global Christianity, and interfaces with emergent Christianity and culture. Looking more deeply, we find historical-theological debates about the very definition of *evangelical* and whether it reflects—still, or ever—a shared gospel, a shared doctrine of God, and a theological method that can operationalize our shared commitment to Scripture's authority.

In response, prompted by James 1:22-25, our proposal develops the metaphor of a mirror for clarifying evangelical theology's relation to Scripture.

The reality behind the mirror is the gospel of God and the God of the gospel: what is revealed in Christ. In disputes about whether to focus on a center or boundaries, it may seem as if evangelicalism has no doctrinal core. But we propose treating what is revealed in Christ—the triune God and the cross of Christ, viewed in the mirror of Scripture—as an evangelical anchor, a center with a certain range of motion. Still, it may seem as if evangelicalism has no hermeneutical coherence, as if interpretive anarchy nullifies biblical authority. But we propose treating Scripture as *canonical testimony*, a God-given mirror of truth that enables the church to reflect the wisdom that is in Christ. The holistic and contextual character of such wisdom gives theology a dialogic character, which requires an evangelical account of the church's catholicity. We need the wisdom to know the difference between church-destroying heresy, church-dividing disagreements that still permit evangelical fellowship, and intrachurch differences that require mutual admonition as well as forbearance.

Volumes in the SCDS series will not necessarily reflect the views of any particular editor, advisory board member, or the publisher—not even concerning "evangelical" boundaries. Volumes may approach perceived boundaries if their excellent engagement with Scripture deserves a hearing. But we are not seeking reform for reform's sake; we are more likely to publish volumes containing new explorations or presentations of traditional positions than radically revisionist proposals. Valuing the historic evangelical commitment to a deeply scriptural theology, we often find that perceived boundaries are appropriate—reflecting positions' biblical plausibility or lack thereof.

3. We seek fresh understanding of Christian doctrine **through creatively faithful engagement with Scripture**. To some fellow evangelicals and interested others today, we commend the classic evangelical commitment of *engaging Scripture*. To other fellow evangelicals today, we commend a contemporary aim to engage Scripture with *creative fidelity*. The church is to be always reforming—but always reforming according to the Word of God.

It is possible to acknowledge *sola Scriptura* in principle—Scripture as the final authority, the norming norm—without treating Scripture as theology's primary source. It is also possible to approach Scripture as theology's primary source in practice without doing that well.

The classic evangelical aspiration has been to mirror the form, not just the content, of Scripture as closely as possible in our theology. That aspiration has potential drawbacks: it can foster naive prooftexting, flatten biblical diversity, and stifle creative cultural engagement with a biblicist idiom. But we should not overreact to these drawbacks, falling prey to the temptation of paying mere lip service to *sola Scriptura* and replacing the Bible's primacy with the secondary idiom of the theologians' guild.

Thus in *Theology and the Mirror of Scripture* we propose a rubric for applying biblical theology to doctrinal judgments in a way that preserves evangelical freedom yet promotes the primacy of Scripture. At the ends of the spectrum, biblical theology can (1) rule out theological proposals that contradict scriptural judgments or cohere poorly with other concepts, and it can (5) require proposals that appeal to what is clear and central in Scripture. In between, it can (2) permit proposals that do not contradict Scripture, (3) support proposals that appeal creatively although indirectly or implicitly to Scripture, and (4) relate theological teaching to church life by using familiar scriptural language as much as possible. This spectrum offers considerable freedom for evangelical theology to mirror the biblical wisdom found in Christ with contextual creativity. Yet it simultaneously encourages evangelical theologians to reflect biblical wisdom not just in their judgments but also in the very idioms of their teaching.

4. We seek **fresh understanding of Christian doctrine**. We do not promote a singular method; we welcome proposals appealing to biblical theology, the history of interpretation, theological interpretation of Scripture, or still other approaches. We welcome projects that engage in detailed exegesis as well as those that appropriate broader biblical themes and patterns. Ultimately, we hope to promote relating Scripture to doctrinal understanding in material, not just formal, ways.

As noted above, the fresh understanding we seek may not involve altogether novel claims—which might well land in heresy! Again, in *Theology and the Mirror of Scripture* we offer an illustrative, nonexhaustive rubric for encouraging various forms of evangelical theological scholarship: projects shaped primarily by (1) hermeneutics, (2) integrative biblical theology, (3) stewardship of the Great Tradition, (4) church dogmatics, (5) intellectual history, (6) analytic theism, (7) living witness, and (8) healing resistance. While some of these scholarly shapes probably fit the present series better than others, all of them reflect practices that can help evangelical theologians to make more faithfully biblical judgments and to generate more creatively constructive scholarship.

The volumes in the SCDS series will therefore reflect quite varied approaches. They will be similar in engaging one or more biblical texts as a key aspect of their contributions while going beyond exegetical recital or descriptive biblical theology, yet those biblical contributions themselves will be manifold.

5. We promote scriptural engagement **in dialogue with catholic tradition(s)**. A periodic evangelical weakness is relative lack of interest in the church's shared creedal heritage, in churches' particular confessions, and more generally in the history of dogmatic reflection. Beyond existing efforts to enhance understanding of themes and corpora in biblical theology, then, we hope to foster engagement with Scripture that bears on and learns from loci, themes, or crucial questions in classic dogmatics and contemporary systematic theology.

Series authors and editors will reflect several church affiliations and doctrinal backgrounds. Our goal is that such commitments would play a productive but not decisive hermeneutical role. Series volumes may focus on more generically evangelical approaches, or they may operate from within a particular tradition while engaging internal challenges or external objections.

We hope that both the diversity of our contributor list and the catholic engagement of our projects will continually expand. As important as those contextual factors are, though, these are most fundamentally studies in Christian *doctrine* and *Scripture*. Our goal is to promote and to publish constructive evangelical projects that study Scripture with creative fidelity and thereby offer fresh understanding of Christian doctrine. Various contexts and perspectives can help us to study Scripture in that lively way, but they must remain secondary to theology's primary source and soul.

We do not study the mirror of Scripture for its own sake. Finding all the treasures of wisdom in Christ to be reflected there with the help of Christian doctrine, we come to know God and ourselves more truly. Thus encountering God's perfect instruction, we find the true freedom that is ours in the gospel, and we joyfully commend it to others through our own ministry of Scripture's teaching.

Abbreviations

CD	Karl Barth, *Church Dogmatics*
De. Doc. Chr.	Augustine, *De doctrina Christiana*
De Trin.	Augustine, *De Trinitate*
GD	Karl Barth, *Göttingen Dogmatics*
Tr. in Io. Ep.	Augustine, *Tractatus in Iohannis Epistulam*
Tract.	Augustine, *Tractatus in Iohannis Evangelium*

ONE

Seeing by the Light

A S IS WELL KNOWN, the twentieth century elevated the doctrine of revelation to a kind of first theology.[1] It did not, however, extend the same courtesy to the doctrine of illumination. And yet, if God is light (1 John 1:5), illumination is not a marginal theological issue. Illumination is at the core of God's self-communication to us. It is God's loving call "out of darkness into his marvelous light" (1 Peter 2:9). Moreover, if we do not *understand* God's revelation and how we receive it, what good does revelation do us in the first place? The doctrine of illumination is the solution to this problem precisely.

With such a crucial aspect of the divine-human relationship before us, the commitment of the task before us is to provide an exegetically faithful dogmatic account of illumination. In so doing, we will draw out all that is entailed in this proposal for a new definition: *illumination is human participation in the Son's knowledge of the Father by the power of the Holy Spirit.* In language more attuned to the language of illumination, it is *human participation in the light of the divine life.*

A review of the literature reveals that a treatment like the present one is long overdue. Full-length monographs on the doctrine of illumination number in the single digits and the little attention that illumination has received has focused narrowly on its purely cognitive dynamics. Possibly the greatest offense has been neglecting to incorporate the pre-Reformation

---

[1]"First theology" according to Kevin Vanhoozer, is what one considers a first and most important question for all else that one does in a field of investigation. This is because the conclusions one draws in this domain will ripple throughout the rest of one's thought. Kevin J. Vanhoozer, *First Theology: God, Scripture & Hermeneutics* (Downers Grove, IL: InterVarsity Press, 2002), 15-16.

contribution to illumination. Both Lydia Schumacher's *Divine Illumination* and Ronald Nash's *The Light of the Mind* make great strides toward understanding the Augustinian theory of illumination but neither are dogmatic constructions. Bernard Ramm's *The Witness of the Spirit* may very well be our closest comparable work, though some may distinguish illumination from the internal witness of the Holy Spirit.

John Owen's magisterial *Pneumatologia* (or, *A Discourse Concerning the Holy Spirit*), which John Webster praises as "the greatest Reformed treatise on the Spirit," remains among the most influential works on the doctrine of illumination today.[2] Owen's work, published in 1674, addresses the doctrine of illumination as an aspect of regeneration, as preparatory for conversion, as supernatural revelation, and as enlightening our minds to the understanding of Scripture. As a result of his comprehensive approach, his work is often taken as the benchmark in terms of theological development around the Holy Spirit in general and the doctrine of illumination in particular.

In spite of all that Owen contributes to the discussion, a tenuous point of Owen's proposal is the distinction between illumination and revelation. Within two paragraphs of one another, he writes both that Scripture is "the only external means of divine supernatural illumination" and that Scripture is "the only external means of divine revelation." The context of these statements suggests the two terms are being used synonymously and interchangeably. However, Owen communicates that revelation is both a cause of illumination, and at the same time, that revelation comes under the "denomination of illumination."[3] There is a lack of clarity in his thought around the relationship of illumination and revelation that demands the kind of clarity this treatment will offer.[4]

What we need is an account of illumination that fully incorporates both its cognitive and its affective implications, includes both the regenerative

---

[2]John Webster, "Illumination," *Journal of Reformed Theology* 5 (2011): 328.

[3]The complete sentence is: "Fifthly, in asserting the Scripture to be the only external means of divine revelation, I do it not exclusively unto those institutions of God which are subordinate unto it, and appointed as means to make it effectual unto our souls." John Owen, *Pneumatologia* (Grand Rapids: Sovereign Grace, 1971), 459.

[4]Michael Seaman's dissertation, "The Indispensability of the Holy Spirit for Biblical Interpretation: A Proposal for the Concept of Transformative Illumination" (PhD diss., Southeastern Baptist Theological Seminary, 2010), gives a short section on illumination and revelation, but it is impossible to do justice to this question in just seven pages.

and the revelatory aspects of illumination, and retrieves a fuller voice from the theological witness prior to the Reformation. Augustine, in particular, helps us understand that illumination transcends modernity's preoccupation with cognition and knowledge—it is about more than understanding and application. Augustine helps us understand that illumination is about *participation* in the "Divine Light."[5]

In order to address this vacuum and the underappreciation of the doctrine of illumination in contemporary theology, I intend to construct an "economy" around illumination—an economy that gives an account of the divine light's being, action, and effects in the world. Fortunately for us, at the beginning of the twentieth century, the German Protestant theologian Franz Overbeck located just such an economy in the Gospel of John. There is an "economy of divine light in the world" that captured for Overbeck the entirety of the divine light's being, actions, and effects in the world.[6] It also accounted for a system of witnesses and relationships that the Fourth Gospel suggests is necessary for communicating that divine light.

From the very beginning of John's Gospel, this economy of divine light is front and center as the light of the world dwells among us in the flesh of the Logos. This economy expands to capture the full range of implications in the Johannine confession, "God is light and in him is no darkness at all" (1 Jn 1:5). These implications are: (1) The nature of God's being is light. (2) The communication of this divine light to his creatures involves the whole community of divine persons. (3) Given that the nature of God's being is light, then in this economy his actions are illumining, and its effect is illumination. This economy of light and what it means for God's creatures captures the subject matter of this book.

The term *economy* will be deployed both according to its theological definition and its more general sense. In its theological usage, "economy" encompasses the works of God in his dealings with his creatures. In its more general sense, an economy orders all the components comprising a system. In this sense, an "economy" of the divine light must properly order both the

---

[5]Augustine, *Homilies on the Gospel of John*, Nicene and Post-Nicene Fathers 7 (Peabody, MA: Hendrickson, 1994), 39.

[6]Franz Overbeck, *Das Johannesevangelium: Studien zur Kritik seiner Erforschung* (Tübingen: J. C. B. Mohr, 1911), 416-17. Cited and translated in Karl Barth, *Witness to the Word: A Commentary on John* (Eugene, OR: Wipf & Stock, 1986), 14.

cognitive and affective aspects of illumination.[7] Drawing on the work of Karl Barth, we will make the case that subjective revelation is inextricably bound up with Christ's work of reconciliation and the Spirit's work of regeneration.[8] In this way, illumination is not purely epistemological. Illumination is also a matter of cognitively *and* affectively "coming to see the light of Christ" and, ultimately, participating in it.

In order to fully clarify the intersection of revelation and regeneration at illumination, I will bring together Augustine's work on illumination with Barth's work on revelation. Both emphases are necessary to rightly handle the issues of Word and Spirit involved in the economy of divine light. More specifically, Augustine's and Barth's concerns converge in their readings of the Gospel and letters of John. They intersect here because both expressed immense interest in John and offered sustained theological treatment of his Gospel and letters. Moreover, Augustine exercised tremendous influence over Barth's own interpretation of John. Case in point, almost the entirety of Barth's introductory lecture is a rehearsal and reflection upon Augustine's own Tractates. Finally, Augustine and Barth intersect here with illumination because the writings of John are themselves permeated by the language of light and present matters of regeneration and revelation as integral to the economy of divine light.[9]

The Gospel and letters of John are of particular interest here for two key reasons. First, John is unique in his focus on so many of Jesus' encounters with individuals. In fact, compared with the other Gospels, much more of

---

[7]This language of "economy" is substantiated in Owen's reference to a "denomination" of illumination that encompasses the many dynamics of illumination—revelation, regeneration, etc. (Owen, *Pneumatologia,* 156).

[8]John Webster acknowledges this doctrinal intersection of revelation and regeneration at illumination when he writes, "Illumination is subjective revelation in its reconciling and regenerative effectiveness" ("Illumination," 338).

[9]As a project addressing questions of how humanity receives knowledge of God, the Gospel and letters of John are among those texts that are most immediately relevant. Without a doubt, all types of literature in both the Old and New Testaments address questions of knowledge and revelation, but few do so as explicitly and with such sustained reflection as John. To the point, Gail R. O'Day has commented on this phenomenon, suggesting that the nature of revelation in the Gospel of John has become "one of the most basic questions in Fourth Gospel study." *Revelation in the Fourth Gospel: Narrative Mode and Theological Claim* (Philadelphia: Fortress, 1986), 34. D. Moody Smith agrees, suggesting that revelation—God's making himself known—is "precisely the theme of this Gospel." *The Theology of the Gospel of John,* New Testament Theology (New York: Cambridge University Press, 1995), 24.

John's Gospel is consumed with long narratives of engagements with single individuals. Many of these passages present us with an individual encountering Jesus in life-transforming ways. Second, this Johannine material places a strong emphasis on Jesus as the light (Jn 1:9) and as the light of the world (Jn 8:12). This challenges us to consider the christological and trinitarian aspects of illumination in addition to its grounding in pneumatology.

Augustine's and Barth's exegesis of John will show that illumination, in its intersection with revelation and regeneration, is ultimately about divine self-communication. This self-communication happens through our participation in Christ—the light of the World. This participation in Christ is made possible in the power of the Holy Spirit. Thus, as stated at the outset, *illumination is a participation in the Son's knowledge of the Father by the power of the Holy Spirit.*

The practical theological upshot of this definition is its bearing on the human experience of illumination. The denial of such a human experience in illumination implies a theological anthropology in which humanity does not really participate in the divine life. On the other hand, the affirmation of human experience of the divine risks a headlong fall into the absolute subjectivity and relativism (my experience of the divine vs. yours). The objective is to chart a way between the Scylla of dismissing human experience and the Charybdis of rampant subjectivity. In doing so, we will articulate an account of illumination in the reading of Scripture and in human experience that charts just such a course.

Through this engagement with Augustine's and Barth's theological exegesis of the Gospel and letters of John, we see their understandings of how God makes himself known. The most relevant texts are those that depict in dramatic fashion the event of coming to see the light of the Logos (Jn 1:1-18; 3:1-21; 4:1-42; 9:1-41; 20:11-18; 21:12-13). In understanding the biblical text to be a witness to "God's presence and action in history," it follows that these encounters give us a view into the ways and works of God in the events of revelation, illumination, and regeneration.[10]

The intent here is to uncover and comprehend that moment when someone "gets it"—the aha moment, as it were. The Spirit works in these

---

[10]Kevin J. Vanhoozer, ed., *Theological Interpretation of the New Testament: A Book-by-Book Survey* (Grand Rapids: Baker Academic, 2008), 16.

events of illumination to enlighten humankind by healing fallen intellectual faculties, pouring light into darkened understanding, and rescuing humanity from ignorance toward the things of God. In this way, the economy of divine light involves the work of regeneration because the Spirit works to heal, repair, and renew human faculties and capacities in order to restore them fellowship with God the Father. Facilitating this fellowship with the Father is precisely the work of the Son in the Gospel of John. This is where the concept of economy comes into its own. God executes his decree to enlighten a person in the Son through the Spirit. Ultimately, the aim here is to understand what it means for someone to come to see the light of God, revealed in Christ, through the Gospel and letters of John. Through a treatment of the economy of light as it is depicted by the conversion narratives and the language of light in the Gospel and Letters of John, and particularly through the eyes of Augustine and Barth, we will arrive at a more robust account of illumination. It is an account in which we see God by means of his own light.

STRUCTURE

The first part of this book (chaps. 2–4) will focus intently on Augustine. Chapter two will lay out Augustine's hermeneutical method with respect to the Gospel and letters of John. This includes the role of the letters in his interpretation of the Gospel, hermeneutical practices and presuppositions, and, where applicable, the role of the larger canon, the *regula fidei*, creeds, and Christian doctrine. Chapter three directly engages Augustine's theological interpretation of the relevant passages of John. Chapter four concludes the section on Augustine by considering his theology of illumination and participation in the divine light. The second part of the book (chaps. 5–7) then engages Barth's reading of John in precisely the same manner and order, exploring his methodology, interpretation of relevant passages, and theology of illumination. The final part (chaps. 8–10) begins by providing a Johannine account of illumination as a way of rooting this project in biblical theology. Then follows the culminating dogmatic account of illumination as it is informed by Augustine, Barth, and most foundationally the Gospel and letters of John. This will include articulating what it means to "come to see the light" of the Logos, the nature of our participation in the Divine Light, and the Trinitarian work of the Father, Son, and Spirit in illumination.

Finally, a concluding chapter will address the human experience of illumination in reading Scripture and in encountering God.

TWO MOMENTS OF ILLUMINATION

It is important to clarify from the beginning that we distinguish and develop two "moments" of illumination in the economy of divine light as attested in John. First, events such as Jesus' encounters with Nicodemus, the woman at the well, and the man born blind are marked by a genuinely confounding experience in which something inexplicable is said or done and yet for the individual it is undeniable and unforgettable.[11] In striking resemblance to this, Barth states that illumination "is an event of revelation and knowledge by which the being of man is not only affected but seized and refashioned so that it becomes his new being."[12] As a result, this study argues for an *effectual* (i.e., definitive) illumination.[13] I have referred to it as such primarily because of its close theological connection with what in traditional Reformed theological terms is referred to as the "effectual call." This is the calling whereby "the Spirit of God illumines the minds and softens the will of the elect, thus enabling them personally to respond to the external call of the gospel."[14] As Barth states, and as we see in John, coming to see the light is more than a cognitive recognition and acceptance; it is a being "seized and refashioned." This effectual illumination is a penetrating reorientation and renovation. As one participates in this light, it is determinative for one's new being.

Second, in addition to this *effectual illumination*—the initial "coming to see the light"—we also see an ongoing illumination in the Gospel of John. Christ's followers (his disciples or figures such as Mary Magdalene or Lazarus) experience a progression in their understanding of who this man is as the Gospel unfolds. In particular, Jesus' identity is shrouded in mystery

---

[11]For Nicodemus, he is informed that he must be born again (Jn 3:3); for the woman at the well, she has been told everything she has ever done (Jn 4:29); and for the man born blind, he has received sight with mud and water and all he knows is that though he was blind, now he sees (Jn 9:25).

[12]*CD* IV/3.2:519.

[13]John Owen used the language of "effectual illumination" speaking "of an internal, effectual work of the Holy Spirit, in the illumination of our minds . . . enabling us to believe with faith divine and supernatural" (*Pneumatologia*, 487).

[14]Bruce A. Demarest, *The Cross and Salvation: The Doctrine of Salvation*, Foundations of Evangelical Theology (Wheaton, IL: Crossway, 1997), 39.

as those whom he encounters often ask, "Who are you?" or "Who is he?"
(e.g., Jn 8:25; 9:36). However, by the end of the Gospel, we hear the Evangelist make the perplexing observation, "None of the disciples dared to ask
him, 'Who are you?' because they knew it was the Lord" (Jn 21:12).

In other words, the Gospel of John also displays a sort of *progressive* illumination.[15] This progression is not only a progression in knowledge. It is
also a progression in obedience. Progressive illumination is a way of life that
is developed in the economy of divine light. Those who come to see the light
of life are made able to *walk in that light* also (Jn 8:12; 12:35-36; 1 Jn 1:5-10;
2:7-11). Faith and obedience thus appear in conjunction with each other
throughout this project. Intimate knowledge of the divine light and walking
in the sphere illumined by that light are indivisible. As one comes to know
the light, they are compelled also to walk in it.

Objectives

An exegetically based, dogmatic account of divine light addresses the relationship of illumination to revelation and regeneration. The account does
so by incorporating Augustine's voice into the discussion and by attending
to the Johannine depictions of "coming to see the light." Augustine writes in
his homilies on John, "When the soul receives from God the elements of its
goodness it becomes good by participation, just as by participation thine eye
seeth. For it sees not when the light is withdrawn, while so long as it shares
in the light it sees."[16] The notion of participation itself has received significant attention in recent theological discourse.[17] A first major objective is to

---

[15]For more on the distinction between initial and progressive illumination, see Seaman, "Indispensability," xiv.

[16]Augustine, *Homilies on the Gospel of John*, 224.

[17]The concept of participation is complicated by a variety of proposals for the nature of this participation. Such models on offer include covenantal, historical, missional, ontological, sacramental, and theodramatic construals of participation. See, for example, J. Todd Billings, *Calvin,
Participation, and the Gift: The Activity of Believers in Union with Christ* (New York: Oxford
University Press, 2007); J. Todd Billings, *Union with Christ: Reframing Theology and Ministry
for the Church* (Grand Rapids: Baker Academic, 2011); Constantine R. Campbell, Michael J.
Thate, and Kevin J. Vanhoozer, eds., *"In Christ" in Paul: Explorations in Paul's Theology of Union
and Participation* (Tübingen: Mohr Siebeck, 2014); Michael J. Gorman, *Becoming the Gospel:
Paul, Participation, and Mission* (Grand Rapids: Eerdmans, 2015); Keith L. Johnson, "Karl
Barth's Reading of Paul's Union with Christ," in Campbell, Thate, and Vanhoozer, *"In Christ" in
Paul*, 453-74; and Adam Neder, *Participation in Christ: An Entry into Karl Barth's Church Dog-
matics* (Louisville, KY: Westminster John Knox, 2009).

engage such conversations here also. In this engagement with participation, we hope to illumine the participatory nature of our redemption in Christ. That is to say, illumination is not given by the distribution of individual lights but through the invitation to see by the one light of Christ.

A second major focus will be a systematic treatment of Augustine's homilies on the Gospel and letters of John. We will engage these texts both as they relate to his doctrine of illumination in particular and his theory of knowledge in general. That is not to say these works have not been considered but to acknowledge that his homilies have only been referenced anecdotally and unsystematically. In this way, we will attempt to retrieve the contribution of Augustine's homilies on John.

A third major objective is to engage Barth's untranslated lectures on the Gospel of John. John Webster has recently noted that, "In spite of the fact that they constituted a considerable share of his teaching in the 1920s, Barth's exegetical lectures have had remarkably little impact on the interpretation of his work."[18] Though there are a variety of reasons for this,

> one is the assumption that all that needs to be known about Barth's exegetical work can be found in *The Epistle to the Romans*; another is a concentration on Barth's supposed general hermeneutical principles or on his attitude to historical criticism, particularly in the prefaces to the various editions of *Romans*, to the neglect of detailed attention either to his doctrine of Scripture or to his exegetical practice.[19]

The engagement with Barth's exegetical work in John will draw out the implications of his interpretation for his larger dogmatic work, especially at the points of revelation and redemption.

Finally, there is the crucial question of illumination and religious experience. A discussion on the role of an individual's experience in coming to see the light of Christ is not without its challenges. How does such an event remain a valid event in the realm of human experience without being reduced to and dismissed as subjective relativism? And yet that is the crucial pastoral question of this conversation: How do we come to see the light of Christ and what role do we play in it? I seek here to offer a

---

[18]John Webster, "Witness to the Word: Karl Barth's Lectures on the Gospel of John," in *The Domain of the Word: Scripture and Theological Reason* (New York: T&T Clark, 2012), 66.
[19]Webster, *Domain*, 67.

robustly theological and practical account of human experience while recognizing that such an experience is ultimately inaccessible from the standpoint of a "spectator" to the event.

A FINAL NOTE

The economy of divine light in the world is an expansive and therefore challenging concept to capture in its fullness. This is due in part to incorporating the whole triune economy into the conversation. Moreover, there is much to consider in offering a robust account of all that the divine light entails by its being, actions, and effects. Nevertheless, a dogmatic account of illumination demonstrates a phenomenon that is rooted in the nature of God (God is light, 1 Jn 1:5), that proceeds through the Son (the true light coming into the world, Jn 1:9), and that is executed or completed by the Holy Spirit (Jn 14:26). In light of the triune economy's activity here, the entire project might be best summarized as explicating the drama of illumination in the theater of God's creation.

PART ONE

AUGUSTINE'S
READING OF JOHN
AND DOCTRINE
OF ILLUMINATION

◆◆◆◆◆◆◆◆◆◆◆◆◆◆◆◆◆◆◆◆◆◆◆◆◆◆

TWO

Augustine's Method of Theological Interpretation

T HE FOLLOWING THREE CHAPTERS are an "excavation" of Augustine's homilies on John. As themes of light, illumination, and enlightenment abound in Augustine's homilies, his text provides a rich resource for clarifying the doctrine of illumination implicit in John's Gospel and letters. In order to properly interpret Augustine's thoughts on illumination here, we must begin with the proper tools. These proper tools include a thorough knowledge and understanding of Augustine's interpretive method. How does he go about making exegetical decisions? What contributes to his understanding of the biblical text itself? Given Augustine's considerable premodern influence on the practice of the theological interpretation of Scripture and his contribution to the doctrine of illumination, it follows that we would clarify his method and its implications for illumination.[1] Furthermore, as a project that attempts to envision systematic theology as a discipline dependent on the conclusions of other theological tasks (biblical interpretation and theology, church history and historical theology, and philosophy), this chapter is a first step in the interdisciplinary tasks of constructing a dogmatic account of illumination.

---

[1] In her exceptional work on Augustine's theory of knowledge, Lydia Schumacher narrates every major contributor to the discussion of illumination in the medieval period (Anselm, Bonaventure, Aquinas) as attempting to align their view with Augustine or demonstrate Augustine's support for their position. *Divine Illumination: The History and Future of Augustine's Theory of Knowledge*, Challenges in Contemporary Theology (Malden, MA: Wiley-Blackwell, 2011).

AUGUSTINE'S THEORY OF REPRESENTATION

Interestingly enough, the language of the Fourth Gospel is foundational to Augustine's theory of signs—a theory that is essential to Augustine's theological hermeneutic. In particular, the Word's descent into the flesh is the preeminent model for God's condescension to humanity.[2] Augustine finds this model paradigmatic for God's condescension to humanity in the inspiration of Scripture also. With this in mind, this chapter lays open both the contribution of John's Gospel to Augustine's interpretive method and the application of his interpretive method to the Gospel and letters of John as demonstrated in his homilies.

Augustine's homilies may be best conceived of as a complex tapestry. It is a tapestry that weaves together Old and New Testament typology, figurative reading, intertextuality, philosophical reflection, theological and doctrinal exposition, and refutation of heresy. As Pamela Bright indicates, attempting to understand Augustine's method for teaching on Scripture is not so much the work of articulating a systematized process as it is ordering Augustine's "pattern of thought directed toward the contemplation of the Incarnate Word."[3] Augustine's hermeneutical approach to the Gospel and letters of John is no exception. The most well-known aspects of Augustine's interpretive method have been thoroughly discussed: the purpose of Scripture is the increase of charity and destruction of cupidity; Scripture interprets Scripture; read of all Scripture; read different translations; and be knowledgeable of the languages (Hebrew and Greek) and images used by Scripture.[4] The task here is to understand these aspects as Augustine applies them to the Johannine writings.[5] Thus this chapter seeks to understand Augustine's interpretive method for the Gospel and letters of John by

---

[2] John M. Norris, "The Theological Structure of Augustine's Exegesis in the 'Tractatus in Euangelium Ioannis,'" in *Augustine: Presbyter Factus Sum*, ed. Joseph T. Lienhard, Earl C. Muller, and Roland J. Teske, Collectanea Augustiniana (New York: Peter Lang, 1993), 385.

[3] Pamela Bright, "St. Augustine," in *Christian Theologies of Scripture: A Comparative Introduction*, ed. Justin S. Holcomb (New York: NYU Press, 2006), 41.

[4] Richard N. Soulen, *Sacred Scripture: A Short History of Interpretation* (Louisville, KY: Westminster John Knox, 2009), 92.

[5] More than a few theologians and biblical scholars, especially those invested in the project of theological interpretation of Scripture, have suggested that the sermon itself is the true culmination of the theological task. See, e.g., Stanley Hauerwas, *Unleashing the Scripture: Freeing the Bible from Captivity to America* (Nashville, TN: Abingdon, 1993); and Ellen F. Davis and Richard B. Hays, *The Art of Reading Scripture* (Grand Rapids: Eerdmans, 2003).

considering the interpretive practices demonstrated in these texts them-selves.[6] Understanding Augustine's method in exegeting these texts will re-quire engaging his theology of Scripture, the history and development of his interpretive method, the relationship of history and allegory, his work of exegesis and combating heresy, and finally the relationship of the Gospel to the letters in his homilies. All of this will be treated here and then brought to bear in the next chapter on those passages pertinent to Augustine's doc-trine of illumination.

THE INSPIRATION OF SCRIPTURE, THE COMMUNICATION OF ILLUMINATION

Coming to grips with how Augustine makes use of Scripture inevitably in-volves understanding what kind of text Augustine considers the Bible to be. Augustine develops his compelling vision for the inspiration of Scripture at the very outset of his homilies on John. His theology of inspiration con-fronts us with a most eloquent vision of the interplay of divine discourse, human witness, and biblical record.[7] For Augustine, the prologue of John is from beginning to end a deeply rich theological introduction to God's rev-elation in Christ—the Word made flesh.[8] John Norris writes, "In the incar-nation, the Word accommodates himself to humanity's capacity for knowledge, dwelling beneath the cover of flesh so that humanity can progress from a knowledge of Christ in the flesh to a knowledge of the Word in the beginning."[9] As with the incarnation of the Word, the inscripturation of the Word is a movement of God toward humanity, aimed at humanity's understanding and thus its healing and restoration.[10]

---

[6]The work that has been done on Augustine's method, and in particular on *De doctrina Chris-tiana*, will be considered, but only as it aids in understanding what Augustine is doing with John. George Wright Doyle has done the invaluable service of evaluating Augustine's instruction on rhetoric in *De doctrina Christiana* with Augustine's implementation of that instruction in the tractates on John, defending Augustine's consistency between his theory and his practice. "St. Augustine's 'Tractates on the Gospel of John' Compared with the Rhetorical Theory of 'De Doctrina Christiana'" (PhD diss., University of North Carolina at Chapel Hill, 1975).

[7]Augustine, *Tractates on the Gospel of John 1–10*, Fathers of the Church 78 (Washington, DC: Catholic University of America Press, 1988), *tracts.* 1, 2, though this is not his most thorough treatment of the subject.

[8]Maico Michielin, "Augustine's Interpretation of John's Prologue," *Theology Today* 67, no. 3 (Oc-tober 2010): 302.

[9]Norris, "Theological Structure," 385.

[10]Bright, "St. Augustine," 44.

In this way, the inspiration of Scripture is bound up with its ministry. The ministry of Scripture is its communication of the salvation accomplished in Christ. Augustine illustrates his doctrine of inspiration using the imagery of Psalm 72:3. In Augustine's vision the mountain—the Evangelist—is illuminated with the message of peace in order that the hills—the readers of his text—may receive justice.[11] The justice we "hills" receive is, of course, our justification.[12] Augustine insists the Evangelist speaks because he is given a word, he is a lamp lit by another light.[13] In view of Augustine's theory of signs, the incarnation is paradigmatic for God's condescension to humanity in the inspiration of Scripture. *Signum*—"signs," which in the case of Scripture are words—are God's adaptation to humanity's cognitive limitations in communicating the *res*—the thing or reality—of God's being and actions.[14] As the Evangelist is illuminated by wisdom itself, he shines a light apart from which we could never imagine such lofty ideas as "in the beginning was the word, and the Word was with God, and the Word was God."[15] In this sense, the inspiration of Scripture is a tension that works in opposing directions. On the one hand, our hope is the Lord, the maker of heaven and earth, not the mountains. On the other hand, apart from these "mountains," we could not see the one from whom our hope comes.[16]

Augustine's theological convictions regarding the text are indispensable to his hermeneutical method. The nature of God's communicative action and presence, in and with the Word, is indivisible from Augustine's method for reading the text. Both Augustine's theory of signs and his understanding

---

[11]*Tract.* 1.2.1.

[12]Or justifying faith, "Because the just man lives by faith" (*Tract.* 1.2.1; cf. Hab 2:4, Rom 1:17, Gal 3:11; Heb 10:38).

[13]Augustine, *Tractates on the Gospel of John 1–10*, 4.

[14]"God is obliged to communicate with signs, to make use of concrete terms to explain higher realities, to use objects which are manifest to the senses to describe invisible things, because the darkened understanding of sinful man cannot grasp truth directly." John M. Norris, "Augustine and Sign in *Tractatus in Iohannis Euangelium*," in Schnaubelt and Van Fleteren, *Augustine: Biblical Exegete*, 217.

[15]*Tract.* 1.7.1.

[16]"Therefore, let us lift our eyes to the mountains from which help shall come to us; and yet it is not the mountains themselves in which our hope is to be placed, for the mountains receive what they may present to us" (*Tract.* 1.6.2). The inspiration of the text is "dialectical" in the sense that there are forces at work in opposing directions. On the one hand, we are not to hold the source of our hope in humanity but in the divine. On the other hand, we are compelled to place some reliance on the human vessel because this human vessel of the text is the means by which we receive our help from God.

of the ministry of the text reinforce the way in which inspiration is not first and foremost an abstract theory. Rather, inspiration is ultimately about the communication of salvation.

Augustine's Priorities in Interpretation

A profitable means of organizing Augustine's interpretive method in John is to speak of his interpretive "priorities." The pastoral context of Augustine's reflections on John suggests that his priorities are the intellectual, moral, and spiritual exhortation of his church. Augustine is concerned about their right thinking, right disposition, and right practice.[17] It is readily apparent that Augustine's intellectual concerns include combating heresy, defending the theological consistency and accuracy of the Bible, and demonstrating the intellectual feast that the Scriptures afford the learned mind. The moral dimensions of Augustine's interpretation pertain primarily to our human disposition toward the text—namely, humility and love.[18] That is to say, pride regarding one's own interpretation and the love of one's own opinion are inimical to interpreting the text well.[19] Finally, his spiritual priorities in interpreting the text pertain to understanding the way of life that leads to right thinking and right disposition. Though ostensibly circular, the core of Augustine's thinking on this is his distinction of the *uti* and the *frui*. Clarity of mind and proper disposition of humility to the text are the products of properly ordered love for things of *use* and love for things of *enjoyment*. To love for the sake of pleasure what was intended for use is tantamount to the

---

[17]Thomas Williams, "Biblical Interpretation," in *The Cambridge Companion to Augustine*, ed. Eleonore Stump and Norman Kretzmann (New York: Cambridge University Press, 2001), 59-70.

[18]Williams, "Biblical Interpretation," 66.

[19]Augustine places pride and disordered love among the chief dangers of mistaken interpretation, "For if he takes up rashly a meaning which the author whom he is reading did not intend, he often falls in with other statements which he cannot harmonize with this meaning. And if he admits that these statements are true and certain, then it follows that the meaning he had put upon the former passage cannot be the true one: and so it comes to pass, one can hardly tell how, that, out of love for his own opinion, he begins to feel more angry with Scripture than he is with himself. And if he should once permit that evil to creep in, it will utterly destroy him. 'For we walk by faith, not by sight.' Now faith will totter if the authority of Scripture begins to shake. And then, if faith totter, love itself will grow cold. For if a man has fallen from faith, he must necessarily also fall from love; for he cannot love what he does not believe to exist. But if he both believes and loves, then through good works, and through diligent attention to the precepts of morality, he comes to hope also that he shall attain the object of his love. And so these are the three things to which all knowledge and all prophecy are subservient: faith, hope, love" (*De doc. Chr.* 1.37.1).

fiancée who forsakes her paramour for the ring he gave her.[20] Although an interpretation that builds up the twofold love of God and neighbor is not necessarily proof of accuracy in interpretation,[21] a way of life that is enamored with creation for its own sake and not for the sake of the one who created it is certainly indicative of some distortion.[22] The disorder of one's interpretation is demonstrated in the disorder of one's loves and vice versa.

HISTORY AND SPIRITUAL INTERPRETATION

A challenging component of Augustine's hermeneutical method is accounting for what seem to be arbitrary exegetical conclusions. Such arbitrary decisions include the conclusion that the "sixth hour" when Jesus takes a rest by the well in Samaria signifies the sixth age of history which is enacted in the incarnation, or that the Samaritan woman's previous five husbands refer to the five senses (touch, taste, smell, hear, see). Such readings present challenges to constructing a systematic Augustinian methodology for arriving at the divinely intended meaning of the text.

However, the arbitrariness of his conclusions ought not surprise us. Rather, his conclusions are coherent when considered in the sphere of his exegetical practices. To this point, we make the case that Augustine's methodology is to exegete Scripture in light of three histories. The first *literal-historical* meaning, that is, clarifying what is in the text. The literal-historical conclusions are informed by Augustine's understanding of history, science, philosophy, and philology, and accounts for his Platonist bent when matters turn toward philosophical reflection. The second *salvation-historical* meaning, which locates the text within the history of redemption and discerns its implications

---

[20] *Tr. in Io. Ep.* 2.11.2.

[21] "If, on the other hand, a man draws a meaning from them that may be used for the building up of love, even though he does not happen upon the precise meaning which the author whom he reads intended to express in that place, his error is not pernicious, and he is wholly clear from the charge of deception" (*De doc. Chr.* 1.36.40).

[22] "We are to love the things by which we are borne only for the sake of that towards which we are borne" (*De doc. Chr.* 1.35.39). See also where Augustine writes that there is a way of life lived in respect of the Creator such that desires of the flesh, lust and ambition "do not shackle you by your love [for them]," and "love for enjoyment what you ought to love for use" (*Tr. in Io. Ep.* 2.12.1). In contemporary theology, Kevin Vanhoozer has referred to these as "interpretive vices"—habits that lead interpreters away from contact with authorial meaning and truth. *Is There a Meaning in This Text?: The Bible, the Reader, and the Morality of Literary Knowledge*, 10th anniversary ed. (Grand Rapids: Zondervan, 2009), 376-77.

for our understanding of God's redemptive work in the world. This includes understanding its location within the canon and is disciplined by the *regula fidei*. It gives credence for the kinds of typological and figurative work that Augustine performs, both intertextually between Old and New Testaments, and in locating ecclesial realities within the text itself (i.e., Augustine's identification of the woman at the well as figurative of the church). The most "arbitrary" conclusions, however, arise out of the third history that Augustine considers, which is the *rhetorical-historical* meaning. This level of reading interprets the text in light of the historical situation to which Augustine himself is speaking. These are the conclusions that cannot be systematized into predictable categories simply because the variety of rhetorical audiences and contexts are infinite and never-ending. This does not justify every arbitrary rhetorical-historical conclusion but gives intelligibility to the occurrence of all seemingly arbitrary exegetical conclusions.

With these three histories in mind, we delve deeper into the historical and spiritual aspects of Augustine's interpretation. The predominant characteristic of his "spiritual interpretation"[23] is the way in which he follows the narrative logic of the text while also projecting the story in light of salvation history.[24] In this way, Augustine's spiritual interpretation follows from his theology of Scripture, namely, that the human author only understands in part what the divine author is doing in whole.[25] Spiritual interpretation is about fleshing out the static image captured in the text, giving it depth and

---

[23] Augustine's interpretation is being referred to as "spiritual interpretation" here both because it allows for the greatest breadth of diversity in encompassing all that is involved in Augustine's interpretation, and because it possesses the greatest freedom from prejudice among the alternatives (allegorical, figurative, typological, symbolic, etc.). Within the scholarly literature, however, profound disagreement exists regarding the proper language for describing Augustine's approach to the Gospel and letters of John and his interpretation in general—whether it is allegorical, figurative, symbolical, typological, etc. The concern here is not with determining the right term but with faithfully representing Augustine's method (cf. Van Fleteren, "Augustine's Hermeneutic").

[24] This is evident, for instance, in his homilies on John the Baptist, the woman at the well, and the man born blind.

[25] That is not to say that the Evangelist misunderstands his own work or produces an incoherent text. Rather, if as Augustine suggests, the Evangelist speaks only because he is given something to say, the giver's use is not thereby restricted only to the narrow intent which the Evangelist understands in relaying the message. As with a mirror which reflects only what is placed before it, so the human author's reflection can only be a static image of a more dynamic revelation. The implication is that as a human being, the Evangelist "did not express the entire reality, but said [only] what a human being was capable of saying" (*Tract.* 1.1.2).

dimension, breath and life. As an object caught in the mirror is not in contradiction to its own image, neither is the spiritual fleshing out of a text necessarily in contradiction to the surface-level, literal-historical depiction offered by the text. Rather, the human author's literal-historical message stands as a static reflection of a far greater reality, as a history within a history—the history of salvation. Augustine's spiritual interpretation is about locating the text's reflection and history within the reality and history of salvation.

As it pertains to the literal/allegorical divide, the accuracy of the classic division between the literal-historical emphasis of the Antiochene school and the allegorical emphasis of the Alexandrian school has been challenged. If this divide between these two schools is not as disjunctive as previously thought, this may open a way for us to understand how the literal-historical and the allegorical function for Augustine.[26] Without renarrating the entire development of Augustine's interpretive method, it can be said that Augustine developed a unique approach by amalgamating the various influences he encountered. This began with his early tutelage among the Manichaeans, and continued through to the lofty and eloquent allegorical interpretation of Ambrose in Milan. Although Augustine vigorously rebuts the Manichaean brand of literal interpretation in his *De Genesi contra Manichaeos*, it is clear that Augustine maintained an important space for a properly literal interpretation.[27] Augustine's literalism has the letter of the sacred text as its norm, not the prevalent contemporary thought external to the text.[28] The space Augustine carved out for the literal interpretation of

---

[26]See Donald Fairbairn, "Patristic Exegesis and Theology: The Cart and the Horse," *Westminster Theological Journal* 69 (2007): 1-19; and Charles Kannengiesser, "A Key for the Future of Patristics: The 'Senses' of Scripture," in *Dominico Eloquio—In Lordly Eloquence: Essays on Patristic Exegesis in Honor of Robert Louis Wilken*, ed. Paul M. Blowers, Angela Russell Christman, and David G. Hunter (Grand Rapids: Eerdmans, 2002), 90-106. Fairbairn argues that the division breaks down when one evaluates three faulty assumptions: (1) that the Antiochene and Alexandrian schools had internal uniformity; (2) that "the Antiochenes were the 'good guys' who took Scripture seriously, and the Alexandrians were the 'bad guys' who paid little attention to the text itself but instead treated the passage as a jumping off point for philosophical speculation"; and (3) that "different theologies and homiletic emphases of Antioch and Alexandria were the result of different exegetical methods" ("Patristic Exegesis," 3). It is also interesting to note that several of the Antiochene school's major representatives (Paul of Samosata, Theodore, Diodore, and Nestorius) were condemned by the church. Finally, given that Origen was condemned, Fairbairn questions whether Origen should really be considered the "Alexandrian *par excellence*" rather than perhaps a Cyril of Alexandria or Athanasius.

[27]Van Fleteren, "Augustine's Hermeneutic," 3.

[28]Charles Kennengiesser writes that Augustine's *De Genesi ad litteram* "was literal because it was

Scripture, then, is granted based on the recognition of an important distinction between a literal and a *literalistic* interpretation.[29]

Augustine's appropriation of allegory underwent a similar evolution. In meeting Ambrose while serving as professor of rhetoric in Milan, Augustine discovered a powerful mind and eloquent tongue that did not conform to his long-held image of an anti-intellectual Christianity.[30] Ambrose's figurative exegesis provided a robust defense against the Manichaeans' most devastating criticisms of the Old Testament. Augustine began to understand the logic of a truly defensible Christianity. Not only did Augustine find Ambrose's allegorical interpretation a convenient means of dealing with difficult texts (à la *De doctrina Christiana*). Augustine was himself convinced by its explanations. Although Augustine ultimately adopts a more tempered approach to allegorical or figurative interpretation, it must be acknowledged that in Augustine's relentless pursuit of truth, it was an allegorical interpretation of Scripture that gave rest to his soul. In this way, alongside of literal interpretation, allegorical interpretation is another aspect of interpretation under the broader umbrella of Augustine's spiritual interpretation.[31]

Allegorical interpretation was particularly persuasive for Augustine because it offered a fundamentally different orientation toward the nature and authorship of the biblical text. Donald Fairbairn writes,

> In interpreting the Bible, we [moderns] start with the immediate context of the passage in question, and we generally refuse to allow any interpretation of that passage that cannot be drawn from the passage itself. In sharp contrast, the church fathers started with the whole Bible, with its entire message, and they read each passage in light of that message.[32]

It is not as though the Fathers did not recognize the human authorship in all its diversity. Rather, viewing the text first and foremost as the work of a single divine author invited an underlying, unifying thread to the text not

---

to the letter of the sacred text." "Augustine of Hippo," in *Dictionary of Major Biblical Interpreters*, ed. Donald K. McKim (Downers Grove, IL: IVP Academic, 2007), 135.

[29]Kevin Vanhoozer develops this distinction within the context of modern debates over the literal interpretation of Scripture (*Is There a Meaning?*, 310-12).

[30]Christopher A. Hall, *Reading Scripture with the Church Fathers* (Downers Grove, IL: InterVarsity Press, 1998), 119.

[31]Van Fleteren, "Augustine's Hermeneutic, 8-10."

[32]Donald Fairbairn, *Life in the Trinity: An Introduction to Theology with the Help of the Church Fathers* (Downers Grove, IL: IVP Academic, 2009), 111.

permitted by modern critical scholarship. Fairbairn continues, "as the church fathers drew numerous connections between the Testaments, they relied on their perception of what the Holy Spirit meant, not what the human author could have known or intended."[33] A "preoccupation with the human author's intent" paired with the pervasive influence of the idea that the Bible is primarily a human book has produced an interpretive culture whereby entering into the logic of the Fathers is nearly unconscionable. Augustine's fundamentally different orientation toward the nature and authorship of the biblical text is a logic in which God as a single divine author transcends the diversity of human authors, contexts, and time periods without destroying the polyphony of their voices.[34]

Augustine's forty-ninth tractate on the Gospel of John provides a compelling instance of this logic. Augustine draws on a diverse spectrum of the canon in expounding the episode of Jesus raising Lazarus from the grave.[35] In the passage Jesus has asked Mary a question to which Augustine believes a theological answer is demanded: "Where have you laid him?" As it was theologically unsatisfactory to suggest that Jesus does not actually know, Augustine argues that the far more robust explanation is to understand the way in which God *does not know* something. Lazarus functions as a sign for the lost person to whom the Lord, in Matthew 7:23, speaks in judgment: "I do not know you, depart from me." Informed by the teaching of the church—namely, affirming the omnipotence of God—the "I do not know you" is not the expression of a deficiency in God's knowledge. Rather, it is the matter of God knowing an individual to be, or not to be, in his justice.[36] The "where have you laid him?" is the call of God to Adam in the garden, "Adam, where are you?" It is not the expression of God's ignorance but the invitation to God's mercy. The Lord comes to see Lazarus as he came to see Adam, "for when he has mercy the Lord sees," and for this reason the psalmist pleads,

---

[33]Fairbairn, *Life in the Trinity*, 113-14.

[34]Fairbairn adds, "Moreover, we are also influenced by the modern idea that the Bible is not so much a single book as it is a collection of unrelated or scarcely related human accounts of the human experience of God" (*Life in the Trinity*, 114).

[35]In the single paragraph of the *Tractates* engaged here, Augustine cites Genesis, Psalms, and Matthew, a "diverse spectrum" in that it engages texts of significantly different genres, time periods, and contexts, spanning the two Testaments.

[36]Augustine, *Tractates on the Gospel of John 11-27*, tran. by John Rettig. Fathers of the Church 79 (Washington, DC: Catholic University of America Press, 1988), *Tract.* 15.20.

"*See* my lowliness and toil and take away all my sins."[37] Without a doubt Augustine's exegesis leaves the surface level of the text but not by disconnecting from it. His exegesis leaves the surface not by lofty flights of the imagination but by deeply conditioned interpretive moves informed by the theological judgments of the church and the larger message of the Bible.[38]

The way in which Augustine's spiritual interpretation of the text follows the narrative logic of the passage even as it transcends its strictly literal-historical dimensions is paradigmatic of Augustine's interpretation of John. In Augustine's *Tractates*, this practice: (1) is rarely performed at the expense of the integrity of the historical account; (2) permits for the entire canon to speak into Augustine's interpretation; (3) often reads the narrative in light of the history of salvation; and, most importantly for understanding Augustine, (4) is both informed and disciplined by the *regula fidei*.

William Wright's work *Rhetoric and Theology* offers a compelling account of the way Augustine's interpretive method appropriately adheres to a history in the text without becoming enslaved to it. That is to say, more often than not, the "historicity" of the text is simply assumed. In his discussion of Augustine's forty-fourth tractate on John 9, Wright argues that although the blind man is a sign signifying the human race, the man's function as a sign does not thereby dismiss his historical existence or the episode itself. Rather, "according to Augustine, the deed, the actual event of Jesus healing the man born blind, is a thing that signifies. This historical event is a sign."[39] Van Fleteren agrees, suggesting that "for both Paul and Augustine, allegory lies not only in words, but more importantly in events themselves."[40] "History and allegory are not antithetical, but complementary. The latter often presupposes and builds upon the former."[41] Wright offers his example by way of a comparison with J. Louis Martyn's two-level reading of John 9. In so

---

[37]*Tract.* 15.20, emphasis mine.

[38]Commenting on Augustine's *De doc. Chr.* 3.2.2, Fairbairn writes, "notice that when there is ambiguity about a certain passage, one should first consult the rule of faith (which he describes as both the clearer passages of Scripture and the church's authoritative statements about it)" (*Life in the Trinity*, 112-13).

[39]William M. Wright, *Rhetoric and Theology: Figural Reading of John 9* (New York: Walter de Gruyter, 2009), 80.

[40]For this reason, it may be more accurate if Van Fleteren used "typological" rather than "allegorical" to describe this aspect of Augustine's and Paul's interpretive methods.

[41]Van Fleteren, "Augustine's Hermeneutic," 7.

doing, Wright demonstrates modern interpretation's congruence—in method, not in content—with Augustine's approach to the text. Namely, within a modern two-level reading of John 9 "the reconstructed [Johannine] community's history functions analogously to a figural or spiritual sense of Scripture, in which difficulties at one level of the text are interpreted to make theological sense at another."[42] Wright is "concerned with the way in which both of these exegetes read the Gospel to mean something other than that which the text ostensibly claims."[43] Martyn is interested in the way the text functions as a window into the Johannine community. Augustine is concerned with the way the text figurally depicts Christ and his body, the church.[44] In terms of specific hermeneutical practices, Wright observes four similarities, two of which are significant to the purposes of this chapter.[45]

First, "both exegetes discern in John 9 multiples levels of meaning." For Martyn, there is not only the level of the text that depicts the "persons and events in Jesus's day (i.e., the *Einmalig* level)" but also the level that "simultaneously refers to persons and events in the history of the Johannine community." As for Augustine, the text depicts not only the events in the life of a specific individual, the man born blind, but also "Christians at various stages of spiritual development." Wright adds the further observation that "both Martyn and Augustine think that these different levels or modes of signification are inscribed in the Gospel itself and are not the creation of the reader."[46]

The second point of comparison that Wright identifies is the way in which Martyn and Augustine both interpret characters and events in the story in

---

[42]Wright, *Rhetoric and Theology*, 93. Wright's example here is the anachronistic use of ἀποσυνάγωγος in John 9.

[43]Wright, *Rhetoric and Theology*, 76.

[44]Wright, *Rhetoric and Theology*, 76.

[45]In light of Wright's third observation, I posit that Augustine's interpretation of the text is actually *more* historically charitable to the text than Martyn's. Wright's third observation is a bit more dubious because he suggests that a third similarity exists in "how both Martyn and Augustine use figural reading to deal with what they perceive to be problems in the text" (*Rhetoric and Theology*, 88). However, in reality Augustine does not use figural interpretation to address possible problems in John 9 because he does not perceive there to be any. As a result, Wright goes to Augustine's explanation of this found in *De doc. Chr.* 2.6.7 in order to produce points of comparison with Martyn. Nonetheless, Wright is correct in his observation that "both Martyn and Augustine hold that problems at one level of the text can be resolved or explained at another level" (*Rhetoric and Theology*, 88-89).

[46]Wright, *Rhetoric and Theology*, 86.

light of these multiple levels.[47] For example, "Martyn holds that the man born blind in the narrative refers to both a man who was healed by Jesus and a Johannine convert, who was excommunicated from the synagogue for his belief in Jesus."[48] In Augustine's case, "the man born blind is both a real individual in his own right and also a sign for something else, i.e., the sinful state of fallen humanity."[49] Wright concludes that the comparative analysis of Martyn's and Augustine's approaches to John 9 proves that a category mistake has been made. What Martyn has done in the interest of historical reconstruction is in fact a figural reading of the text. It is figural in that the man born blind stands as a representative of someone beyond the narrative —a convert to the Johannine community. For Augustine, spiritual interpretation has been employed not to escape the problems of the historical account; rather, it is Augustine's attempt to showcase the rich theological treasures of the text lying beyond the average layperson's grasp.[50] It is the pursuit of the mystery in the history.

CONCLUSION

These reflections on Augustine's method of theological interpretation will serve as a guiding light for reading Augustine's homilies on the Gospel and letters of John. By drawing out the particularities of Augustine's method, we gain insight into what we must understand of Augustine in order to read Augustine's homilies well. These aspects include the conclusion that Augustine's spiritual interpretation is a method that pursues the literal-historical, salvation-historical, and rhetorical-historical meanings of the text. These "histories" give us categories for organizing Augustine's often wandering exegetical and theological reflections in the homilies. This chapter has given necessary justification on modern and contemporary terms (i.e., Wright's comparison of Augustine with J. Louis Martyn) for Augustine's multilevel

---

[47] Wright, *Rhetoric and Theology*, 87.

[48] Wright, *Rhetoric and Theology*, 87.

[49] Wright, *Rhetoric and Theology*, 87.

[50] "The preacher is not a reasoner who proceeds from arguments but is in the service of the Word of God as he is in the service of the sacraments. He is the mediator between the text and the faithful, and he knows his authority comes from the Word of God upon which he comments and which he himself listens to in prayer and reflection. The preacher searches the Scriptures to apprehend the voice of God speaking to his people rather than apprehending the human voice of the inspired author" (Norris, "Theological Structure," 387).

readings of the text and articulated a coherent coordination with Augustine's method. Therefore, when it comes to articulating a dogmatic account of illumination on the basis of Augustine's work, it can be seen clearly that the illumination—inspiration—of the biblical authors too falls within the economy of the divine light. This is because the communication of divine light to human beings entails this first communication of light to the biblical authors. Finally, there is no coincidence that Augustine's priorities in interpretation themselves reflect the ends which we will argue are illumination's effects: the intellectual (enlightening the mind), moral (walking obediently in the light), and spiritual (communion with the divine light) exhortation of the church. The previous discussion will help us in the following chapter by providing familiarity with Augustine's progression as he moves through a passage and by understanding the aspects of the text that move toward theological construction for him. In movement toward articulating a robust trinitarian doctrine of illumination, the next chapter will bring Augustine's theology of Scripture and his method of interpretation to bear on the text's witness to the location of illumination in the triune economy.

THREE

Illumination in Augustine's Theological Interpretation of John

W E NOW TURN TO THE NARRATIVES in the Gospel of John where Augustine's exposition intersects with the notion of illumination. The aim is to retrieve Augustine's thought on illumination from those texts in which an individual has an encounter with Christ—the light of the world. The one exception is the ever-important prologue (Jn 1:1-18). Though it is not the narration of an individual's encounter with the light of the world, the prologue does narrate the light of the world's encounter with the world. In the following chapters these reflections will be employed in order to construct a sort of Augustinian-Johannine doctrine of illumination.

This chapter limits the breadth of Augustine's work to his homilies on the Gospel of John for several reasons. First, as it is the desire of this project to remain as close to the text and the practice of interpretation as possible, Augustine's homilies give the best opportunity to do so because Augustine is expounding the text itself, he is not deploying it for other purposes such as warding off heresy (*Contra Manichaeos*), countering poor teaching (*De Spiritu et littera*), articulating doctrine (*De Trinitate*), offering philosophical (*De Natura Boni*) or Christian instruction (*Enchiridion*), and so on. Second, the homilies afford us an opportunity to work in as direct parallel to Karl Barth as possible by surveying extended reflections on John from both theologians. Third, it is believed that Augustine's homilies on John were written over the course of Augustine's life, therefore providing insight into the development of his thoughts on illumination over a long period of time.

Finally, we will frequently place alongside Augustine's homilies his most sustained reflection on the interpretation of Scripture, *De doctrina Christiana*. *De doctrina Christiana* is also believed to have been developed in incremental stages throughout Augustine's life.[1] By bringing these two works into conversation, we are able to bring the method of his interpretation and its practice together.

PHILOSOPHICAL CONSIDERATIONS

It would be unacceptable to overlook the philosophy informing Augustine's thought on illumination in the Gospel of John. Étienne Gilson argues in his seminal work on Augustine's philosophy, *Introduction à l'étude de Saint Augustin*, that Augustine formulated his doctrine of illumination through merging a philosophical metaphor with the texts of Scripture.[2] In this philosophical metaphor, light is figurative for God, eyes are the soul, and sight is the soul's receptivity of truth. The way the mind knows truth is comparable to the way the eye sees an object. As the physical sun is the source of light that renders things visible to the eye, God is the source of spiritual light that renders truth intelligible to the mind.[3] Diogenes Allen refers to this metaphor as the "germ" of Augustine's doctrine of illumination. The influence of Platonist and Neoplatonist philosophy is unmistakable at this point. Augustine himself even acknowledges agreement with Plotinus and the Platonist.[4] He writes in *De civitas Dei*, "Plotinus asserts, often and strongly, that not even the soul which the Platonists believe to be the soul of

---

[1] Books one and two of *De doctrina Christiana* were completed by 396 CE, and books three and four by 426–27. The first sixteen homilies were given by 406–7 and the remaining were most likely completed between 418 and 422. See George Wright Doyle, "St. Augustine's 'Tractates on the Gospel of John' Compared with the Rhetorical Theory of 'De Doctrina Christiana'" (PhD diss., University of North Carolina at Chapel Hill, 1975), 9; and Eugene Kevane, "Augustine's *De Doctrina Christiana* in World-Historical Perspective," in *Collectanea Augustiniana*, ed. B. Bruning, M. Lamberigts, and J. Van Houtem (Leuven: Leuven University Press, 1993), 1013-14.

[2] Étienne Gilson, *Introduction à l'étude de Saint Augustin*, Études de Philosophie Médiévale 11 (Paris: J. Vrin, 1949), 103; cf. Marie Comeau, *Saint Augustin: Exégète du Quatrième Évangile*, 2nd ed. (Paris: Gabriel Beauchesne, 1930), 305.

[3] "L'act par lequel la pensée connaît la vérité soit comparable à celui par lequel l'oeil voits les corps . . . comme le soliel est la source de la lumière corporelle qui rend visibles les choses, Dieu soit la source de la lumière spirituelle qui rend les sciences intelligibles à la pensée" (Gilson, *Introduction à l'étude de Saint Augustin*, 103).

[4] Augustine, *The City of God Against the Pagans*, ed. R. W. Dyson (New York: Cambridge University Press, 1998), 393-94 (10.2).

the world derives its blessedness from any other source than . . . the light which is different from it, which created it, and by whose intelligible illumination the soul is intelligibly enlightened."[5]

Augustine bolsters his argument by referencing Plotinus's own analogy in his *Enneads* between knowledge and the celestial bodies.[6] Plotinus likens

> God to the sun and the soul to the moon; for the Platonists suppose that the moon derives its light from the sun. This great Platonist therefore says that the rational soul . . . has no nature superior to it except God, Who made the world, and by whom the soul itself was made. Nor, he [Plotinus] says, can these heavenly beings receive a blessed life, and the light by which the truth is understood, from any other source than that which we too receive it.[7]

Lest we endorse the Hellenization narrative of Christian history,[8] Gilson is right to acknowledge that though there is little doubt regarding the inspiration of Augustine's metaphor, Augustine only accepts tenets of Platonist doctrine because of their harmony with Scripture.[9]

Plato's well-known cave metaphor depicts human liberation from the deception of sensual reality as liberation from a shadowy "cave." Individuals are set free from the dark cave as they are propelled into the full light of day. The metaphor demonstrates how a vision of the good, attained by the intellect alone, far surpasses sensual perception. Through our "conversion"—a renunciation of sensual delights and gratification—we are at last led into reality by the intellect rather than away from it by the senses.[10] As Plato narrates the progression toward reality of those bound in the cave, they are at first repelled due to the brightness of the light and the stubbornness of their hearts. They must not only be turned toward the light but also dragged up the steep and rugged incline to the mouth of the cave.

> Forced into the presence of the sun . . . when he approaches the light his eyes will be dazzled, and he will not be able to see anything. . . . First he will see the shadows best, next the reflections of men and other objects in the water,

---

[5] Augustine, *City of God*, 393 (10.2).
[6] Plotinus, *The Enneads*, trans. Stephen Mackenna, 3rd ed. (London: Faber and Faber, 1962), 417 (5.6.4).
[7] Augustine, *City of God*, 393 (10.2).
[8] Most famously, Adolf von Harnack, *History of Dogma*, 7 vols. (New York: Dover, 1961).
[9] Gilson, *Introduction à l'étude de Saint Augustin*, 104.
[10] Allen, *Philosophy for Understanding Theology*, 54.

and then the object themselves, then he will gaze upon the light of the moon and the stars and the spangled heaven; and he will see the sky and the stars by night better than the sun or light of the sun by day. . . . Last of all he will be able to see the sun.[11]

Though not explicitly referenced in the homilies, the Platonic depiction of "the ascent of the soul from sense perception (the cave) to a vision of the Good" functions significantly in Augustine's construal of those illuminated in the Gospel of John.[12] In particular, there is the sense in which, for Augustine, the Christian life parallels this ascent of the soul, but in this case, from sensual perception to a "vision" of *God*.

Alongside the soul's ascent toward reality as depicted in the allegory of the cave, there belongs also, in Allen's words, the "moral improvement or purification of the soul [which] is achieved with the increasing knowledge of reality." Augustine's own depictions of illumination demonstrate the way "the increase in knowledge of God goes hand in hand with moral improvements." His homilies on John will demonstrate the Platonic-Augustinian epistemological tradition in that "there is no intimate knowledge of God without such a moral change in the knower."[13] In Augustine's own metaphor, although the sun, may be present to the blind man, the blind man is "absent" from the sun. Analogically speaking, the light may be present with the immoral person, but the immoral person is absent from the light because the eyes of their heart are sullied and darkened by sin. The moral trajectory of their life prohibits their reception of the divine light.[14] In this way, divine illumination, moral purification, and human understanding function in a necessary conjunction.[15] It will, therefore, be imperative of this project to return to this philosophical metaphor of sight and knowledge at crucial junctures in the relevant homilies to inform our understanding of Augustine's interpretation as it pertains to light and illumination.

This is all said with an important caveat. Augustine's doctrine of illumination was not the platonic doctrine in terms of the platonic reminiscence.

---

[11]Allen, *Philosophy for Understanding Theology*, 54.

[12]Allen, *Philosophy for Understanding Theology*, 49.

[13]Allen, *Philosophy for Understanding Theology*, 49.

[14]*Tract.* 1.19.1.

[15]These are the seeds of justification for incorporating sanctification into the economy of divine light as will be developed in the more constructive portions of this project.

Gilson rightly states that according to Augustine, "we discover truth not in the memories deposited previously in the soul, but in the divine light which is constantly present there."[16] Gilson concludes that "although he used Platonic language at first, he restricted its meaning later on, and in a way to remove all doubt, made it serve to express his own doctrine of illumination."[17] That is to say, illumination is not recalling knowledge previously deposited. Rather, as a doctrine oriented toward knowledge of God, illumination is the means by which we attain knowledge and sight of the one who is present among us. Augustine's homilies on John will continually return to the theme of God's presence among us and the need for illumination in order for humanity to perceive it. This perception of his presence is the illumination of one's initial reception of the light of life.

INCARNATION AND ILLUMINATION: AN INTRODUCTORY NOTE

Augustine's homilies on John's prologue are among his most dense discussions of illumination in the Gospel. The language of light, enlightenment, and illumination are essential to capturing the message of John's prologue. In Augustine's mind, John's prologue sets the agenda for the Fourth Gospel: the prologue is a theological reflection on the Word's becoming flesh and dwelling among us. Thus, prior to coming to terms with the true light's encounter with individuals, John must first narrate the true light's encounter with the world.

In the previous chapter we maintained that Christ's incarnation was for Augustine, the example *par excellence* of his sign theory. That is to say, the incarnation was God's condescension to humanity in God's self-communication. As we begin to engage Augustine's exegesis of John, it becomes evident that for Augustine, God's self-communication in Christ is about more than the communication of information. God's self-communication demands a discussion of the manifold work God intended in the revelatory, regenerative, therapeutic, and transformative work of the incarnation. As indicated in the introduction, we are proposing that illumination is best conceived of as a complex economy incorporating both revelation and regeneration. The prologue of John contains the germ of these doctrinal relationships

---

[16]Gilson, *Introduction à l'étude de Saint Augustin*, 82.
[17]That is, in terms of revelation, not ratiocination; Gilson, *Introduction à l'étude de Saint Augustin*, 82.

(illumination, revelation, and regeneration, Jn 1:12-13). In both the Gospel and Augustine's expositions, it is evident that the incarnation and illumination are indivisible—but not indistinguishable—concepts as well. The incarnation and two-natures Christology are essential to Augustine's doctrine of illumination. The intolerable brightness of God's light is incomprehensible to our dim, weak, human eyes. Therefore, in the incarnation, the light clothes itself in flesh as the Son of Man in order that dim eyes may gaze on him, know him, be healed by him, and, finally, behold his glorious light as the Son of God.[18]

JOHN 1:1-18

Augustine's homiletical concern in John's prologue was to address how God is present and communicative to Augustine's own parishioners. This required first confronting a significant paradox in the prologue, the paradox that the Logos/true light was both in the world (Jn 1:10) and was also coming into the world in the incarnation (Jn 1:9, 11). Augustine argues that the incarnation was more about the nature of the Word's presence in the world than it was about the Word's movement from absence to presence in the world. He who was already here according to his divinity came here according to the flesh so that he could be seen by the foolish, blind, and the wicked.[19] The incarnation of the Logos was the divine being's self-communication in a medium accessible to those in darkness.

John 1:1-3. "In the beginning was the Word, and the Word was with God, and the Word was God. He was in the beginning with God. All things were made through him and without him was made nothing."[20] The content of

---

[18]The Son of Man/Son of God distinction is important for Augustine throughout the course of the *Tractates* because the distinction communicates the two forms of the Word's existence among men. Furthermore, the distinction represents the natural progression of human knowledge of the Word. Augustine routinely describes the individuals whom Jesus encounters as moving from a knowledge of the word as the Son of Man to a knowledge of him as the Son of God. This is synonymous with Augustine's description of their movement from a knowledge of the word in the flesh to a knowledge of the Word who was in the beginning. Cf. Keith E. Johnson, "Augustine's 'Trinitarian' Reading of John 5: A Model for the Theological Interpretation of Scripture?" *Journal of the Evangelical Theological Society* 52, no. 4 (2009): 799-810.

[19]*Tract.* 2.8.1.

[20]Unless otherwise stated, the translation of Scripture cited in this section is John W. Rettig's translation of Augustine's Latin. This allows us to maintain continuity with the language of the text Augustine was expounding.

revelation in these initial verses of John is the clarity that this Word who would descend into human flesh, was first with God and was God. Moreover, what the remainder of this Gospel will unveil is how it is that this Word in whom we have been made, is the Word in whom we must be remade.[21] In a brilliant turn of phrase, Augustine exhorts his congregation, "Let the one who created you re-create you."[22] Augustine read these words as a confession so lofty, it could only be the product of illumination.[23] John had ascended beyond all things that are made in order to gaze on the Word through whom all things are made.[24] And yet, due to his limited capacity as a *created* medium, he could not communicate the entirety of the divine reality.[25]

John's illumination here mirrors what contemporary theology would categorize more narrowly as the work of inspiration. However, interestingly, Augustine does not mention the Spirit in these first three homilies. This may be due in part to the absence of the Spirit in the prologue of John. Rather, what is spoken of in John 1 is not the inspiration of human beings by the Holy Spirit, but their enlightenment by the Word of God. Consequently, Augustine identifies the inspiration of the biblical authors as an element of our illumination as readers of the text. In this way, the inspiration of the biblical authors is drawn into the economy of divine light as the divine light is applied with particularity to the biblical author so as to inspire in them a witness to this divine light shining. *Inspiration*, then, is an aspect of the divine light communicating itself in the world.

John 1:4-5. "That which was made, in him is life. and the life was the light of men. And the light shines in the darkness, and the darkness did not comprehend it." These verses are the first to introduce the language of light in the prologue and thus also in the Gospel of John. In order to accurately interpret this first epithet, "the light of men," Augustine insists that, "that which was made in him is life" means not that all created things are the source of life, but that all things, by their life, are *reflective* of the one, uncreated source of

---

[21] *Tract.* 1.12.1.

[22] *Tract.* 1.12.1. This statement is aimed particularly at the mistaken sense of the Logos held among the Arians.

[23] *Tract.* 1.5.2; 1.7.1; 1.18.1; 2.3.1.

[24] *Tract.* 1.5.2.

[25] "Because he [John] was inspired, he said something; if he had not been inspired, he would have said nothing. Now since he was an inspired human being, he did not express the entire reality, but said what a human being was capable of saying" (*Tract.* 1.1.2).

life.[26] Augustine's point is to clarify that all things that have life, have life because they are created *in him*.

John's Gospel narrates how this Logos, which gives life in creation, will also give life in salvation. This life—the Logos—is the light of people. Augustine takes "this life" at the very least as a reference to the person of Jesus Christ, who is the light of people. He is the light of people in that he is the interior master, "the ultimate giver of illumination."[27] In Augustine's own words, it is "from this very life men are enlightened."[28] Humanity, being made in the image of God and therefore possessive of a rational mind, is made capable of recognizing wisdom by this interior master.[29]

Nevertheless, Augustine suggests there are those who cannot yet receive that light. This would be those whose hearts—the eyes by which the light is seen—are weighed down by their sin.[30] Here Augustine offers a fundamental metaphor for sin and its interference with illumination: "Just as when a blind man is placed in the sun, the sun is present to him, but he is absent to the sun, so every slow-witted person, every evil person, every ungodly person is blind in his heart."[31] Dirty and sore eyes, tainted and irritated by the filth of iniquities, obstruct the blind man's vision when wisdom is present. The remedy? "Let him cleanse that by which God can be seen" for "blessed are the clean of heart, for they shall see God."[32] Two initial conclusions can be drawn here. First, it is not simply the mind that receives the light, but the heart also. Second, sanctification is drawn into the economy of divine light as the eyes of the heart are cleansed to see the light. There is a correspondence between what the mind can recognize and the purity of the heart's desires. The mind cannot recognize and pursue what the heart does not

---

[26] *Tract* 1.16.2-3.

[27] Rettig, "Introduction," 4.

[28] *Tract*. 1.18.1.

[29] *Tract*. 1.18.1. This is to distinguish men from animals, which are not made in God's image, do not possess rational faculties, cannot receive illumination, and consequently cannot recognize wisdom.

[30] "Perhaps there are slow-witted hearts that cannot receive this light because they are weighed down by their sins so that they cannot see it." These are not to think that the light is absent because they cannot see it. Rather, "they themselves, because of their sin, are darkness" (*Tract*. 1.19.1). It is about such people that the Scriptures say, "And the light shines in the darkness, and the darkness did not comprehend it" (Jn 1:5).

[31] *Tract*. 1.19.1.

[32] *Tract*. 1.19.2; Mt 5:8. The implication here is that the light is seen with the heart (cf. Rettig, "Introduction," 58n44).

desire. Consequently, it is not only the mind that must be enlightened but the heart also. This is the rhetorical-historical application of the salvation-historical observations grounded in the literal-historical data of the text.[33]

John 1:6-8. "There was a man sent by God whose name was John. This man came for a witness, to give witness concerning the light, that all might believe through him. He was not himself the light, but he came to give witness concerning the light." In the midst of his second sermon on the Gospel, Augustine develops the proper *disposition* for illumination. In so doing, Augustine likens reaching life and intimacy with God with reaching a distant shore. Augustine presses the point that it is by imitation of the humility Christ demonstrated on the cross that we are carried across the "sea of this world." In his incarnation, the Word "came from him to whom we desired to go" like a vessel that will make its return trip. If we do not depart from Christ's lowliness, if we are not too proud to identify with Christ's humiliation, we might join him in reaching the shore, which we now only see from afar. Christ's crucifixion was a pedagogical demonstration of humility. The instruction is given under the cover of flesh because he came to those who could not *see* God. Therefore, John the Baptist's witness was intended to help those who could only see the flesh to see the one hidden beneath the flesh.[34]

In expounding John 1:6-8 and John's witness to the light, Augustine develops how human witness—the word of God *proclaimed*—may also be incorporated into the communication of divine light in the world. John the Evangelist and John the Baptist are "mountains" which have been "bathed" in light and thereby reflect or witness to the divine light. However, these men are not lights in themselves. They are not the source of their own illumination. They are lights enlightened by another: *lumen, sed illuminatum, non illuminans.*[35] These mountains, apart from the light shed on them, stand in darkness.[36] The hope is that those who see these illumined "mountains"

---

[33]To recap, the "literal-historical data of the text" refers to the literal or verbal sense of Scripture (see chap. 2 above).

[34]"Because, then, he [Jesus] was a man in such a way that God lay hidden in him, there was sent before him a great man through whose witness he might be found to be more than man" (*Tract.* 2.5.1).

[35]Comeau, *Saint Augustin,* 306 (cf. *Tract.* 14.1).

[36]"For a mountain is in darkness unless it is clothed in light" (*Tract.* 2.5.1).

might then raise themselves up to him who gives light to the mountain. John was sent in order to receive the rays from the true light and report them to others' eyes. In proclamation, the Evangelist becomes a vessel of light.

Marie Comeau, however, raises a curious question: Why it is that the true light who enlightens all people must enlighten these two (the Evangelist and the Baptist) as witnesses to himself?[37] Could not this light, which has no need of another light in order to shine, enlighten others without these intermediaries? Augustine provides a compelling response referring back to these verses in a later homily. He writes, "But he [Christ] was himself a greater testimony which he bore to himself. But they with their weak eyes were seeking lamps because they could not bear the day."[38] Comeau comes to this conclusion herself:

> "The light that created the sun" covered itself with a created body, veiled itself
> under the "cloud of the flesh," less to hide than to soften its too bright splendor
> that weak human eyes cannot bear. And now men, whom the testimony of
> God to himself exceeds, can rely on the testimony of other men. They need a
> lamp, a torch to find the day.[39]

The sun's illumination of the earth's terrain is a consistent metaphor for his doctrine:

> For even those who have injured eyes are able to see a wall which has been
> clearly and brightly lighted up by the sun; or they are able to see a mountain
> or a tree or anything of the sort. And through that irradiated object the rising
> of the sun is shown to them even though they still have insufficient sharpness
> of eye to see it. So, then, all those to whom Christ had come were less able to
> see him; he shed his rays upon John.[40]

Plato's cave metaphor is conceptually helpful here. Those with *weak* eyes, newly emancipated from the dark depths of the cave, are not yet able to look into the full light of day. In the same way, humanity undergoes a gradual progression from self-inflicted darkness to a perception of shadows, to lamps, and ultimately, the full light of day, the divine light himself. The true

---

[37]Comeau, *Saint Augustin*, 306.

[38]Augustine, *Tractates on the Gospel of John 28-54*, trans. by John Rettig. Fathers of the Church 88 (Washington, DC: Catholic University of America Press, 1993), *Tract.* 35.3.1. "The day" here is a reference to Christ as developed in his homily on John 9 where Jesus is contrasted with the night.

[39]Comeau, *Saint Augustin*, 307.

[40]*Tract.* 2.7.2.

light has enlightened other people as lamps—that is, made them witnesses—on humanity's behalf. There is an embedded theology of evangelism here that is first rooted in the work of the Johannine evangelist himself. It is in the incarnation that the true light transforms his own presence among us in order that we may see him also.[41] Because weak eyes could not yet handle the full light of day, they must first be given such lamps. These lamps are enlightened in that by their life, their love, their knowledge, and their speech, they reflect the true light of life.

John 1:9-11. "It was the true light which enlightens every man who comes into the world. He was in this world, and the world was made through him, and the world knew him not. He came unto his own and his own received him not." Augustine's exposition of the true light now turns to address its contact with the doctrine of sin. Augustine contends here that in its original condition, humankind dwelled in a perpetual state of enlightenment. Humanity was free of sin's obstruction to vision of the light and was bathed as with a light in the knowledge and radiance of God.[42] Humankind could always have been enlightened because the true light has always been present among them. They could always have had knowledge of the divine, participation in its life, and proper ordering of their loves. In this way, human blindness to God was not due to the light's absence from humankind, but humankind's absence from the light.[43] The true light shines on all people, but as with the blind man in the sun, the human eyes of the heart are corrupted by sin and cannot see it. Therefore God has not abandoned humanity, humanity has departed from the light. In speaking of the true light's presence, the incarnation once again comes to the fore. Augustine writes brilliantly, "He both was here and he came here. He was here by his divinity; he came here by his flesh because when he came here by his divinity, he could not be seen by the stupid and the blind and the unjust."[44] As John writes, "The light

---

[41]They are given a knowledge of Christ, a conviction of his truth, a recognition of his nature such that they may communicate this to others who cannot yet look directly into the full light of Christ.

[42]The ensuing statements confirm this as a reference to the fall: "Do not fall and the sun will not set for you. If you have caused your fall, he causes his setting for you; but if you stand upright, he is present to you" (*Tract.* 2.8.2).

[43]"If man had not departed from that light, he would not have to be enlightened; but he must be enlightened here precisely because he departed from that light whereby mankind could always have been enlightened" (*Tract.* 2.7.2).

[44]*Tract.* 2.8.1.

shines in the darkness [of stupidity, blindness, and unrighteousness] and the darkness did not comprehend it" (Jn 1:5). In this way, Augustine's own words indict humanity in its responsibility for clouding the light.[45]

John 1:12-13. "But as many as received him, he gave power to be made sons of God to these who believe in his name, who were born, not of blood or of the will of the flesh or of the will of man, but of God." Augustine's exegesis of the current passage is relevant given the relationship of illumination and conversion. Augustine understands that this "born of God" is a birth by adoption, not a "birth" parallel to that of the only-begotten Son. In the work of the Son, he loosens our sin in such a way that our adoption effectively reconstitutes the history and direction of our lives. Now as sons and daughters, those who believe are heirs of God and coheirs with Christ.[46] This produces an entire reorientation of human existence. In this adoption, Augustine identifies a mutual possession, not simply God's possession of humanity. In Augustine's language, "Let us possess him and let him possess us. Let him possess us, as the Lord; Let us possess him as salvation; let us possess him as light."[47] The incarnation is operative for Augustine here also: "But that men might be born of God, God was first born from among them. . . . He was born of God, that we might be made through him; and he was born of a woman, that we might be *remade* through him."[48] Augustine will elaborate on the birth from God in his exposition of John 3, but we see here again the correlation of the incarnation with illumination. In this instance, the correlation articulates how the incarnation makes possible human illumination: by being born of God. In his first tractate he addresses his congregation with a message of sanctification and illumination. Here he addresses them with a message of illumination and regeneration.

John 1:14. "And the Word was made flesh and dwelt among us and we saw his glory." John 1:14 is the culmination of the light and Logos language. In this verse, Augustine brings the incarnation and illumination together most

---

[45]In a note, translator John Rettig writes, "The enlightening God never stops shining on men; but a person's sin blocks out that light and, so to speak, God the sun sets on that person," in Augustine, *Tractates on the Gospel of John 1–10*, trans. John Rettig (Washington, DC: Catholic University of America Press, 1988), 67n20.

[46]*Tract.* 2.13.3. Augustine references Gal 4:7 and Rom 8:17 here.

[47]*Tract.* 2.13.3.

[48]*Tract.* 2.15.1, emphasis mine.

explicitly. Under the cover of flesh, the light of the world is uncovered: "Thus, 'the Word was made flesh, and dwelt among us.' He healed our eyes. And what follows? 'And we saw his glory.' His glory no one could see unless he were healed by the lowliness of his flesh."[49]

On Augustine's reading of John 1:14, Christ's incarnation was like a salve that cleansed the eyes of our hearts. As Christ became flesh and dwelt among us, we were made able to behold his glory. We could not see him in his divinity so he became flesh, so that people of flesh may behold his divinity.[50] Augustine demonstrates the fittingness of Christ's healing methods: as "dust" or "earth"—metaphorical of the filth of humanity's fleshly desires—"wounded man's eyes so that he could not observe the light, so the wounded eye is anointed as earth [referring to salves and medicines derived from earth] is applied to it for healing. Flesh wounded you, flesh heals you. He came by flesh to extinguish the vices of the flesh, and by his death he killed death. He became flesh so that we might be able to say, 'We have beheld his glory.'"[51] Human eyes are cured by means of Christ's flesh.

In an article on Augustine's *Homilies on John*, Eoin Cassidy concludes that Augustine most comprehensively considers the mediatory work of Christ "under the twin images of Christ as Physician and Christ as Teacher."[52] Christ's healing work as physician is comprehensive, addressing not only the human need of salvation but also the darkness of our intellection. The physician heals rational faculties of our mind in order that the teacher may then instruct our understanding. The incarnation of Christ, explicated in terms of physician and teacher, among others, is a malleable concept in Augustine's thought, but not because it is void of content, waiting to be filled. Rather, the expansive doctrine of the incarnation informs Augustine's interpretation at every turn of John's Gospel because John the Evangelist himself is a light enlightened to witness to the events of the Word's becoming flesh and dwelling among us. In tractate two in particular, Augustine demonstrates most explicitly the remedial work of the incarnation in answering humanity's

---

[49] *Tract.* 2.16.2.
[50] *Tract.* 2.16.
[51] *Tract.* 2.16.2.
[52] Eoin Cassidy, "Per Christum Hominem ad Christum Deum: Augustine's Homilies on John's Gospel," in *Studies in Patristic Christology*, ed. Thomas Finan and Vincent Twomey (Dublin: Four Courts, 1998), 135.

self-inflicted blindness, his self-excommunication into darkness. This blindness/darkness is humanity's ignorance toward the things of God and the incapacity to love rightly due to the elevation of fleshly things above love of God. Christ's life is the light of people not only as it shines light but as it uncovers our eyes to *see* the light. Here we encounter a message of illumination and glorification. The human heart and mind cannot glorify what they cannot recognize. The light of this life disperses the darkness cast on our hearts by sin in order that we may recognize his glory and offer him praise.

John 1:15-18. In the final tractate of the prologue, Augustine expounds the text in light of the full theological force of the Word's eternal coexistence with the Father, the Word's role as agent of creation, revelation, salvation, and illumination.[53] Nonetheless, as evidenced by many works and the general discussion around Augustine's doctrine of illumination, one of the more convoluted aspects of his doctrine is what "the light of men" refers to.[54] In his third tractate he states that there is a certain light of men that differs from beasts—that light is the intellect. It is in the intellect alone that humanity is greater than animals (cattle are stronger, flies swifter, the fan of peacocks more beautiful). Humanity is better only in its bearing the image of God, and the image of God is on the mind, the intellect.[55] He concludes then that, because it is in the mind that human beings are greater than animals, "the light of men is the light of minds."[56]

It is unclear, however, to what extent Augustine is here equating *lux hominum*—the light of men—with *lux mentium*—the light of minds. There are two possibilities: there are two "lights," the mind being a second, weaker light in addition to the true light, who is Christ; or Christ is the one true

---

[53]In this third tractate, Augustine circles back to every verse of the prologue except Jn 1:2. In so doing, the verses of the prologue mutually inform one another as the true light's encounter with the world unfolds. Augustine's theological interpretation of Scripture is repetitive in such a way that his interpretation expands as he comes back around. Though Augustine may have offered extensive reflection on a particular text, the verse takes on new light when referenced and addressed in a new context.

[54]Caroline Eva Schuetzinger, *The German Controversy on Saint Augustine's Illumination Theory* (New York: Pageant, 1960); Lydia Schumacher, *Divine Illumination: The History and Future of Augustine's Theory of Knowledge, Challenges in Contemporary Theology* (Malden, MA: Wiley-Blackwell, 2011); Ronald H. Nash, *The Light of the Mind: St. Augustine's Theory of Knowledge* (Lexington: University Press of Kentucky, 1969).

[55]R. Willems, ed., *Sancti Aurelii Augustini In Iohannis Evangelium Tractatus*, Corpus Christianorum Latina 36 (Turnhout: Brepols, 1954), 3.4.

[56]*Tract.* 3.4.3.

light who illumines the image-bearing minds of human beings. In this case, there are not two lights but only one—the light of Christ, which enlightens humanity's mind. Augustine's concluding statement may help clarify the issue: "The Light of minds is above minds and transcends all minds. This was that life through which all things were made."[57] As a preliminary conclusion, it seems Augustine comes back around to the notion that Jesus, as the light of humanity, grants humanity knowledge and understanding, and heals the eyes of the heart so as to see Christ properly. Even so, we will return to this especially important clarification in the following chapter after his relevant homilies have been considered.[58]

LIGHT AND LOGOS IN THE PROLOGUE: SOME PRELIMINARY OBSERVATIONS

Across the span of Augustine's first three tractates, we see that "light" functions in at least three ways as it pertains to the nature of light and the work of the Logos: (1) The life of the Logos is the light of men in that by his life it purifies humanity's vision. It is both life in creation and life in salvation. An aspect of this salvation is the salve that purifies our hearts of their corrupt and disordered desires. Such corruption and disordered loves darken our eyes and blind us to the light in our presence. (2) The Logos is the light of the mind in that he is an interior master who makes us capable of recognizing wisdom of God (the way in which he effects this capacity in us will be the subject of the next chapter). (3) The Logos is himself the light which we long to gaze upon. When our hearts have been cleansed and we have been taught by the interior master to recognize the wisdom of God, we see the Light in all of his glory. The life of the Logos is both the light we see, and the means by which we are made able to see it. In this way, we see the Light, by the Light.

John 2:23–3:36. Augustine's exposition of John 2:23–3:21 spans two homiletical reflections (Jn 2:23–3:5 and Jn 3:6-21). It is evident that Augustine

---

[57] *Tract.* 3.4.3.

[58] It is the ambiguity of Augustine's discussions similar to this one that drive much of the debate regarding his doctrine of illumination. The major thrusts of disagreement are along the lines of whether the mind is itself a light in addition to God's divine light and how illumination takes place (direct divine communication, divinely enabled capacity for understanding, or a purely natural conceptual process). These are the strands of contention that will be addressed in the following chapter by considering what Augustine's homilies contribute to these debates.

has two primary pastoral concerns in mind as he makes his way through the passage: the baptism/confirmation of the catechumens and the heresy of Donatism. These homilies demonstrate well the way Augustine's pastoral concerns direct his interpretation without absolutely determining it (see discussion in chap. 2 above).

Methodologically speaking, we have noted Augustine's practice of locating the congregation within the biblical narrative as an aspect of his rhetorical method. By identifying subsets of his congregation with characters or groups in the text, Augustine draws his congregation more intimately and personally into the exegesis and exposition of the text. John 2:23–3:21 is no exception. Along with most modern commentators, Augustine takes Nicodemus in the episode of John 3:1-21 to be illustrative of the Evangelist's commentary in John 2:23-25. On this reading, Nicodemus was one who supposedly believed in Jesus' name, but one to whom Jesus would not entrust himself.[59]

As the Evangelist identifies an individual (Nicodemus) who believes in Jesus but to whom Jesus does not entrust himself, so Augustine identifies a corresponding subset in his congregation as well: the catechumens.[60] Like Nicodemus, the catechumens are among those who believe, but have not yet been born again of water and the Holy Spirit—they have not yet been baptized.[61]

Augustine acknowledges the metaphorical significance of Nicodemus's coming at night and writes that "he came to the Lord but he came at night, he came to the Light but he came in darkness."[62] To be precise, he came in the darkness of his flesh.[63] When Nicodemus asks how a man can be born when he is old, Augustine interprets in a brilliant turn of phrase, "The Spirit speaks to him, and he understands his *own flesh* because he does not yet understand *Christ's flesh*."[64] This was the hard teaching to which many could not listen. Because Nicodemus had not yet savored the flesh of Christ in his mouth,

---

[59]Augustine takes Jn 3:2 as evidence of this (*Tract.* 11.3.1).

[60]This is one example of Augustine grounding the rhetorical-historical in the literal-historical.

[61]*Tract.* 11.1.2. Taking his cue from Jn 3:3, 5, Augustine instructs, "Jesus trusts himself to those who have been born again" (*Tract.* 11.3.3). Christ only entrusts himself to those who have passed through the waters of baptism. In their passing through the waters, Christ entrusts himself to them and thus are they invited to partake of his flesh and blood.

[62]*Tract.* 11.4.1.

[63]*Tract.* 11.5.1.

[64]*Tract.* 11.5.2, emphasis mine.

> He knew only one birth from Adam and Eve, he did not yet know [the birth] from God and the church. He knew only the parents who beget for death, he did not yet know the parents who beget for life . . . although there are two births, he knew one. One is from earth, the other from heaven; one is from the flesh, the other from the Spirit; one from mortality, the other from eternity, one is from male and female, the other from God and the church.[65]

In the rise of Augustine's arguments regarding those to whom Christ entrusts himself, it becomes clear that though Nicodemus is among those who believe because of the signs Jesus has done, he remains shrouded in darkness. Though he stands in the presence of the day (cf. *Tract.* 44), it is as though it is night to him. Building on the imagery he developed in the prologue, Augustine says that the light is present to Nicodemus, but because he has not been born of water and spirit, he himself is absent from the light. In this way, Nicodemus is *not* merely the illustration of John 2:23-25, but of the prologue also: "He came to that which was his own, but his own did not receive him." Indeed, Augustine points out, "Yet to all who received him, to those who believed in his name, he gave the right to be children of God— children born, not of blood or of the will of the flesh or of the will of man, but of God" (Jn 1:11-13). He entrusted himself to those born of God; Nicodemus was not (yet) one of them.

In Augustine's exposition of John 3:5, the birth of water and Spirit corresponds directly to the sacrament of baptism performed by the church. The church, being pregnant with catechumen, brings them forth: "They have been conceived; let them be brought forth into the light."[66]

Essentially, this draws the event of baptism into the order of salvation. With respect to illumination in the *ordo salutis*, it is helpful to understand that for Augustine, baptism is not the demonstration of one's faith or one's public profession of Christ's lordship. Rather, according to the language of Augustine's eleventh tractate, in baptism, the believer's sins are crossed over and their enemies destroyed.[67] Most importantly, like Moses and the Israelites who crossed over the Red Sea and partook of the manna, those who have crossed through the waters of baptism are granted to partake of the

---

[65] *Tract.* 11.6.1.
[66] *Tract.* 12.3.2.
[67] *Tract.* 11.4.3.

living bread which has come down from heaven. Interpreting John 3 in light of John 6, he makes clear, "Unless a man eats my flesh and drinks my blood, he will not have life in him."

The Gospel continues: that which is born of spirit is spirit (Jn 3:6); for Augustine, we are born in the Spirit through word and sacrament.[68] The *ordo salutis* in this rendering is not a purely invisible course of events. The spiritual and physical aspects of regeneration—that which God works by his Spirit and that which we participate in with our bodies—are complementary. By human bodily participation in such sacramental activity of baptism and Eucharist, God effects spiritual transformation. The Spirit's work in a Christian's spiritual birth is, however, invisible and mysterious. As the Gospel insists, "Do not wonder that I have said to you, you must be born again. The Spirit breathes where he will, and you hear his voice but do not know where he comes from or where he goes."[69] The upshot of this participation in sacrament activity is our being and walking as children of light. This comes front and center in Augustine's concluding section on John 3:6-21.

Though Nicodemus does not experience illumination here, the episode remains instructive for our understanding of the relationship of illumination and regeneration. First, Augustine most often speaks of regeneration in analogy to natural human birth.[70] In natural generation, humanity is born with the stain of original sin. Those who believe are reborn into the absolution of their sin's guilt.[71] Second, it follows that for Augustine regeneration pertains to the communication of baptismal grace, which is primarily the remission of sins.[72] Regeneration is a metaphorical "laver" for washing that is accomplished in the literal laver of the baptismal waters. Third, there is a correlation in the economy of divine light between regeneration and comprehension of the Logos.[73] Those who believe and have been reborn are made able to understand what the light who enlightens all people is saying.

---

[68] *Tract.* 12.5.2.

[69] *Tract.* 12.5.2.

[70] *Tract.* 12.2.1.

[71] Regeneration is a "laver" in which a person is "washed" for the remission of its sins. *Tract.* 12.4.5.

[72] *Tract.* 11.4.3. See also J. I. Packer, "Regeneration," in *Evangelical Dictionary of Theology*, ed. Walter A. Elwell (Grand Rapids: Baker Academic, 2001).

[73] *Tract.* 11.5.2. Reading John 3 in light of John 6, Augustine takes it that those to whom Christ entrusts himself are those who have consumed the body and blood of Christ and who understand what the light who enlightens all men is saying.

Finally, therefore, the language of light remains an integral aspect of rebirth as those who have been born again, were of the night and now are of the day; they were darkness and now are light.[74] In darkness the nature of sin and its destructive effects are obscured. For those who are reborn, an aspect of their illumination is an illumination to the true nature of sin. Due to regeneration, light shines, exposes sin, and reveals sin's nature as evil.[75] For Augustine, this illumination does not transpire without regeneration.

John 4:1-42. Some context and explanation of Augustine's exposition of John 4 has already been given in chapter two above. Therefore, we endeavor here only to articulate how it is that Jesus' encounter with the woman at the well informs Augustine's doctrine of illumination. At the outset of his exegesis, Augustine again quickly locates his congregation in the narrative. He instructs his congregation to identify itself with the Samaritan woman. From the very introduction of the woman into the narrative, Augustine refers to her as a form (*forma*), type (*typum*), and figure (*figura*) for the church. In this narrative the event of this woman's justification will signify the justification of the church.[76] Once again he has projected the narrative into its salvation-historical context: Christ's journey into the flesh for the justification of his church. Augustine instructs his congregation, "Let us hear ourselves in that woman, let us recognize ourselves in that woman, and let us give thanks to God for that woman for ourselves."[77]

As the meandering conversation develops, Jesus asks for a drink of water and promises the Holy Spirit—a fountain of living water welling up to eternal life. Unfortunately, the woman is preoccupied with the physical implications of Jesus' words. Captivated by the possibility of not having to return to the well or to draw out water, she latches on to his words. Jesus' promise of "abundant nourishment of the Holy Spirit" was lost on her.[78]

---

[74]*Tract.* 4.3.2.

[75]In light of John's teaching in Jn 3:19-21, Augustine insists that he who confesses his sins and accuses his sins acts with God and becomes a partner of God. In partnership with God human beings begin to experience the distaste and revulsion of sin. The moral component of the light's illuminating work is this exposure of sin; our sin begins to displease us as God sheds his light on us (*Tract.* 12.13.4). The true light's work is not only to uncover sin but also to judge sin for what it is: evil (Jn 3:19).

[76]*Tract.* 15.10.1-2.

[77]*Tract.* 15.10.2.

[78]*Tract.* 15.17.1.

"Wishing her to understand," Augustine writes, "Jesus says to her, 'Go, call your husband and come here.'" Jesus instructs her to go call her husband not because he wants to give her water through him or because she must learn through her husband (cf. 1 Cor 14:34-35). Rather, the two-level discourse so common to John is at work here also: *Jesus longs to speak to her soul.* In order to do so, the "husband" of her soul, her "understanding," must be present.[79] It is a complicated interplay of metaphors, but in Augustine's spiritual reading of this text, this woman's literal historical five husbands represent the five human senses. These senses have dominated her understanding and have continually led her away from the true light. The man she is with now is an illegitimate master of understanding because he does not submit to the lordship of this one true light.

Recalling his theological interpretive method of reading the text in light of its salvation-historical significance, Augustine's narration considers not only the progression of the church from its fallen, sinful condition to its justification and salvation but also the deep-seated intransigence of the human condition that must be overcome in the process. In particular, this intransigence pertains to human preoccupation with the sensual.[80] Jesus longs to speak to the woman about the things of the Spirit, which pertain to the soul. These can be grasped by understanding (*intellectus*) alone, which belongs to the soul.[81] Augustine explains, "When life has been well ordered, the understanding rules the soul while belonging to the soul itself."[82] This launches Augustine's investigation into the various components of the soul.

He draws out his explanation of the relation of understanding (*intellectus*) to the soul (*anima*) by means of comparison with the eye and its relationship to the flesh. As the eye is itself something of the flesh, so understanding is properly a part of the soul. However, it is the eye alone that receives and fully enjoys the light: "The remaining members of the flesh can be flooded with

---

[79]Let us be clear: this was not a commentary on female intellect or subservience. It is not instruction for women to learn through their husbands. Augustine was utilizing a familiar relationship— husband and wife in marriage—to illustrate the relationship of the intellect and the sensual in the soul. The intellect must inform the sensual parts of the soul in order for proper understanding and illumination to have its effects.

[80]Étienne Gilson, *The Christian Philosophy of Saint Augustine*, trans. Lawrence E. M. Lynch (New York: Random House, 1960), 14.

[81]*Tract.* 15.19.3; cf. 2.14.

[82]*Tract.* 15.19.3.

light [but] cannot receive it . . . the eye alone is both flooded by it and enjoys it fully."[83] In the same way, the understanding is the part of the soul that is enlightened by a higher light, namely, God.[84] Understanding "rules from above the impulses of the soul" in order that the soul might not be driven by the lower, carnal, immoderate desires of the flesh.[85] Christ was such a light to illumine the woman's understanding and this light was speaking with her. If her understanding had been present with her, she could "be enlightened by that light, and not only be flooded by it, but also enjoy it."[86] Augustine concludes, "Therefore the Lord, as if he were saying, 'I wish to enlighten, and the one whom [I wish to enlighten] is not here,' said, 'call your husband.'"[87]

ILLUMINATION AND *INTELLECTUS*: REORDERING THE SOUL

Augustine's theological exegesis of John 4 brings us directly into contact with the cognitive aspects of Augustine's doctrine of illumination. When the woman confesses that Jesus is a prophet, Augustine detects a progression in or toward her illumination, noting that her 'husband' is beginning to come, but is not yet fully present.[88] That is to say, as she emerges from the cave of sensual preoccupation, her intellect begins to take control of the lower components of the soul and properly reorients them. It is only with Jesus' full self-disclosure as the Messiah that the woman's "husband" is said to have come (Jn 4:25-26). Her understanding is now firmly established and ordered by Christ. Augustine writes, "Now the woman is constituted by faith, and ruled, as about to live rightly."[89] That is, "having received Christ the Lord into her heart, what could she do but now leave her water-pot, and run to preach the gospel? She cast out lust [in leaving her water jar behind] and hastened to proclaim the truth."[90] For this woman, her illumination was a gradual progression of understanding, corresponding to Christ's simultaneous gradual unveiling. The overcoming of this woman's sensual preoccupations

---

[83] *Tract.* 15.19.3.
[84] *Tract.* 15.19.3.
[85] "*Motus enim animae secundum carnem se mouentis, et in delicias carnales immoderate diffluere cupientis, regit desuper intellectus*" (*Tract.* 15.19.3).
[86] *Tract.* 15.19.3.
[87] *Tract.* 15.19.3.
[88] *Tract.* 15.23.1.
[89] *Tract.* 15.28.1.
[90] *Tract.* 15.30.1.

and the gradual recognition of the man speaking with her signified the breaking in of Christ's light, the true light that enlightens all people.

Augustine's theological and philosophical elaboration on the events of this encounter helpfully unveil the inner workings of illumination. At least as it pertains to this woman, illumination takes place as light shines on and is received by the *intellectus,* the higher portion of the soul. In illumination, understanding is firmly established and ordered by Christ, and thereby properly ordering the remainder of the soul, its passions, and the remainder of the entire person. Augustine's reflection also opens the door for a sort of gradual illumination, however instantaneous or prolonged it may be. In any case, this progression of illumination corresponds with the word's simultaneous self-revelation.

John 8:12-14. With John 8:12 we arrive at Jesus' self-proclamation as the "light of the world." Augustine's homily on this verse, however, betrays an important consideration in his theory of illumination. In addition to the influence exerted by Platonism on Augustine's theory of illumination, it is also clear that Augustine's nine years as a disciple of the Manichees has informed his concept of the divine light. This is evident even as he works rigorously to rebut much of Manichaeism's physical, material construal of God's light.[91]

In speaking of Christ as the light of the world, the Manichees tragically mistook this designation as Jesus' profession to be the *physical* light of the world, the sun. Augustine condemns this as a "fabrication" and a "diabolical doctrine."[92] Augustine finds John himself to address the matter in John 1:3: "The Lord Christ is not the sun [which was] made, but [he is the one] through whom the sun was made. For 'all things were made through him and without him was nothing made.'"[93] The doctrine of creation, grounded in such biblical data as John 1:3, exerts a regulative force for Augustine at this point. If Christ is the wisdom of God, and if it is through wisdom that God created all things, it follows that a created object—such as the physical sun—could not be the means by which all other things are made. The light of the sun was made through the true light of the Son.

---

[91]Robert Dodaro, "Light in the Thought of St. Augustine," in *Light from Light: Scientists and Theologians in Dialogue,* ed. Gerald O'Collins and Mary Ann Meyers (Grand Rapids: Eerdmans, 2012), 197-98.
[92]*Tract.* 34.2.2.
[93]*Tract.* 34.2.2.

The connection between the doctrines of creation and salvation should not be lost here either. Regarding the true light through which the sun was made, Augustine adds, "We may sometime come to it itself and may so live in it that we may never at all die."[94] It was about this light that Augustine believes the psalmist sang, "You will save men and beasts, O Lord, as your mercy has been multiplied, O God."[95] Psalm 36 (35 LXX) informs Augustine's whole approach to this aspect of the matter. After quoting John 1:3, Augustine writes, "Therefore, there is a light which made this light [that we see]. Let us love this Light, let us desire to understand this Light. Let us thirst for it that under its guidance we may sometime come to it itself and may so live in it that we may never at all die." Following his praise of God's mercy and the refuge that may be found in his wings, the psalmist celebrates the drink he provides from his river of delights, because the fountain of life is with God: *in his light we see light.* It is this river and this fountain of life for which we ought to thirst, for this life was the light of humanity. The doctrine of illumination, in Augustine's estimation, hangs together both with the doctrine of creation as well as the doctrine of salvation—this light, through whom all things are made, is also the one who brings (eternal) life. Seeing by the light means knowing God cannot be dissected from *life* with him.

"He who follows me will not walk in darkness, but will have the light of life" (Jn 8:12). Augustine's exposition of John 8:12 frames illumination within the context of a lifelong practice of discipleship. Unlike the sun, which people can chase from east to west and never attain, the light of the world never sets on those who do not fall from him. Augustine discerns in this verse both a command and a promise. The command is "follow me"; the promise is the light of life. The future tense of ἔχω indicates for Augustine that the promise is not fulfilled as the command is obeyed. The fulfillment of the promise is delayed: "Now he follows, later he will have, now he follows by faith, later he will have by sight."[96] The life of discipleship is lived by faith,

---

[94] *Tract.* 34.3.1.

[95] *Tract.* 34.3.1. "Your righteousness is like the mighty mountains, / your judgments are like the great deep; / you save humans and animals alike, O Lord. / How precious is your steadfast love, O God! / All people may take refuge in the shadow of your wings. / They feast on the abundance of your house, / and you give them drink from the river of your delights. / For with you is the fountain of life; / in your light we see light" (Ps 36:6-9 NRSV).

[96] *Tract.* 34.7.1. Augustine draws on Paul's words in 2 Cor 5:6-7 here for explanation and justification of this interpretation.

not by sight, in order that on that day when the night of this age and its terror of temptations has passed, we shall have the light of life. In this way, the earthly life of discipleship is thus one long, torturous night awaiting the light of the morning.[97]

THE SALVE OF ILLUMINATION

In Augustine's reflection on John 8:12-14, Christ as the light of the world does not only function as an interior master who enlightens minds. As the light of the world, Christ is also a physician of light who heals eyes, enabling humanity to "see" him. In this regard Augustine makes five further points clear about his doctrine of illumination: (1) As it is the one Logos who gives life in both creation and salvation, it is the same Logos who gives *light* in both creation and salvation. In this way, (2) salvation is therapeutic for humanity's eyes. The "salve of faith" as Augustine puts it, gradually heals our sight. In the progression of loving this light, increasing in desire to understand it, and obeying its guidance, a process of healing is always in progress, aimed at living in it for eternal life. Therefore, (3) we see here again how it is that the Logos is both the light we see and the light by which we see. The light progressively heals our eyes, and by its very shining reveals something about itself. (4) Christ's self-proclamation to be the way, the truth, and the life (Jn 14:6) means for us progressing through life in light—humanity is given light on *the way*, so that we may in eternity live in the full light of *the truth* and *the life*.[98] Finally, then, (5) illumination is not only this process of healing by which the salve of faith is applied to the eyes of our heart. Illumination is also the culmination of lifelong discipleship—a life of obedience lived in faith. Illumination in its fullest measure is to behold the eternal brilliance of the glory of God itself (Rev 21:23).[99]

---

[97]"When the night of this age is passed, when the terrors of temptations have been traversed, when that lion has been overcome which 'goes about at night, roaring, seeking someone to devour.' . . . In the morning I shall stand before you, and I shall see" (*Tract.* 34.7.1, citing 1 Pet 5:8; Ps 5:3).

[98]Jn 14:6 is the clarifying text for Augustine here. "The way, the truth, and the life" is a progression of faith in Augustine's view that begins in this life and extends into eternity. Jesus is "the way" in the sense that he is the way to the truth and the life. The Son is the way, the Father, the truth and the life. "Abiding with the Father, the truth and the life; clothing himself with flesh, he became the way" (*Tract.* 34.9.3).

[99]"[When] the day dawns and the morning star rises in our hearts . . . when our Lord Jesus Christ has come . . . you will come to the fountain; from where the ray has been sent to your shadow-filled heart by a winding and oblique path, *you will see the naked light itself*; and to see and

John 9:1-41. From the beginning of homily forty-four, Augustine recognizes the magnitude of John 9 and the impossibility of treating all of it in a single sermon, so he narrows his aim accordingly. His intent stated from the start is to "present briefly the mystery of the enlightenment of this blind man."[100] As discussed in chapter two, John 9 is an exceptional instance of Augustine interpreting on multiple levels. Augustine insists that in this mystery, both the words and deed of Jesus ought to "produce astonishment and wonder: the deeds because they were done, the words because they were signs."[101] George Lawless speaks of this episode and Augustine's exposition as three overlapping transparencies, laid over one another "in the manner of an overhead projector." The first "transparency" is the level of the historical event and the healing itself. The second is that of the tension near the end of the first century regarding Christians' exclusion from the synagogue. The third is Augustine's early fifth-century interpretation of the two previous layers in light of his North African milieu. In Augustine's spiritual interpretation of Scripture, the narrative is cast in light of its salvation-historical context and implications. He introduces the sermon with creation and fall and concludes with judgment.[102] As the things done and said are signs, Augustine indicates that which they represent. The production of the mud paste recalls God's creation of humanity from clay and dirt, and the man's blindness naturally represents the corruption of human race whose blindness was induced through the sin of the first human.[103] Augustine's hamartiology naturally informs his exegesis at this point. If humans are by nature children of wrath as the apostle suggests, then in the first human's sin,

---

endure [it] you are being cleansed" (*Tract.* 35.9.1, emphasis mine). "But we could not see. He became weak for the weak; through weakness he healed weakness, through mortal flesh, he took away the death of flesh. From his body he made a salve for our lights" (*Tract.* 35.6.2).

[100] *Tract.* 44.1.1. George Lawless writes, "From the outset of the tractate Augustine opts for a figurative interpretation without forfeiting the *sensus litteralis* generated by the wording of the original account." "The Man Born Blind: Augustine's Tractate 44 on John 9," *Augustinian Studies* 27, no. 2 (1996): 72.

[101] *Tract.* 44.1.1.

[102] Lawless agrees, "Within the compass of seventeen sections of the tractate, some of which are fairly short, Augustine transports his hearers from the moment of creation to the final judgment, graciously and generously guided by God throughout the entire range of what we have come to know as 'salvation history'" ("Man Born Blind," 64).

[103] "The mud paste produced from Jesus' spittle recalls the fact that in the beginning God formed a human being from the clay/dirt of the earth, an exegetical tradition which goes as far back as Irenaeus" (Lawless, "Man Born Blind," 61-62).

a flaw (*vitium*) grew in place of nature. If the flaw has grown in place of nature, every man is born blind as regards his mind. With the context depicted as such, the mystery of this man's enlightenment demonstrates how Christ heals this intractable infirmity of the human condition.

Augustine begins by summarizing the episode so as to focus in on and specify the mystery. The Word who was made flesh spat on the ground and made mud from his saliva, but the besmearing of the mud on his eyes was not sufficient for his healing. Rather, the man was commanded to go and wash in order that he then may be enlightened. Augustine suggests that in this besmearing the man is made a catechumen, and in his washing he was baptized, enlightened, and counted among the faithful. As the mud paste is preparatory for healing and illumining the man's eyes, so catechesis is preparatory for illumination, which was closely identified with baptism in the early church. Augustine instructs his catechumens: "Let them hurry to the baptismal font if they seek light."[104]

Due to the length of the episode Augustine elects to "run rapidly through the words of the Lord and of the whole reading itself."[105] Having clarified that this man was born blind due to no sin of his own or that of his parents but so that the works of God might be displayed in him, Jesus begins to explain what that work is and what it means for the sight of this man.

"I must work the works of him who sent me while it is day. The night comes when no one can work. As long as I am in this world, I am the light of the world" (Jn 9:4-5). This verse is the primary source of a third characteristic of Augustine's view of illumination, the metaphor of the "day." One may recall that throughout his homilies, Augustine commonly describes the relationship of John the Baptist to Christ as the lamp by which we seek the day. Or, in terms of the weakness of human eyes, humanity needs a lamp because it cannot yet bear the full brightness of the day.

From Jesus' self-witness "as long as I am in this world, I am the light of the world," Augustine derives that Jesus himself is this *day.* Thus "the blind man will wash his eyes in the day that he may see the day."[106] As the narrative unfolds, the man born blind undergoes his own transformation in the

---

[104]*Tract.* 44.2.2.
[105]*Tract.* 44.1.1; 44.2.2.
[106]*Tract.* 44.5.1.

brightness of this daylight. In the man's response to the Pharisees' inquiry as to how his eyes were opened, Augustine observes that this man has now become a proclaimer of grace.[107] As was demonstrated by the woman at the well, illumination leads naturally to proclamation.[108] It also leads naturally to discipleship. When called to account a second time by the Pharisees (Jn 9:24) the man responds sarcastically. And yet the content of his sarcasm suggests to Augustine that the man's illumination has now led him to follow Jesus. As the man chides the Pharisees, "Do you *also* want to become his disciples?" Augustine wonders whether "also" implies that this man already is.[109]

Augustine affirms the Pharisees' interpretation of the man's condition as one "wholly born in sins"—*wholly*, in Augustine's understanding, as one with closed eyes. But it is not an irreparable condition. Rather, "he who opened the eyes also heals the person wholly, he who has given enlightenment to the face will also give resurrection at his right hand."[110] The close association of enlightenment and physician is once again signified. The physician of our soul is the one who heals the eyes of the heart so that we may see.

CONCLUSION

We have gathered from Augustine's exegesis of John that the divine light touches on many of the major doctrines, and rightly so. The *Tractates* articulate a vision of illumination that begins with regeneration and progresses in sanctification as the purifying of our hearts renders possible the clarity of our vision. Our vision is clarified in order to recognize and know the wisdom and nature of God. Christ the Logos is both the light we see and *the means by which* we see it. Christ applies the healing salve of faith, granting us vision (a type of illumination in itself) and then also is the light on which our vision is to be fixed. Illumination takes place as the divine light shines on and is received by the *intellectus*—our understanding. In doing so, this illumination reorders our soul and its passions under the lordship of Christ. According to Augustine, the Logos gives light both in creation and in the

---

[107]"He preaches the Gospel, seeing, he confesses" (*Tract.* 44.8.1).

[108]If faith comes by hearing (Rom 10:17), her faith is at least in part due to this prophet who has *told* her everything about herself. Furthermore, he has spoken the words, "I am," after the hearing of which she runs to proclaim this prophet to the people of her town.

[109]*Tract.* 44.11.1, emphasis mine.

[110]*Tract.* 44.14.1; cf. Mt 25:31-34.

healing work of salvation. In the growth of our love for this light, of our desire to understand and obey this light, we live the life of discipleship. The life of discipleship culminates in the fullest measure of its expression, beholding the eternal glory of God. In living on this "way" of faith and obedience, guided by the shining of this light, then in eternity we live in the *full* light of its truth and life. Jesus' own later teaching about the work of the Spirit incorporates and indicates the Spirit's ongoing action of sustaining men and women in this knowledge, faith, and obedience (see Jn 14–16).

Though Augustine does not here expound the relation of every doctrine to the light of Christ, the fact that light belongs to the nature of God himself suggests it has also to do with all aspects of God's activity. Augustine shows the light's relevance to the intra-trinitarian dynamics of the Father and the Son, its significance for creation, as well as its importance for the incarnation, salvation, judgment, and eternal life. The next chapter will synthesize this exegetical data and systematize Augustine's doctrine of illumination, thus tying up the loose ends of this chapter. In particular, it will bring the economy of the Trinity into conversation with the theme of divine light. The economy of the Trinity and the economy of divine light will be placed in conversation in order to articulate Augustine's understanding of the divine light and its communication via the Son and the Spirit. The next chapter will therefore clarify precisely what for Augustine is the communication of God's light, how illumination occurs, and which person(s) of the Trinity makes it happen.

FOUR

Augustine's Doctrine of Illumination

T HE JOHANNINE NARRATIVES in which an individual encounters
Christ indicate that Christ himself is the true light in illumination. In
the prologue, John the Evangelist gives us the foreword to the individual
accounts of illumination in the Gospel—the incarnation. The relation of
illumination and incarnation has already been developed: the true light was
coming into the world as the Word became flesh. This life was the light of
all humankind. It was the *possibility* for humanity to recognize wisdom and
to know God. Then, in the encounters themselves, there is illumination—
the *reality* of humans knowing God.[1]

In the event of illumination as depicted in these narratives, Augustine
uncovers not so much a formula for *inducing* illumination as a way of life
that is *conducive* for it. As right interpretation depends on virtuous life and
proper loves (cf. *De doctrina Christiana*), this ethical component of illumination reinforces the Augustinian epistemological tradition already mentioned. Humility and love of truth resurface repeatedly as the determinative
disposition for receiving illumination. As sin defaces and deforms the image
of God in humanity, it obscures our vision of the divine light.[2]

---

[1]"For this follows: And the life was the light of men: From this very life men are enlightened.
Cattle aren't enlightened because cattle do not have rational minds capable of seeing wisdom.
But man, made in the image of God, has a rational mind through which he is capable of recognizing wisdom. Therefore, that life through which all things were made, that very life is light, and
not the light of every living being but of men. Wherefore, a little later, [Scripture] says, 'It was
the true light which enlightens every man who comes into this world'" (*Tract.* 1.18).
[2]Herman Somers, "Image de Dieu et Illumination Divine," in *Augustinus Magister* (Paris: Études
Augustiniennes, 1954), 457.

As for "economy," Augustine himself does not employ such language with respect to illumination. Nevertheless, a brief survey of Augustine's homilies demonstrates the fittingness of *economy* as a term for encompassing all that light and illumination do in illustrating a broad range of theological foci. The language of economy provides the grammar to speak about the interrelation of these concepts in Augustine's thought.

One of the more intractable issues regarding Augustine's doctrine of illumination is whether the light that illumines is a created light belonging to the human mind itself or if it is an uncreated light belonging to God alone. In Augustine's philosophical metaphor, light, eyes, and sight correspond to God, the soul, and the soul's conception of truth, respectively. What we can conclude is that what Augustine calls the "eye of the soul"—the *intellectus*—is only a light insofar as the divine light enlightens it. The intellect is a lamp lit by another light. It is derived and dependent.

To this extent, illumination as humanity's capacity to see wisdom is special. It is general for Augustine in that wisdom shines on all humanity. It is special in that, for some, sin has so thoroughly darkened their vision, it is only through the gracious, purifying work of sanctification that humanity can be made to see the light of wisdom shining.[3] Once one is enlightened however, the intellect still does not possess light in itself. Based on the apostle Paul's words, Augustine insists that though we were once darkness, we are now light *in the Lord* (Eph 5:8). Therefore, there is darkness in us and "light in the Lord."[4] There is an embedded notion of participation present here. Augustine concludes, "By *participation* in that light, you are light. But if you withdraw from the light by which you are enlightened, you return to your darkness."[5] This participation is a participation made possible only by grace. As Darren Sarisky explains, humanity participates by *grace* in what God is by nature, namely light.[6] According to Augustine's homilies on John, "participation" comprehends all that pertains to how God's light is communicated to those in darkness. This chapter will work to clarify the nature of

---

[3] *Tract.* 1.19.1.
[4] *Tract.* 22.10.2.
[5] *Tract.* 22.10.2, emphasis mine.
[6] Darren Sarisky, "Augustine and Participation: Some Reflections on His Exegesis of Romans," in *"In Christ" in Paul: Explorations in Paul's Theology of Union and Participation*, ed. Constantine R. Campbell, Michael J. Thate, and Kevin J. Vanhoozer (Tübingen: Mohr Siebeck, 2014), 364.

this participation in the divine light. We will engage with more comprehensive accounts of Augustine's doctrine of illumination, but the aim here is to focus narrowly on the contribution of Augustine's tractates on John in the hope that this will bring some clarity to the larger discussion.

PROPOSALS FOR AUGUSTINE'S DOCTRINE OF ILLUMINATION

A handful of works in the past few decades have outlined the major positions on Augustine's doctrine of illumination.[7] In each case, there is both congruence and divergence regarding the major positions and their tenets. Moreover, some books have taken very different approaches, most notably Lydia Schumacher's book *Divine Illumination*.[8] Rather than outline major positions on Augustine's theory of knowledge, Schumacher details the historical reception of Augustine's theory as it is appropriated by the major figures following him (Anselm, Aquinas, and Bonaventure). In order to accurately locate the theory demonstrated in Augustine's homilies on John, it will be helpful to first give a brief survey of the most important interpretations.

Ronald Nash and C. E. Schuetzinger each outline four major interpretations of Augustine's theory of illumination. However, they are not the same four. Nash divides the camps into the Thomists, the Franciscans, the formalists, and the ontologists. Schuetzinger divides the camps into ontologist, concordant, historical, and existential interpretations. Schuetzinger subdivides the concordant into three: the Aristotelian-Thomistic, the Aristotelian-Arabic, and the Franciscan. The historical and existential interpretations are not really interpretations at all, but rather approaches to reading Augustine on illumination that don't necessarily entail a systemization of his thought.

The Thomist interpretation arose out of Aquinas's attempt to harmonize Augustine's theory of illumination with Aristotelian philosophy.[9] Aquinas

---

[7]Johannes Hirschberger, *Geschichte Der Philosophie*, vol. 1 (Freiburg: Herder, 1949); Ronald H. Nash, *The Light of the Mind: St. Augustine's Theory of Knowledge* (Lexington: University Press of Kentucky, 1969); Caroline Eva Schuetzinger, *The German Controversy on Saint Augustine's Illumination Theory* (New York: Pageant, 1960); Lydia Schumacher, *Divine Illumination: The History and Future of Augustine's Theory of Knowledge* (Malden, MA: Wiley-Blackwell, 2011).
[8]Schumacher, *Divine Illumination*.
[9]"Saint Thomas' goal was the reconciliation of the teaching of Saint Augustine and that of Aristotle in such a way that his contemporaries might accept his interpretation as true. Reason and revelation were to be shown to be not contradictory, but complementary" (Schuetzinger, *German Controversy*, 39).

accomplishes this synthesis by identifying the Aristotelian "agent intellect," with the illuminating light of Augustine's theory of illumination.[10] For Aristotle, the "agent intellect" in humanity processes sensory knowledge gathered from the material world and renders it intelligible to the human mind.[11] This "processed" knowledge is known as intellectual knowledge. Intellectual knowledge is then kept in the "possible" or "passive" intellect. In Aquinas's appropriation of Aristotle, the agent intellect belongs to the mind but is separate from it in the sense that it does not act because of any organ of the body as the possible intellect does.[12]

This agent intellect is a "natural light"; but, at the same time this light has a divine origin.[13] In Thomas's thought, the agent intellect *is* the light that God impresses immediately on us.[14] Consequently, it is a faculty of the human mind and its function is to illumine our perception of objective reality. "By this light," Thomas writes, "we discern truth from falsity, and good from evil."[15] Because sensible things do not have subsistence on their own, Aristotle must posit the agent intellect as the power by which sensible things are made intelligible. Intelligibility refers to the common properties shared among a class of sensible objects (i.e., all chairs manifest the property of "chairness"). This is made possible by the process of abstraction. The agent intellect is the power by which intelligibility is abstracted from sensible realities. Aquinas, in accordance with Aristotle, asserts that this agent intellect resides above the human soul and is what every soul's understanding of itself depends on.[16] Insofar as the human soul is intellectual, its understanding is

---

[10]The "agent intellect" is also referred to as the "active intellect."

[11]Aquinas comments on the difference between Plato and Aristotle at this point, "Not, indeed, in the sense that the intellectual operation is effected in us by the mere impression of some superior beings, as Plato held; but that the higher and more noble agent which he calls the active intellect, of which we have spoken above (Q[79], AA[3],4) causes the phantasms received from the senses to be actually intelligible, by a process of abstraction." Thomas Aquinas, *Summa Theologica, Prima Pars*, trans. Fathers of the English Dominican Province, first American edition (New York: Benziger Brothers, 1947) 1.84.a6.

[12]Thomas Aquinas, *Disputed Questions on Spiritual Creatures (De Spiritualibis Creaturis)*, trans. Mary C. Fitzpatrick and John J. Wellmuth (Milwaukee: Marquette University Press, 1949), 10.

[13]Aquinas, *Spiritual Creatures* 10; Nash, *Light of the Mind*, 94.

[14]"It is proper to God to enlighten men by impressing on them the natural light of the agent intellect, and in addition to this the light of grace and glory. But the agent intellect lights up the phantasms, as a light that is impressed by God" (Aquinas, *Spiritual Creatures* 10).

[15]Aquinas, *Spiritual Creatures* 10.

[16]Aquinas, *Spiritual Creatures* 10.

derived from this agent intellect. In this way, the agent intellect is both present among the multiplication of souls and yet remains above them. The agent intellect is present among the multiplication of souls by means of its light.[17] Aquinas, however, does not identify the agent intellect with Christ. This will be the contribution of the Franciscans, as will be discussed shortly.

There are at least two points that complicate this synthesis, if not prohibit it altogether.[18] First, Augustine's theory of illumination provides no place for an agent intellect. The difference of philosophical schools informing Augustine and Aquinas is at the center of this problem. Augustine's Platonism has no need for an agent intellect who gives intelligibility to sensible objects because these objects are reflections of the forms which reside in the mind of God. They have intelligibility already. Aristotelian philosophy, however, demands an agent intellect in order to resolve the issue of how to move from the sensible to the intelligible. In Aristotelian philosophy, abstraction is the process by which one reasons from sensible objects of matter to a concept of the essence which the object manifests (e.g., a chair manifests "chairness," but for Aristotelian philosophy, "chairness" does not exist apart from its manifestation in particular chairs). Sensible objects are not copies of the forms as they are for Platonism. Rather, in Aristotelian thought such "forms" do not exist except as they are manifest in sensible objects. "Forms" are thus the essence of things extracted from the similarities among all objects of that class. The agent intellect is the means by which the mind produces such categories or concepts by abstraction.

The second complication is that Augustine leaves no place for this process of abstraction. Some have argued that because Augustine discards the platonic notion of reminiscence as a means for bridging sensible reality to the realm of the forms, his account demands the work of an agent intellect.[19] Thus it is argued that by replacing reminiscence with divine illumination, Augustine is making room for the agent intellect as agent of illumination.

---

[17]"The light of the agent intellect is multiplied immediately through the multiplication of the souls, which participate in the very light of the agent intellect" (Aquinas, *Spiritual Creatures* 10).

[18]Étienne Gilson, *The Christian Philosophy of Saint Augustine*, trans. Lawrence E. M. Lynch (New York: Random House, 1960), 85.

[19]E. Portalié, "Saint Augustin," in *Dictionnaire de Théologie Catholique* 1/2 (Paris: Letouzey et Ané, 1909): 2336-37. Reminiscence is Plato's theory that our knowledge of the forms is innate from birth and that we come to a knowledge of them by removing the obfuscation of sensual perception and remembering them.

However, Gilson makes the point that although this is a problem for Aristotelians, it is not a problem for Augustine if he is read on his own account.[20] Although Augustine does discard the theory of reminiscence, he does not discard the theory of forms underlying it—he only amends it. The forms remain in a higher realm of reality, but for Augustine the higher realm is the mind of God. Humanity does not access these forms by remembering, but by God's illumination of our minds. Consequently, humanity does not need to abstract the essence of substance in order to attain knowledge of the forms, or divine ideas.

The Franciscan interpretation of Augustine's theory of illumination differs from the Thomist by identifying the agent intellect with God. The illuminating light no longer belongs to the human mind or a sphere just above it but is "God's production, infusion or impression of the divine forms upon the mind of men."[21] Étienne Gilson is among the most notable representatives of this view.[22] Gilson contends that the identity of the light that illumines with the divine light, or God himself, is established by Augustine's own comments in *De Genesis ad litteram*: "Different is the light itself by which the soul is illumined that it may see everything it apprehends with truth through the intellect, either in itself or *in this light*; for the light is God himself, and the soul a creature although made rational and intellectual in his image."[23]

In conjunction with this, it is not uncommon for the Franciscan or Thomist interpretations to be coupled with another prominent vein of thought in Augustine's theory—the formalist view. Gilson is among those who couple these theories. The formal view argues that divine illumination only provides the ability to make proper judgments regarding the truth, beauty, goodness, and justice of a concept. Divine illumination does not

---

[20]"It seems to me that there is a simpler hypothesis to consider, namely that there is no lacuna here provided we look at things from Augustine's point of view and refuse to base our arguments on principles he did not accept. Actually in Augustine there is no problem involving an *Umsetzung* (transformation) of the sensible into the intelligible. If he did not solve this problem, the reason was that he had no such problem to solve. If we insist that he solve it, then we do not fill a lacuna in his doctrine but change it into something else and in doing so take on ourselves the responsibility of foisting it on him" (Gilson, *Christian Philosophy*, 84).

[21]Nash, *Light of the Mind*, 97.

[22]Schuetzinger, *German Controversy*, 19; Étienne Gilson, *Introduction à l'étude de Saint Augustin*, Études de Philosophie Médiévale 11 (Paris: J. Vrin, 1949).

[23]Gilson, *Christian Philosophy*, 93.

communicate content, ideas, or concepts themselves.[24] Nash summarizes the view this way: "We do not see beauty itself. Instead, the idea of beauty illumines our minds so that we are able to judge beautiful objects."[25] For example, using a common metaphor, a person does not need illumination to know what an arch looks like. What illumination enables is the person's ability to know what a *perfect* arch looks like. As Gilson puts it, "Experience and not illumination tells us what an arch or a man is; illumination and not experience tells us what a perfect arch or a perfect man ought to be."[26]

Finally, according to Nash's broad definition, the ontologist view advocates that in some way humanity "can have a direct knowledge of the divine ideas, that man 'sees' the ideas that subsist in the mind of God."[27] However, the proposal that humanity sees the ideas that subsist in the mind of God is a controversial one. This view is controversial because it entails the problematic notion that humanity sees the mind of God itself. This is problematic because of the ontological distance between humanity and the mind of God. Nash argues that the resolution to this problem lies in the distinction between contemplation and mysticism.[28] Although Gilson conflates the two, Nash argues that the equation is doubtful because "Augustine teaches that 'something divine and unchangeable is *learned*' in contemplation."[29] Although contemplation is a profound experience, this description seems a large step short of the ineffable experience of mysticism.[30] Furthermore, Nash avoids the problematic aspects of ontologism by distinguishing between the revelation of universal and particulars in illumination. Gilson charges that if God reveals knowledge of particular copies of the forms, then there is no need for sense perception. But Augustine clearly leaves important space for sense perception in attaining knowledge. Therefore, Nash contends that for Augustine, God only reveals the universal forms (such as goodness, beauty, truth, love) in illumination, not the particulars. The particular copies of such forms are learned as an aspect of *scientia* (knowledge)

---

[24]Étienne Gilson and Frederick Copleston are primary proponents of this view.
[25]Nash, *Light of the Mind*, 98.
[26]Gilson, *Christian Philosophy*, 90.
[27]Nash, *Light of the Mind*, 102.
[28]Nash, *Light of the Mind*, 116.
[29]"*Dividum et incommutable aliquid discritur*" (Nash, *Light of the Mind*, 116, quoting Augustine, *Contra Faustum Manichaeum*. XII, 54, emphasis mine).
[30]Nash, *Light of the Mind,* 102.

and on the basis of reason, not illumination. Consequently, Augustine's is a modified ontologism.[31] Humanity does not see all there is to know in the mind of God. Humanity attains that which pertains to *sapientia* (wisdom) insofar as it accords with human capacity to do so.[32] Augustine identifies truth with God, and thus a vision of truth with a vision of God. But he does not discount the diminution of truth due to our infirmities. A vision of truth is still seen with dim eyes, as through as glass darkly (cf. 1 Cor 13:12). Nash argues that just as Augustine sees levels of goodness in God's creation, there are degrees of truth as well.[33] He writes, "True things partake of more or less truth, depending upon their participation in the absolute truth, which is God."[34] Although the divine ideas are themselves unchanging and eternal, human conception of them may participate in them to varying degrees of perfection.[35] Ultimately though, humanity will not see them as they are because humanity does not exist in equality with God's being.

The complexity of the debate is obviously unending. Lydia Schumacher, however, has offered a constructive way forward by suggesting that Augustine's theory of knowledge ought to be understood in *theological* rather than *philosophical* terms.[36] She writes,

> The impasse in the interpretation of Augustine's account is attributable to the fact that there seems to be no philosophically viable way to interpret illumination that remains faithful to Augustine's intentions. The scholar must opt to construe illumination in a manner that undermines the mind's integrity or to preserve that integrity at the high cost of denying that God interferes in human cognition in the ways Augustine seems to imply that He does.[37]

It is evident from our survey that Augustine's doctrine of illumination is customarily treated in terms of a philosophical inquiry into human knowledge and its relation to capacity for knowledge of God. This conversation regularly

---

[31]Nash, *Light of the Mind*, 121.

[32]Ultimately, what people see in illumination "is qualitatively and quantitatively different from the beatific vision, but it is nonetheless a vision of God" (Nash, *Light of the Mind*, 121).

[33]Nash contends, "Gilson confuses the distinction between immutable truth and the reception of truth. That truth is grasped incompletely or inadequately does not affect truth itself" (*Light of the Mind*, 122).

[34]Nash, *Light of the Mind*, 122.

[35]Nash, *Light of the Mind*, 121-22.

[36]Schumacher, *Divine Illumination*, 17-18.

[37]Schumacher, *Divine Illumination*, 13.

invokes the language of cognition, intuition, perception, and so on. That is to say, the discussion is often quite theoretical and philosophical in nature, neglecting to fully consider the very *theological* and *christological* nature of the question itself: How does *God* work in, through, or with the human nature and cognitive structures such that human beings have knowledge of God?[38] Inescapably, the question involves issues of cognition and intuition. However, the advantage of approaching it by means of Augustine's homilies is the explicitly biblical and theological grounding of his reflection. The homilies bring us back to biblical theology. They help us to recenter Augustine's doctrine in its proper theological context as Schumacher recommends. It is to this theological contribution of the homilies that we turn now.

THE BIBLICAL/SYSTEMATIC THEOLOGICAL CONTRIBUTION OF THE HOMILIES

The question before us is this: "What does illumination look like in the event of an individual's encounter with Christ?" To answer the question is not to give a theoretical discussion per se, but to reflect upon a narration of the event itself. Augustine presents such a reflection on the prologue, the episode with Nicodemus, the woman at the well, Jesus' confrontation with the Pharisees, and the healing of the man born blind. In each case Augustine gives insight into his theory of illumination, as investigated in the previous chapter. This attempt to give a coherent account of his doctrine will bring clarity to the intransigent debate over Augustine's theory of illumination.

Light. Let us begin with a review of how Augustine uses some important terms. Augustine uses the term *light* and its various forms (*lumen, lux, lumine, lucem*) extensively throughout his homilies, and in diverse ways. Augustine invokes the term and its opposite, darkness (*tenebrae*), as an analogy for everything from the illumination of the biblical authors to the brightness of eternal life and the darkness of sin and eternal perdition.[39] With the survey of the previous chapter in mind, there are several conclusions that can be drawn about Augustine's use of the term.

---

[38]Schumacher writes, "Any given theory of knowledge by *divine* illumination derives its meaning from the *theological* assumptions that underlie it and must therefore be read in its proper theological context" (*Divine Illumination*, 1-2).

[39]*Tract.* 44.6.3-4.

First, light refers to the means by which other things are made visible and clear, that is, *intelligible*. Augustine's analogy here is the sun. By the light of the sun, other objects are made visible. Light disperses the darkness and fog of our fallen minds. It might also be included here that light is an agent of judgment. In the process of making visible or bringing clarity, light makes visible the justness or unjustness of human lives and actions.[40]

Second, light refers to truth. Light is not only the means by which to see the truth of reality for Augustine, it is itself the truth. Augustine writes that although the Word was in the world by his divinity, the Word had to come in his humanity in order for it to be seen by the dim eyes of humanity.[41] The light here is not only the means to make other objects visible but is itself to be an "object" of our vision. Augustine writes in his thirty-fifth homily, "The light bears testimony to itself, it opens healthy eyes, and is itself a witness to itself that it may be recognized as light."[42] He is the way and the *truth* (Jn 14:6). Nash puts it well when he concludes that the reason illumination is not simply formal, as Gilson suggests, is that "while light illumines other objects, it also reveals something about its own nature."[43] As the true light comes into the world, his enlightenment of human beings says something about the *true* light himself.

Third, light refers to humanity's own capacity for understanding. Unlike the rest of creation, humanity is set apart in that it bears the image of God by means of its intellect. This is the unique light that humanity alone possesses.[44] Although the image of God functions prominently in some of Augustine's other discussions of illumination, he does not give it great attention in the homilies.[45] Herman Somers makes the case, as others have, that Augustine's doctrine of the image of God is integral to his doctrine of

---

[40]Augustine's reflections on Jn 3:20-21: "The beginning of good works is the confession of evil works. You do the truth and you come to the light. What does it mean, you do truth? You do not caress yourself, you do not flatter yourself, you do not fawn upon yourself. You do not say, 'I am just,' although you are wicked, and you begin to do truth. But you come to the light that your works may be made manifest, because they have been done in God, because also this very thing which displeases you, your sin, would not displease you unless God were shedding his light upon you and his truth showing it to you" (*Tract.* 12.13.4).

[41]*Tract.* 2.8.1.

[42]*Tract.* 35.4.3.

[43]Nash, *Light of the Mind*, 117.

[44]*Tract.* 3.4.2-3.

[45]Somers, "Image de Dieu," 453.

illumination, and in particular, by means of a discussion of *catroptromancy*, or "mirror divinization."[46] Drawing from Paul's language in 1 Corinthians 13:12, "now we see in a glass darkly," Somers suggests that Augustine understands illumination to occur as we look at the mirror of God's image in our soul. In these individual encounters with Christ depicted by John's Gospel, when individuals come to see the light of Christ, or are given eyes to see Christ for who he is, they are looking into the image of God himself, Jesus Christ.

Fourth and finally, light refers to the radiance of the divine perfections. Augustine speaks frequently of the light of divine justice or the light of wisdom and of truth.[47] The radiance of the divine perfections themselves illumine as humans participate in them and are transformed by them. Although wisdom, truth, and justice can all refer to forms or ideas in the divine mind, Augustine also speaks of them in ways that suggest that they have agency.[48] This complicates the strictly formal view of illumination but does not dismiss it altogether. As God is the light of divine justice in himself, so God can illumine humanity with an understanding of perfect justice also. The question that naturally leads out of this is, how does this light get communicated to those in the darkness? The answer has been anticipated: by participation in the divine light.

Participation. Divine illumination for Augustine is accomplished by means of human participation in the divine light. Agostino Trapé writes that participation is a principle "which enters into the essential nucleus of Augustine's thought" and that "its role is so central . . . that in order to understand creation, illumination and beatitude in Augustine, one must view them as 'three modes of expressing the one doctrine of participation.'"[49]

---

[46]"*Il suffira d'identifier le miroir avec l'âme humaine pour obtenir la présentation augustinienne de la doctrine: Dieu, Lumière, éclaire l'âme, miroir, qui reçoit donc l'image de dieu, et dans lequel l'esprit peut contempler par une réflexion totale sur soi, indirectement, mais distinctement, l'image trinitaire de Dieu*" (Somers, "Image de Dieu," 453).

[47]*Tract.* 2.3.2; 1.2.1.

[48]"The lesser souls, however, would not receive faith if the greater souls, who were called mountains, were not *illuminated by wisdom itself*, so that they can convey to the little ones what the little ones are able to grasp, and so that the hills can live by faith because the mountains receive peace" (*Tract.* 1.2.1).

[49]Agostino Trapé, *Patrology*, ed. Angelo Di Berardino, vol. 4 (Westminster: Christian Classics, 1986), 408; David Vincent Meconi, SJ, "St. Augustine's Early Theory of Participation," *Augustinian Studies* 27, no. 2 (1996): 79.

The nature of this participation can be articulated in two very different ways: (1) as a metaphysical participation in which all humans share by virtue of being human; or (2) as a soteriological participation in which one shares only by virtue of one's union with Christ through faith and in the Holy Spirit. Here again Augustine's Platonist philosophical background is important but not ultimately so. His indebtedness to Plato has not been overlooked, and Roland Teske goes so far as to identify the particular text of the *Phaedo* that is most influential.[50] However, as with much of what Augustine adopts from philosophy, he radically Christianizes it.[51] One way to think of radical Christianization would be to construe it as the move from the first to the second definition given above. No longer is participation in divinity achieved through rigorous philosophical speculation. Rather, participation in divinity is solely on the basis of the incarnation. By Christ's assumption of humanity, humanity may now participate in divinity.[52] Once again, incarnation and illumination are coordinated.

The passages that invoke the language of participation and illumination indicate the kind of participation Augustine has in mind. First, participation, as Augustine employs the concept, is non-ontological. On a passage regarding the soul's participation in the goodness of God, he writes, "When the soul takes from God that by which it is good, by participation, it becomes good, as your eye sees by participation. For if the light is taken away, it does not see, but being made a participant in it, it sees."[53] That is to say, men and women may participate by justifying faith in the goodness, truth, or light of God and thereby be made good, made to see, made truer in the work of sanctification. Darren Sarisky refers to this as "dynamic participation."[54]

---

[50]See Plato, *Phaedo* 100D-102A. Roland J. Teske, "The Image and Likeness of God in St. Augustine's 'De Genesi ad Litteram Liber Imperfectus,'" *Augustinianum* 30 (1990): 449; see also M. Annice, "Historical Sketch of the Theory of Participation," *The New Scholasticism* 26 (1952): 49-79; Gerald Bonner, "Augustine's Conception of Deification," *Journal of Theological Studies* 37 (1986): 369-86; Juan Pegueroles, "Participación y Conocimiento de Dios en la Predicación de San Agustín," *Espíritu* 27 (1979): 5-26; Patricia Wilson-Kastner, "Grace as Participation in the Divine Life in the Theology of Augustine of Hippo," *Augustinian Studies* 7 (1976): 135-52.

[51]"Augustine takes this essentially philosophical understanding of participation and radically Christianizes it" (Bonner, "Deification," 373).

[52]"Man derives his spiritual life from participation in God, but this participation is made possible only by the incarnation and flesh-taking of Christ the mediator" (Bonner, "Deification," 373).

[53]*Tract.* 39.8.3.

[54]Sarisky, "Augustine and Participation," 364.

Humans participate by grace in what God is by nature. Nevertheless, an individual's departure from the good, light, or truth of God only diminishes the goodness, light, and truth in them. Humanity is included in the experience of the goodness, light, and truth of God, but not in such a way as to contribute to or detract from the goodness, light, and truth of God by this participation.[55] Human participation in the divine light is sharing in the luminosity of the divine light, producing clarity of understanding and judgment, without contributing ontologically to the divine light itself.

Second, participation does not involve ontological transformation. Deification is present in Augustine's thought but with substantial modification from the Greek fathers' notion of *theōsis*. Gerald Bonner makes a strong case for the centrality of the incarnation for the possibility and reality of deification according to Augustine but comes short of suggesting any ontological transformation. Though Augustine makes such apparently straightforward statements as, "To make gods those who were men, He was made man who is God," it is clear such transformation is by adoption and grace, not by nature.[56] His homily on the prologue of John affirms this: "For we were not born of God as was that only begotten, but were adopted through his grace."[57]

Following this, then, a third central aspect of this participation is its realization by means of our adoption in Christ. Through our adoption in Christ, made possible by the incarnation of the only begotten, we are made coheirs with Christ.[58] Augustine informs us that, in being included in Christ's inheritance, we may take possession of God as God has taken possession of us. God possesses us as our Lord, we possess him as salvation and as light.[59] At the center of this is the New Testament doctrine of *huiothesia,* sonship by adoption.[60] That our adoption invites humanity to take possession of God as light indicates both the gracious nature of the gift and the degree of our

---

[55]"If the soul should withdraw and become evil, goodness is not lessened. If the soul should turn back and become good, goodness does not increase. Your eye has become a participant in this light and you see. Has it been closed? You have not lessened this light. Has it been opened? You have not increased this light" (*Tract.* 39.8.3).

[56]Quoted from Augustine, *Sermons 184-229*, Edmund Hill, OP (Brooklyn: New City Press, 1993) 192.i.1, in Bonner, "Deification," 376. Bonner notes the similarity of this language to that of Irenaeus or Athanasius, but then quickly distinguishes Augustine from them.

[57]*Tract.* 2.13.2.

[58]*Tract.* 2.13.2.

[59]*Tract.* 2.13.3.

[60]Bonner, "Deification," 378.

intimacy with the light. It is given by pure gratuity, but it is possessed and enjoyed as if it were a birthright. To the extent that Augustine does maintain a doctrine of deification, it is only accomplished in the life to come.[61]

Fourth, and closely related to this emphasis on adoption as the means of participation, is this participation's production of our revitalization. That is to say, in Augustine's theology this participation is life giving and life re-newing. Gilson writes, "If we understand Augustinian illumination correctly, we must say that the illuminating action of God is a vitalizing action: Our illumination is the partaking of the Word, namely that Life which is the light of men."[62] In our illumination we participate in the life of the divine light, and this participation not only gives light to humanity, it also gives us life. Given the language of *regeneratio,* it is not surprising that this adoption and life—this participation—begins as a matter of baptism and rebirth.[63]

The origin of this participation is rebirth in baptism. As stated in the pre-vious chapter, Augustine identifies the gracious remission of sin in regener-ation with the baptismal grace that purifies humanity from the guilt of all its sin. This regeneration presupposes a faith only made possible by the grace of God in the first place.[64] Though he does not use such language here, this grace is what Augustine refers to elsewhere as a "prevenient grace" that makes faith itself possible.[65] The illumination that comes to humanity following

---

[61]Bonner, "Deification," 382.

[62]Gilson, *Christian Philosophy,* 105.

[63]A debatable fifth statement that could be made is that this participation is an ecclesial reality for Augustine. Bonner speaks of Augustine's doctrine of deification as an ecclesial process. For Augustine, participation is the means by which deification is accomplished. However, if *deifica-tion* in particular is only accomplished in the redemption of our bodies, it is more precise to say that our *participation* is an ecclesial process or reality commenced in holy baptism (Bonner, "Deification," 382-83). Augustine writes, "Our full adoption as sons will take place in the redemp-tion of our body. We now have the *firstfruits of the Spirit,* by which we are indeed made sons of God; but in other respects we are sons of God as saved and made new by hope" (*De Peccatorum Meritis et Remissione.* II.viii.10). Additionally, the order that Augustine provides for illumination in most cases (i.e., discussion with Nicodemus and the man born blind, but excluding the woman at the well) indicates that baptism and regeneration are prior to illumination. As for "the true light which enlightens everyone," the true light shines his light upon all, but as with the blind man in the sun, the human eyes of the heart are corrupted by sin and cannot see it, and therefore depart from the light (*Tract.* 2.7.2-3; see also discussion on Jn 1:9-11 in chap. 3 above).

[64]"For we were not born of God in the manner in which the Only-begotten was born of Him, but were adopted by His grace" (*Tract.* 2.13.1).

[65]On the basis of John's own words in 1 Jn 4:19 and Jn 15:26, Augustine concludes that human beings are only able to love and choose God because God first loved and chose them. Augustine writes, "It was because they had been chosen, that they chose him; not because they chose him

regeneration is a gratuitous gift of understanding Christ and recognizing his lordship. In short, it is illumination of humanity's own sinful nature and illumination of the nature and being of God. For Augustine, the logical order of this progression is grace, faith, regeneration in baptism, and illumination.[66] The ongoing illumination of humanity that follows is this gracious participation in the divine light.[67]

CONCLUSION: PARTICIPATION IN THE DIVINE LIGHT

To this point we have identified the major strands of interpretation of Augustine's doctrine of illumination, identified the nature of Augustine's language regarding the divine light, and discussed the nature of participation that Augustine speaks about in the homilies. We can now draw the conclusions of these investigations together. Illumination that occurs as one participates in the divine light is accomplished as the divine light disperses the darkness of the human mind and the individual reflects anew and with greater clarity on the Word of God. For those who encountered Christ in the Gospel of John, the Word of God is the Logos, Christ himself. Illumination is formal in the sense that the mind is gifted with a knowledge of wisdom, truth, beauty, and goodness in order to judge rightly the wisdom, truth, beauty, and goodness of particulars in reality. However, the human mind is also illumined with a recognition of Christ's true identity. The woman at the well's confession, "Could this be the Messiah?" and her turn to share with the entire town, and the man born blind's confession, "Lord, I believe," are both expressions of their recognition of who this man is. They were both blind but now they see. They have not only received a knowledge

---

that they were chosen. *There could be no merit in men's choice of Christ, if it were not that God's grace was prevenient in His choosing them.*" Augustine, *On Grace and Free Will*, Nicene and Post-Nicene Fathers 5 (New York: Cosimo, 2007), 38.1, emphasis mine.

[66]In following the narrative of the man born blind, Augustine writes, "Therefore we, brethren, having the eye-salve of faith, are now enlightened. For His spittle did before mingle with the earth, by which the eyes of him who was born blind were anointed" (*Tract.* 34.9.1). Having believed, the man born blind is then illumined. However, between his being smeared with the eye-salve of faith and his illumination, he washes: "Accordingly he washed his eyes in that pool which is interpreted, Sent—*he was baptized in Christ*. If, therefore, when He baptized him in a manner in Himself, He then enlightened him" (*Tract.* 44.2.1, emphasis mine).

[67]"Because in thyself thou wast darkness, when thou shalt be enlightened, thou wilt be light, though in the light. For saith the apostle, 'Ye were once darkness, but now light in the Lord.' When he had said, 'but now light,' he added, 'in the Lord.' Therefore in thyself darkness, 'light in the Lord.' In what way 'light'? Because by participation of that light thou art light" (*Tract.* 22.10).

of the forms in order to judge Christ identity rightly but have been given the power to recognize the Savior. The power of recognition comes not as a deposit of information, but as the spit and mud made a paste for healing the blind man's eyes. In this way, the Word made flesh in the incarnation heals the eyes of human hearts and cleanses them from impurity in order that their vision may be properly restored. This means that the luminosity of the true light is both general and specific. The light shines on all humankind like the sun and thus is *general*, but the luminosity is only received by those whom he has also healed and who are reborn. Consequently, the light is also *special* in its illumination.

The concept of an economy of divine light in Augustine's homilies on John incorporates the communication of the forms to judge rightly, the dispersion of darkness from the mind, and the purification of the heart. The economy of divine light entails both the communication of divine light and the healing of human "eyes." In this economy, incarnation is the possibility of illumination, baptism and rebirth are the initiation of illumination, and participation in the divine light is the realization of illumination. In Augustine's account of illumination as witnessed by his homilies on John, Christ is the one light of illumination as the true light of all humankind.

We began these three chapters on Augustine by elucidating his priorities and common practices in theological interpretation. These priorities and practices have helped to identify and articulate what precisely Augustine is doing in his theological reflection. In particular, understanding these interpretive practices aids us in clarifying what Augustine has to say about illumination in John. Finally, we have brought our findings in the tractates into conversation with the prevailing schools of thought regarding Augustine's theory of illumination. Our conclusions, though helpful in understanding Augustine, are only preliminary. These conclusions will also inform the constructive argument of the overall project. After the next three chapters on Barth, as well as an explicitly theological engagement with the Gospel of John itself, we will draw Augustine back into the conversation. There, we will incorporate what from his theory is essential to our construction of the doctrine of illumination going forward.

PART TWO

BARTH'S READING OF JOHN AND DOCTRINE OF ILLUMINATION

◆◆◆◆◆◆◆◆◆◆◆◆◆◆◆◆◆◆◆◆◆◆◆◆

FIVE

Barth's Method of Theological Interpretation

K ARL BARTH FIRST GAVE HIS LECTURES on the Gospel of John at Münster in the fall of 1925 and the spring of 1926 (published in German as *Erklärung des Johannes-Evangeliums*).[1] Simultaneously, he was completing his first attempt at a dogmatics, *The Göttingen Dogmatics: Instruction in the Christian Religion*.[2] This means we have both Barth's articulation of his interpretive method at that time, and the exercise and illustration of that method in the Gospel of John at precisely the same time. This fortuitous coincidence is a tremendous asset to the current project in that it affords us both stated theory and illustrated practice of his approach. The unique relationship of these two works will be explored here in order to greatly deepen our understanding of Barth's method of theological interpretation.

This first of three chapters on Barth (paralleling the three previous chapters on Augustine) will clarify Barth's method of theological interpretation as it is utilized in his lectures on John. To this end, we will first summarize the

---

[1] Karl Barth, *Erklärung des Johannes-Evangeliums (Kapitel 1-8): Vorlesung Münster Wintersemester 1925/1926, Wiederholt in Bonn, Sommersemester 1933*, Karl Barth Gesamtausgabe 2/9 (Zürich: Theologischer Verlag Zürich, 1976). A portion of this work has been translated into English and published as Karl Barth, *Witness to the Word: A Commentary on John 1* (Eugene, OR: Wipf & Stock, 1986).

[2] Karl Barth, *Unterricht in Der Christlichen Religion* (Zürich: Theologischer Verlag Zürich, 1990); ET: Karl Barth, *The Göttingen Dogmatics: Instruction in the Christian Religion*, ed. Hannelotte Reiffen, trans. Geoffrey W. Bromiley, vol. 1 (Grand Rapids: Eerdmans, 1991). John Webster reports that the lecture series on the Gospel of John "ran from early November 1925 to late February 1926. In the same semester, Barth also completed the cycle of dogmatics lectures which he had begun in Göttingen in the Summer Semester 1924." "Witness to the Word: Karl Barth's Lectures on the Gospel of John," in *The Domain of the Word* (New York: T&T Clark, 2012), 65.

early developments and transitions in Barth's approach to biblical interpretation. This includes the significance of his 1915 theological revolution for his approach to reading Scripture, his critical appropriation of historical-critical methods, and his confrontation with the hermeneutical guild of the early twentieth century. Second, we will expound Barth's understanding of the proper disposition that the reader is to have vis-à-vis Scripture. This is crucial not only for understanding Barth's approach to John, but grasping the entirety of Barth's theological interpretation in general. Finally, we will conclude with a demonstration of Barth's method taken from his lectures on John. However, one caveat is in order. It would be rather unfaithful to Barth to *systematize* his method of interpretation, given his reticence to discuss interpretive methodology apart from the practice of exegesis itself.[3] The advantage of this project's approach is that it attempts to discuss his methodology within the very context of his exegesis itself—his lectures on the Gospel of John.

BACKSTORY: BARTH'S HERMENEUTICAL REVOLUTION

Before Barth's *Romans* commentary "dropped like a bomb on the playground of theologians," it was his 1916 address, "The Strange New World of the Bible" that signaled he was charting a new course.[4] There he asks the programmatic question: "What is there within the Bible?"[5] At least as far back as Johann Gottfried von Herder (1744–1803) the *wissenschaftlich* (scientific) question had been, what is there *behind* the Bible? That is, what are the history, the sources, and the personalities behind this text? It was evident by Barth's time that this question had determined the kinds of answers given. For biblical studies, the question bred a predomination of the field by historical, linguistic, psychological, and inevitably philosophical concerns and agendas.[6]

---

[3]See, for example, Richard E. Burnett, *Karl Barth's Theological Exegesis: The Hermeneutical Principles of the Römerbrief Period* (Tübingen: Mohr Siebeck, 2001), 4-6; John Webster, "'In the Shadow of Biblical Work': Barth and Bonhoeffer on Reading the Bible," *Toronto Journal of Theology* 17, no. 1 (2001): 75-91.

[4]Karl Barth, *The Word of God and the Word of Man*, trans. Douglas Horton (New York: Harper & Row, 1957), 28. Quote from Karl Adam cited by Donald K. McKim, ed., *How Karl Barth Changed My Mind* (Grand Rapids: Eerdmans, 1986), ix.

[5]Barth, *Word of God*, 28.

[6]On Richard Burnett's account, Barth traced modern historicism and psychologism in hermeneutics to Herder: "Barth claimed that 'Herder's significance for those theologians who came after him can scarcely be rated highly enough. Without him there would have been no Schleiermacher

In his *Karl Barth's Critically Realistic Dialectical Theology*, Bruce McCormack explains that the fundamental shift in Barth is toward a notion of God as a "Reality which is complete and whole in itself apart from and prior to the knowing activity of human individuals."[7] This means God was not a Hegelian synthesis or an idealistic notion postulated for the purpose of establishing ethical norms (as with the Ritschlian school). Rather, God is a reality that stands over against the world. Thus, in the text of Scripture, Barth now understood that the complete and whole reality of God is what encounters humanity within the Bible.

The key elements of Barth's radical shift in hermeneutics after 1915 have been well documented in works such as Richard Burnett's *Karl Barth's Theological Exegesis*. The present project only requires a brief review. The most directly relevant exegetical practices include Barth's turn to the "world" of the text and away from the world behind the text that dominated so much of modern biblical scholarship. Barth's disillusionment with his teachers when they aligned themselves with Kaiser Wilhelm prompted him to insist that he must start all over.[8] As we see from his *Romans* commentary, this begins with the Bible itself. One of the great misfortunes surrounding the first edition of *Romans* was Barth's decision to forego including a thorough preface introducing his methodology. The forfeiture of this opportunity exposed him to intense criticism regarding the supposed ineptitude and myopia of his hermeneutics. Although Barth was severely critical of divorcing methodology from the actual practice of exegesis, his preface drafts and later prefaces show that he had a methodology at work.[9] It may have served him well to demonstrate the thoughtfulness of his interpretive method from the outset.

---

or de Wette. Nor would there have been the specific pathos of the course of the nineteenth century. Without Herder there would have been no Erlangen or history of religion schools. But for Herder there would have been no Troeltsch'" (*Barth's Theological Exegesis*, 142).

[7] Bruce L. McCormack, *Karl Barth's Critically Realistic Dialectical Theology: Its Genesis and Development, 1909–1936* (New York: Oxford University Press, 1995), 129.

[8] "As he distanced himself from the theological world of Protestant liberalism, he came to think that the reorientation of theology and the church which he considered necessary must include a reconception of the nature of scripture and its interpretation, a reconception which could, of course, only be achieved in the closest possible connection to actual exegetical work" (Webster, "Witness to the Word," 69).

[9] Burnett, *Barth's Theological Exegesis*, 5. On the basis of unpublished preface drafts, Burnett makes the case that there was a hermeneutic at work in the first edition of the *Römerbrief*.

The methodology demonstrated in these drafts and prefaces was not so much technical and philosophical as it was theological. In particular, Barth expressed a renewed interested in the Scripture principle. He also articulated an intense interest in the readings of Scripture provided by the history of the church and, in particular, John Calvin's exegesis. In Calvin he found an interpretive method that did not disregard historical and linguistic questions but kept them in their proper place as *preparatory* for the task of interpretation.[10] All these elements take a more mature form in his lectures on John's Gospel.

KEY ELEMENTS OF BARTH'S INTERPRETIVE METHOD IN JOHN

First, Barth speaks of historical criticism as prolegomena to understanding. He utilizes historical criticism, including comparative religious studies, as *preparation* for the work of interpretation. Historical criticism is not the work of interpretation itself.[11] It is clear from the reviews of *Romans* that Barth had developed an anti-historical-critical reputation in his early exegetical work,

---

[10]In his *Epistle to the Romans*, Barth writes, "For example, place the work of Jülicher side by side with that of Calvin: how energetically Calvin, having first established what stands in the text, set himself to re-think the whole material and to wrestle with it, till the walls which separate the sixteenth century from the first become transparent! Paul speaks, and the man of the sixteenth century hears. The conversation between the original record and the reader moves around the subject-matter, until a distinction between yesterday and to-day becomes impossible. If a man persuades himself that Calvin's method can be dismissed with the old-fashioned motto, 'The Compulsion of Inspiration,' he betrays himself as one who has never worked upon the interpretation of scripture. Taking Jülicher's work as typical of much modern exegesis, we observe how closely he keeps to the mere deciphering of words as though they were runes. But, when all is done, they still remain largely unintelligible. How quick he is, without any real struggling with the raw material of the Epistle, to dismiss this or that difficult passage as simply a peculiar doctrine or opinion of Paul! How quick he is to treat a matter as explained, when it is said to belong to the religious thought, feeling, experience, conscience, or conviction—of Paul! And, when this does not at once fit, or is manifestly impossible, how easily he leaps, like some bold William Tell, right out of the Pauline boat, and rescues himself by attributing what Paul has said to his 'personality,' to the experience on the road to Damascus (an episode which seems capable of providing at any moment an explanation of every impossibility), to later Judaism, to Hellenism, or, in fact, to any exegetical semi-divinity of the ancient world!" *The Epistle to the Romans*, trans. Edwyn Clement Hoskyns (London: Oxford University Press, 1933), 7-8.

[11]Burnett, *Barth's Theological Exegesis*, 87, 230-40. Barth wrote in his preface to the first edition of *Der Römerbrief*, "The historical-critical method of Biblical investigation has its rightful place: it is concerned with the preparation of the intelligence [or, understanding]—and this can never be superfluous" (Barth, *Romans*, 1). See also *Göttingen Dogmatics*, where after a brief description of the act of historical investigation, Barth writes, "Naturally, this act, which begins with the attempt to relate the different words and word groups of a text, is an absolutely necessary act if I am to have any knowledge of scripture at all" (*GD* 1:256).

even in spite of his insistence that he has "nothing whatsoever to say against historical criticism."[12] Barth simply complained that restating the historical-critical information about the text is not biblical commentary but "merely the first step towards a commentary."[13] Barth's exegesis of John is an excellent demonstration of his intended correction. With tremendous consistency, Barth offers a thorough survey of the relevant historical-critical findings and commentary before moving on to draw his own conclusions regarding the text. He diligently appraises and appropriates higher-critical research for its contribution to correcting inaccurate or misleading images of the historical context. As preparatory, it might be said that historical criticism is a tuning of the instrument in order that, when it is played, we hear it well.

Second, biblical and canonical context takes priority over historical context and the context of comparative religious texts. The privileging of the biblical context arises out of Barth's profound respect for the text, which he grants on the basis of the Scripture principle. The "whole cloth" of the text is a witness to revelation and participates in God's Word and therefore is treated seriously.[14] This is what Barth intended when he insisted that the historical critics need to be more critical—"criticism (κρίνειν) applied to historical documents means for me the measuring of words and phrases by the standard of that about which the documents are speaking."[15] Criticism for Barth meant measuring the words and phrases against the standard presented in the world of the text itself. Barth teaches this on the basis that the world of the text takes precedence over the world behind the text that is reconstructed. This is precisely because the only world we can be sure of as it pertains to the text is the one the text places before us.[16] Most succinctly,

---

[12]Barth writes, "There is no difference of opinion with regard to the need of applying historical criticism as a prolegomenon to the understanding of the Epistle. So long as the critic is occupied in this preliminary work I follow him carefully and gratefully. So long as it is simply a question of establishing what stands in the text, I have never dreamed of doing anything else than sit attentively at the feet of such learned men as Jülicher, Lietzmann, Zahn, and Kühl, and also at the feet of their predecessors, Tholuck, Meyer, B. Weiss, and Lipsius" (Barth, *Romans*, 7).

[13]Barth, *Romans*, 6.

[14]Barth writes in the preface to the second edition, "Jülicher and Leitzmann [two of the most critical reviewers of Barth's *Römerbrief* and his "anti-historical" exegesis,] know far better than I do how insecure all this historical construction is, and upon what doubtful assumptions it often rests. Even such an elementary attempt at interpretation is not an exact science" (*Romans*, 8).

[15]Barth, *Romans*, 8.

[16]Barth, *Romans*, 6.

"Everything in the text ought to be interpreted only in the light of what can be said, and therefore only in the light of what is said."[17]

Third, there is clearly a dialectical relationship of the literal, historical, and grammatical sense with the theological sense of Scripture. The scientific interpretive method of the late nineteenth and early twentieth century largely recognized that the theological sense of Scripture was dependent on the literal, historical, grammatical sense of the text. It was not, however, largely recognized that the literal, historical, grammatical sense could be dependent on the theological sense.[18] By suggesting this, Barth did not mean that an individual passage's theological sense informed the literal, historical, or grammatical findings. Rather, he asserted that the Bible has one, single, indivisible subject matter—the revelation of God in Jesus Christ—thus making a theological claim about the text that is profoundly determinate for all of one's interpretation. The claims we make regarding what the text as a whole is about, whether knowingly or unknowingly, inform what we do with the literal, historical, and grammatical findings of individual texts. In other words, this pertained to the theological presuppositions brought to the text. As Burnett observes, and as we see Barth's lectures on John, "Barth's presupposition was that the Bible was about the self-revelation of God in Jesus Christ." Barth believed this because it was what "the Bible itself bore witness to." Therefore, "those who accuse Barth of imposing a dogmatic *a priori* on the Bible are wrong, . . . not because he does not read the Bible with dogmatic presuppositions, but because his dogmatic presuppositions, at least as he saw it, were established not in *a priori* but in an *a posteriori* fashion." That is to say, his presuppositions were established by what he read to be the subject matter of the text itself: the self-revelation of God in Jesus Christ. Barth admits that we do not know confidently that this is the subject matter of the text until the subject matter makes itself known. And yet we know that the self-revelation of God in Christ is *die Sache des Textes*—the theme of the text—because *Deus dixit*—God has spoken.[19]

---

[17]Barth, *Romans*, 8.

[18]Burnett, *Barth's Theological Exegesis*, 84-86. This remains a controversial notion in many schools of interpretation.

[19]Burnett, *Barth's Theological Exegesis*, 87; Werner G. Jeanrond, "Karl Barth's Hermeneutics," in *Reckoning with Barth: Essays in Commemoration of the Centenary of Karl Barth's Birth*, ed. Nigel Biggar (London: Mowbray, 1988), 90.

Fourth, Barth reads Scripture with the whole history of the church (including but not limited to Justin Martyr, Origen, Athanasius, the Chalcedonian Creed, Augustine, Luther, Calvin, Cocceius, *Synopsis Purioris Theologiae*, and Maresius). He exercises the same critical evaluation and appropriation of those in the tradition as he does of those in modern biblical studies. Barth writes his commentary in such a way that the text's agreement with the orthodox determinations of the early church almost comes *too* easily. And yet, his conclusions seem to be drawn on the basis of the text alone. It is as though the text's agreement with orthodox doctrines is an afterthought while all along the history of interpretation is informing his interpretive moves at every step. This is not because Barth is privileging a particular reading. Rather, he allows the text to speak and the commentary of the fathers to respond "Amen." The fierce christological battles of the fourth century fade into the background, not because they are forgotten, but because for Barth the text so evidently defends the orthodox conclusions that their arguments need not be rehashed. Barth writes in his commentary on John 1:1:

> The Logos, who is three times in this verse described with the definite article, seems perhaps to stand over against this He as a second He who is distinct from the first, but who partakes of the same nature and is thus identical in nature. This would be certain if, as must be shown, we had the exegetical right to assume that the Logos is indeed meant to be characterized as a He by the definite article. I need not say that in this case our position very definitely points us once again (we have already said something of the same relative to the *en archē ēn*) in the direction in which Nicea and the Athanasian Nicenes would later go with their doctrine of the homoousion, of the essential unity of the different persons or hypostases of the Father and the Son. . . . The thought reached with the third sentence in v. 1 is that the Logos can belong to God and can be in the beginning with God, not because he is the person who has the required nature, essence, or operation in the first instance, or, as we should say in the language of dogmatics, is in the mode of the eternal father, but because he is the second person, who as we should say, in the mode of the eternal Son shares the same nature with the person of the Father in the same dignity and perfection. *One must admit that the verse makes sense when it is read thus, with the eyes of what has been called orthodoxy since Nicea. Every word in it is then intelligible in its own place.*[20]

---

[20]Karl Barth, *Witness to the Word: A Commentary on John 1* (Eugene, OR: Wipf & Stock, 1986), 22, emphasis mine.

"Landing" on an Interpretation

Many have given accounts of Barth's interpretive method, and in most cases they follow Barth's own statement of a threefold method of observation (German *Beobachtung*; Latin *explicatio*), reflection (German *Nachdenken*; Latin *meditatio*), and appropriation (German *Aneigung*; Latin *applicatio*).[21] Observation is the task of determining what stands there in the text, investigating its historical references and context, the linguistic nuances in their cultural and temporal location, and the historical figure of the author himself.[22] Respect for Barth's tireless attention to these details in his lectures on John is inescapable.

Reflection, or *Nachdenken*, was an especially significant term for Barth in this process. It is to "rethink the thoughts of the text after it" in such a way that one comes face to face with subject matter of the text itself: the self-revelation of God in Jesus Christ.[23] Bruce McCormack puts it well when he writes that *Nachdenken* is "to penetrate through the text to the mystery which lies concealed within. Exegetes must think along with and after Paul, wrestling with his subject matter until they, too, are confronted by the same object (or Subject!) which once confronted Paul."[24]

Finally, appropriation, or *applicatio,* is the culmination of what is discovered as standing in the text (stage one) and the subject matter who has confronted the interpreter in stage two.[25] It is seeking to understand the text in light of the encounter with the subject matter. Stage three is our attempt to reproduce what we have heard from the Word in the words, in conformity with the grammatical and historical possibilities enumerated by stage one. McCormack explains that Barth's commentaries, as with much of his work, usually only provide us with the results of the third step. A book that included

---

[21]Gregory Bolich, *Karl Barth and Evangelicalism* (Downers Grove, IL: InterVarsity Press, 1980), 118-19; David Ford, *Barth and God's Story: Biblical Narrative and the Theological Method of Karl Barth in the Church Dogmatics* (Eugene, OR: Wipf & Stock, 1985), 24-25; Bruce McCormack, "Historical Criticism and Dogmatic Interest in Karl Barth's Theological Exegesis of the New Testament," in *Biblical Hermeneutics in Historical Perspective*, ed. Mark S. Burrows and Paul Rorem (Grand Rapids: Eerdmans, 1991), 327; Jeanrond, "Barth's Hermeneutics," 88-89.

[22]Barth, *Romans*, 7.

[23]Barth, *Romans*, 7. See also Burnett's excellent discussion of *Nachdenken* in *Barth's Theological Exegesis*, 58-59.

[24]McCormack, "Historical Criticism," 327-28.

[25]McCormack, "Historical Criticism," 328.

the entire interpretive process would be far too long and "unwieldy."[26] This, however, is not entirely the case with the lectures on John. Possibly because it is technically a series of lectures and not a commentary, we are privy to Barth's formal analysis of the best historical scholarship on offer at his time. This, too, is an advantage of engaging Barth's lectures on John: we are able to see when and how Barth makes use of such resources before he arrives at his "final stage" of interpretation.

McCormack makes the case that what links the "revelatory significance" (stage two) of the text to the "historical sense" of the text is Barth's use of the *analogia fidei*.[27] If we cannot make this connection, then the claim that Barth takes "historical-critical study seriously would be rendered hollow."[28] First, the *analogia fidei* is an event in which a human hears *in faith*—that is, hearing with a disposition of belief and trust. This disposition of belief and trust is given to the believer in the event of revelation. Second, in this event an analogical relationship is established between the Word of God and the human words in Scripture. It is an "analogical" relationship in that a *partial* similarity is established between the meaning of human language in its ordinary use and its meaning when adopted by God. Nevertheless, in this *analogia fidei*, God elects to conform our speech to God's speech about himself.[29] In short, the challenge of linking the revelatory significance with the historical sense of the text "is overcome in that God continually takes up the witness of the biblical writers and bears witness to himself in and through their witness."[30] McCormack is clear however, that "the analogy works strictly from above to below. It is not that the divine Word is like our human understanding of it; rather, human understanding is made to conform to the divine word."[31]

---

[26]"The first stage, in which he has listened to the results of the best historical work available, is something which has occurred behind the scenes" (McCormack, "Historical Criticism," 329).

[27]McCormack defines the *analogia fidei* in Barth most fundamentally as "a correspondence between an act of God and an act of the human subject . . . in the event of revelation, an analogical relationship is established between content of the divine speaking and the content of the human hearing in faith. The analogy works strictly from above to below. It is not that the divine Word is like our human understanding of it; rather, human understanding is made to conform to the divine word" (McCormack, "Historical Criticism," 331).

[28]McCormack, "Historical Criticism," 325.

[29]"The biblical language . . . is made to conform to God's speech about himself. It is not that God's speech conforms itself to this language" (McCormack, "Historical Criticism," 332).

[30]McCormack, "Historical Criticism," 332.

[31]McCormack, "Historical Criticism," 331.

METHOD AND MEANING: A DEMONSTRATION

There remains still the question of *meaning*: what does "meaning" mean in Barth's theological interpretation? Let us take Barth's commentary on the all-important John 1:4 as a demonstration: ἐν αὐτῷ ζωὴ ἦν, καὶ ἡ ζωὴ ἦν τὸ φῶς τῶν ἀνθρώπων. Barth's very first step is in the direction of the grammatical and the historical (the first key element of his interpretive methodology in the lectures). Specifically speaking, he undertakes to uncover the significance of John's move from ζωή in the first part of the verse to ἡ ζωή in the second. After scouring the breadth of John's writings for a similar grammatical transition, he concludes that the Logos is not being described as the personification of life as in John 11:25 and John 14:6. Rather, the material point arises from John 5:26, which speaks of the Father having life in himself and giving it to the Son to have life in himself also.[32] The Father is *the* source of resurrecting, everlasting life, and has given it to the Son to be a source of such life also.

Interestingly, it is only now, after these grammatical concerns have been cleared away, that Barth says, "Let us begin." This "beginning" is a consideration of this verse within the context of the prologue (the second key element of Barth's interpretive methodology: biblical and canonical context takes priority over historical context). He proposes that a new train of thought that is carried through the end of John 1:5 is being introduced here in John 1:4: "The life that was in the Logos is the light of men, and it shines in the darkness, but the darkness does not cease to be darkness. This is the point. By life, provisionally and very generally, redemption is meant, and by light revelation." Barth concedes that this interpretation undoubtedly requires some defense against "a whole flock of exegetes" (both modern and precritical: Augustine, Luther, Calvin, Schleiermacher, Holtzmann, Tholuck) who read John 1:4 as the response to the question of John 1:3: How can all things have come into being by the Logos?[33] On this reading, all things have come into being by the Logos in that the life that was in the Logos is the life that gives rise to all natural life. Barth evaluates these interpretations,

---

[32]Barth, *Witness*, 35. The most relevant comparison is with θρόνος and ὁ θρόνος of Rev 4:2. As with Rev 4:2, the definite article carries a demonstrative significance: "*This* life that dwells in the Logos, characterizes it, and is given to it, was as such . . . the light of men" (36, emphasis mine).
[33]Barth, *Witness*, 36.

granting that there is a possible link between the first part of John 1:4 and John 1:3. Nevertheless, he finds no other precedent in John's Gospel for understanding ζωή as the principle being that brings into existence other beings. He contends, "Always in the Gospel of John the term ζωή (with or without the addition αἰώνιος) has soteriological-eschatological significance." He adds, "ζωή in John's Gospel is not the life that is already in us or the world by creation; it is the new and supernatural life which comes to us in redemption and has first to be imparted to us in some way."[34] Barth cast doubt on the likelihood that John would intend a different meaning here in the prologue than it has in every other instance and even questions the methodology of allowing such an exception.[35]

If we are to look forward from John 1:4 to John 1:5 and not back to John 1:3, as Barth argues, then we have before us "the whole complex of reconciliation and revelation."[36] Having established that the Logos mediates God's creation of all things, John can now go on to demonstrate that ζωή and φῶς, redemptive life and revelation, also are mediated by the Logos alone. "This redemptive life, verse 4b explains, was (ἐν αὐτῷ, contained and offered in God's Word) the 'light of men,' the light of revelation which illumined them."[37]

The operative word for much of the prologue is the imperfect ἦν—*was*. This verb appears in this form in seven of the first fifteen verses of the prologue (Jn 1:1, 2, 4, 8, 9, 10, 15). As Barth handles the interpretation of this word throughout the prologue, he demonstrates the dialectic of the grammatical and theological senses of Scripture (the third key element of Barth's interpretive methodology in these lectures: the dialectical relationship of the literal, historical, and grammatical sense with the theological sense of Scripture). To be sure, the imperfect ἦν carries a particular tense, but as such,

---

[34]Barth, *Witness*, 39.

[35]"Is it really permissible to assume that precisely here we have an exception and that what is meant is the natural life that is lent by God to all creatures as such? Is it not more likely that precisely at the point where it occurs for the first time it has to be used in the pregnant sense that it bears in the rest of the Gospel?" Barth follows this discussion with a similar criticism of rendering φῶς as the natural light of reason over against the revelatory connotation that it carries everywhere else in the Gospel (Barth, *Witness*, 39).

[36]Barth, *Witness*, 40. Remarkably enough, Barth acknowledges that this conclusion has support in the findings of the uses of "life" and "light" in comparative religious studies but makes clear that this has very little to do with his reasoning for following in this direction.

[37]Barth, *Witness*, 40-41.

it is not self-interpreting and unequivocal in its meaning. Barth demonstrates how the meaning of ἦν throughout the prologue must be fleshed out
theologically if it is to do justice to the content communicated by the Evangelist in the prologue. It is accurate to translate the ἦν of John 1:1, "In the
beginning *was* the word, and the word *was* with God, and the word *was* God,"
but to truly do justice to the magnitude of the Evangelist's statement, we
must understand its bearing on the level of eternity and time. The ἦν of John
1:1 is an eternal ἦν, and therefore John's statement regarding the relationship
of the Logos to God only reaches its fullest sense when the ἦν of John 1:1 is
understood as communicating the coeternality of the λόγος and the θεός.[38]

The ἦν of John 1:4, 9 must be fleshed out theologically as well. In this case,
the theological context of these verses presses Barth in the direction of another possibility within the grammatical rules of the imperfect tense. As the
imperfect is used to speak about a past action that is in progress, the imperfect verb can carry a present sense if the action has continued into the
present.[39] That life *was* in him, that this light *was* the light of men (Jn 1:4),
and that the true light *was* coming into the world (Jn 1:9) does not preclude
that life *is* in him, that this light *is* the light of men, and that the true light *is*
coming into the world. Grammatically, the imperfect tense allows for ambiguity of interpretation on this point. For Barth, theology informs grammar
by clarifying such inherent ambiguities in language.[40] Therefore, theology
clarifies that this is not the eternal ἦν of John 1:1. It is the more complex imperfect that includes a present sense. For Barth, this is because these verses
speak of "the Word which *is* spoken from eternity into time, and which may
be heard in time with all the seriousness of eternity."[41] The announcement of
the Word's entry into history was more than simply the announcement of his
past physical arrival. It was a declaration of the inbreaking of eternity into
time, of revelation into nonrevelation, of light into darkness. For this reason,

---

[38]Barth, *Witness*, 41.
[39]Barth, *Witness*, 41.
[40]It was not that Barth chose to allow theology to inform his grammar in contrast to other exegetes
  who do not. Rather, Barth insists that we must be cognizant of the presuppositions which inevitably inform interpretive decisions at just such points as these. Barth is acknowledging that
  he is allowing the subject matter of the text—the self-revelation of God in Jesus Christ—to inform his reading of this ambiguity in the grammar. See Barth, *GD* 1:258-60; Burnett, *Barth's
  Theological Exegesis*, 84-87.
[41]Barth, *Witness*, 41.

grammar itself must be interpreted in light of its theological context, lest we fail to communicate the full magnitude of the Evangelist's witness.

Barth lands on his interpretation, indicating that it is the ἐν αὐτῷ that warrants the emphasis in this verse. Barth writes,

> What the author wants to say is that whatever was revelation, the light of life, redemption for men, was so only in him—again not directly or immediately from God . . . but in him, in the same Word that took flesh in Jesus Christ, alongside which there has never been or can be any other Word. In *him* was life, and *this* life was the light of men. . . . Wherever there was light, it was this light. Apart from him there is only witness to the light (v. 8).[42]

In the end, Barth commends Augustine's grasp of the Evangelist in his commentary on the phrase τὸ φῶς τῶν ἀνθρώπων: "John the Baptist was illumined by this light, and so was John the evangelist himself. He was full of this light who said: 'I am not the Christ, but he who comes after me.' . . . He was illumined by this light who said: 'In the beginning was the Word, and the Word was with God, and God was the Word.'" (This is the fourth key element of Barth's interpretive method in his lectures: reading with the whole history of the church).[43]

What then does it mean to be the "meaning" of the text? It is clear that for Barth, the grammatical-historical conclusions regarding the text are not its *meaning*, not least because these are merely the first step toward interpretation. It is equally clear that the meaning is not the analogies made between what John said then and what John says now. In fact, Barth intends rather to defend an identity between what John said then and what John says now. Whatever differences exist between the two are "purely trivial" as they pertain to "the spirit of the Bible, which is the Eternal Spirit."[44] Bruce McCormack has written that the Spirit was for Barth "the creative power of the Word itself that, when spoken, creates faith and obedience."[45] The meaning of Scripture then, was not only interpretation but also the production of faith and obedience in the reader by the Spirit of the Bible. The meaning of

---

[42]Barth, *Witness*, 43.
[43]Barth, *Witness*, 43-44; Augustine, *Tract*. 1.18.1.
[44]Barth, *Romans*, 1.
[45]Bruce McCormack, "The Significance of Karl Barth's Theological Exegesis of Philippians," in *Epistle to the Philippians*, 40th anniversary ed. (Louisville, KY: Westminster John Knox, 2002), xxi.

John 1:4 is not simply that the Word, as life and light, brings reconciliation and revelation. Its meaning is the production of faith in this Word as the one true Word who brings reconciliation and obedience to his revelation.[46]

CONCLUSION

George Hunsinger has famously written that Barth's theological method and practice might best be compared to examining a many-faceted crystal. With each turn of the crystal, Barth reflected on a new dimension of Christian dogmatics.[47] Such a comparison might be rightly made of Barth's hermeneutical method as well. Barth did not find the meaning of text at the end of a linear equation. Rather, the meaning came through reflection on the text from its many facets, and he drew nearer to his conclusions with each revolution. He begins with the grammar and language of the text itself. There he observes what possibilities from historical criticism lie within, or are restricted by, the Hebrew or Greek itself. This itself may entail many revolutions as Barth moves back and forth between theology, the text, and its interpreters. In each turn of the crystal Barth picks up or dispenses with their contributions as they either draw him closer to or further away from hearing the text's witness. In the midst of this circling, Barth brings in the master interpreters of the tradition—the Fathers, the Reformers, and the Protestant scholastics. These masters embody in themselves the hermeneutical dialectic of freedom and authority. They held themselves open to hear what the text had to say. The church has since affirmed that what they heard stands as an authority in our own exercise of this freedom before the Word.

---

[46]It might be said that I have identified the meaning of the text with its "significance" or the perlocutionary effect of language in speech-act theory, but it would at the very least be anachronistic to assign such terminology to Barth's method. See Michael Seaman, "The Indispensability of the Holy Spirit for Biblical Interpretation: A Proposal for the Concept of Transformative Illumination" (PhD diss., Southeastern Baptist Theological Seminary, 2010), 201-8; Kevin J. Vanhoozer, *Is There a Meaning in This Text?: The Bible, the Reader, and the Morality of Literary Knowledge*, 10th anniversary ed. (Grand Rapids: Zondervan, 2009), 427-29. Furthermore, it is not entirely clear that Barth is willing to make such a distinction between "meaning" and "significance" or "perlocutionary effect." At least for the *Erklärung*, if one stops short of the claim the text makes on the reader, it is not clear that one has understood the text at all.

[47]George Hunsinger, *How to Read Karl Barth: The Shape of His Theology* (New York: Oxford University Press, 1991), 28-29.

Theological exegesis for Barth was a constant turning of the crystal involving "a movement from text, to subject matter and back to text again."[48] Theological exegesis as a movement means it never comes to a permanent rest. It is a task that is never finished. For Barth, this is properly so as we do not possess the Spirit of the Bible, the Holy Spirit—it possesses us. Like a leaf that lands when the wind dies down, Barth may come to rest on an interpretation as he does throughout his lectures on John, but only to take flight again as the *pnuema* blows where it wants.[49] Where the Spirit of the Lord is, there is freedom.[50]

---

[48]McCormack, "Barth's Theological Exegesis of Philippians," xxi.

[49]"There is a spirit in the Bible that allows us to stop awhile and play among secondary things as is our wont—but presently it begins to press us on; and however we may object that we are only weak, imperfect, and most average folk, it presses us on to the primary fact, whether we will or no" (Barth, *Word of God*, 34).

[50]"With the mediacy of revelation the scripture principle of Protestantism also proclaims its immediacy. It speaks about scripture and the Spirit, about the Spirit in scripture. Where the Spirit is, there is freedom [2 Cor 3:17]. All freedoms have their source here. They also have their limit here. . . . The immediacy of God in which the Word sets us ends all false immediacies" (*GD* 1:262).

SIX

Illumination in Barth's Theological Interpretation of John

T HE TASK OF THEOLOGICAL INTERPRETATION as Barth performed it took on a definite form. First and foremost, it is evident
from the very beginning of Barth's lectures that as readers of this Gospel,
"We cannot and may not free ourselves from the fact that we are baptized,
that therefore the Gospel of John does not exist for us as other than a part
of the canonical scripture of the Christian church."[1] That is to say, as
Scripture it cannot be treated as other than a word spoken to us in the name
of God.[2] We read from the very beginning within a theological context of
baptism, church, and canon.[3] By defining this interpretive context or location, Barth is working to overcome what John Webster refers to as "one of
the primary commitments of hermeneutics after Spinoza, namely the association of textual inquiry with indeterminacy on the part of the reader."[4]
As located in the context of baptism, church, and canon, "the reader of John's
Gospel is determined by the fact that in this text, she finds herself addressed,
and that this address is constitutive of, not accidental to, both the text and
the reader's situation."[5] In addition to the determination of this theological
context of the reader, Barth's theological interpretation is considerably

[1]Karl Barth, *Witness to the Word: A Commentary on John 1* (Eugene, OR: Wipf & Stock, 1986), 4.
[2]Barth, *Witness*, 4.
[3]John Webster, "Witness to the Word: Karl Barth's Lectures on the Gospel of John," in *The Domain of the Word* (New York: T&T Clark, 2012), 73.
[4]Webster, "Witness," 72.
[5]Webster, "Witness," 72.

informed by a notion that as readers we carry on the witness to that which is first witnessed in the text. That is to say, the heavy emphasis on the motif of "witness" for the nature of Scripture as witness to the Word does not end with the Evangelist. Faithful theological interpretation is listening to the text's humanity *and* to its divinity, and thereby becoming a faithful witness to the Word within the words.

JOHN 1:1-18

As Barth takes up the prologue to John's Gospel, he dedicates over a third of his 398 pages of lectures to these eighteen verses. However, in his extensive engagement with the prologue, there is one theme that runs from beginning to end. More precisely, there are a pair of concepts that run inseparably alongside one another: the Word of God as life and light (Jn 1:4). As he explores the defining nature of these two concepts for John's understanding of the Word, Barth also finds that life and light encompass the relationships of grace and truth, incarnation and illumination, reconciliation (or redemption) and revelation.[6]

As noted in chapter five above, Barth makes the exegetical decision that ζωή refers to a soteriological-eschatological notion rather than a creative and creation-sustaining notion of life. This conclusion is based on John's larger, theological use of ζωή throughout the rest of the narrative. Barth draws a similar conclusion regarding light: "I have still to find in John a passage in which light is the light which is present by creation, which is given in and with the light of creation . . . which does not rather come only with the life of redemption, which is not the light of revelation, which perhaps comes from the very beginning but still comes."[7] All of this works to unveil the robust and multifaceted nature of the relationship we begin to explore now—the relationship between life and light and thus also, between incarnation and illumination, reconciliation and revelation.

John 1:1-5. "In the beginning was the Word, and the Word was with God, and God was the Word. He was in the beginning with God. Everything was

---

[6]There is no dearth of evidence to defend this conclusion (Barth, *Witness*, 36). In a collection of his reflections titled *Christmas* (Edinburgh: Oliver and Boyd, 1959), Barth writes, "The meaning of 'Grace and Truth' can best be understood as a parallel to 'Life' and 'light' (= salvation and Revelation) in v. 4f" (16).

[7]Barth, *Witness*, 39.

made by him, and without him nothing that is was made. In him was life, and this life was the light of men" (Barth's translation).[8] In the midst of Barth's meticulous grammatical and theological exegesis of the prologue, he writes, "God's self-revealing is a separate action that goes beyond creation. … φῶς is a new and different light which is only arising. It is the light of dawn, not the full light of eternity already present."[9] The temptation, Barth suggests, is to correlate life with creation and light with human reason. But read in context, this does not do justice to the "light coming" of John 1:9. That is, "it does not do justice to the strict character of revelation as φῶς ἐρχόμενον."[10]

This unveils an important finding in from Barth's exegesis of the prologue. The conclusions that ζωή looks forward to redemption (not backward to creation) and that φῶς refers to revelation (not human reason) are inseparable for Barth. This is because for Barth ζωή and φῶς are not concepts or ideas, ζωή and φῶς are a person, ὁ λόγος.[11] Φῶς ἐρχόμενον suggests something new is arriving, breaking in; something not previously available. That is not creation or human reason, but reconciliation and revelation communicated by God himself in ὁ λόγος. Barth understands all talk of life and light in John's Gospel as first and foremost the exposition of a person, not of concepts. Though this seems obvious as a text narrating the life of Jesus Christ, Barth is concerned that reading will quickly devolve into the exposition of concepts and their meaning. Instead, Barth is first concerned with readers being encountered by *die Sache*—the subject matter of the text— himself. The prologue introduces the reader to the subject matter—Jesus Christ as the self-revelation of God. The remainder of the Gospel narrate a series of encounters with this life and light *in Jesus* in order that the reader herself might encounter the life and light in this text. "This," Barth writes, "is the radical procedure of the Gospel." The Gospel of John draws us to it in order to point us to the Lord.[12] Exegesis that does not take us to this level

---

[8]Scripture quotations labeled "Barth's translation" are from Geoffrey Bromiley's translation of Barth's German translation from the Greek (see Barth, *Witness*, 11-12).

[9]Barth, *Witness*, 40; *Erklärung*, 48.

[10]Barth, *Witness*, 40.

[11]Barth, *Erklärung*, 34. He grounds this conclusion in his grammatical exegesis of the text itself, but finds support for this way of reading it in the other commentators (Zahn, Schlatter, Thurneysen, etc.).

[12]"The Johannine prologue is not dealing with the general situation of humanity vis-à-vis revelation. It is dealing concretely with the question of the situation that arises when we hear a witness

of confrontation with the text has not done the work of exegesis but only the work of preparing for it.

Barth spends a great deal of time working out the ontological dimensions of the relationship between ὁ λόγος and ὁ θεὸς, and consequently the trinitarian significance of John 1:1-3. While it is unnecessary to go into the minutia of Barth's discussion of these matters, his conclusions do provide important groundwork regarding the relationship of light and life, revelation and redemption, illumination and incarnation. His key conclusions are as follows. First, Barth concludes that the Logos is "as" God. In other words, the Logos is of the same nature as God.[13] Second, the prologue identifies two distinct persons—that is, in terms of the persons of the Trinity.[14] Third, the Logos, who functioned in beginning as agent of creation, is now agent of revelation and redemption.[15] Fourth and finally, as the Logos is that through which all things are made (Jn 1:3), there is no immediacy to God in creation except that of the Logos. This for Barth is not so much a negative statement about creation so much as it is a positive attribution to the Logos.[16]

"And the light shines in the darkness, and the darkness has not comprehended it" (Jn 1:5, Barth's translation). In John 1:5 we encounter for the first time opposition to the light: the light shining in the darkness. In Barth's language, light shining in the darkness is revelation confronting nonrevelation.[17] Barth contests any notion of a dualism between light and darkness in John and poses rather that no origin of darkness is given.[18] In fact, Barth

---

to revelation, when we lift up our eyes to the hills from which our help comes, and yet when we can expect only help from the Lord who made heaven and earth. . . . More plainly than anywhere else in the Bible except in the parallel 1 John 1-4, which is probably by the same author or from the same circle, we are told here what the Bible is, namely, witness to revelation both in relation to revelation and yet also in distinction from it. What might at first seem to be exegetically very remote in the passage from Augustine is in fact typically [*typisch*] Johannine. There is said in it by way of introduction something which has to be said by way of introduction to the exposition of all biblical books as such: the great Yes and No with which these books call us to themselves only to point us to the Lord, as the Baptist pointed his disciples. This is the radical procedure of the Gospel, or at least a distinctive example of it" (Barth, *Witness*, 18; *Erklärung*, 20-22).

[13]Barth, *Witness*, 19-22.
[14]Barth, *Witness*, 28-29.
[15]Barth, *Witness*, 70-71.
[16]Barth, *Witness*, 34.
[17]"*Offenbarung steht gegenüber einem Nichtoffenbarsein*" (Barth, *Witness*, 45; *Erklärung*, 54).
[18]"It has been noted, and quite correctly, that John does not explain why revelation is revelation in the darkness. He has given no origin for this opponent of revelation. He has set it in no rela-

suggests that for John, the riddle of the origin of darkness is a "meaningless question." What matters for John is darkness' reality as it is confronted by light.[19] Moreover, darkness does not only contend against light but also life. Therefore, the coordination of light and life is reflected here also in that which opposes it. Darkness (σκοτία) is the atmosphere out of which Jesus' disciples are called (Jn 8:12; 12:35; 1 Jn 2:11). As Barth reads John, the greatest threat to the ζωή brought by the Logos is not death but darkness. Barth concludes, "This incident [darkness] on the one side and the Word of the revelation of life on the other are what the Evangelist finds to be the determinations of human existence." That is to say, they cannot be held at arm's length and reflected on impartially. This is a conflict within which the Evangelist himself is embroiled. Revelation and darkness are not concepts or "world principles"; they are competing armies approaching from the east and the west.[20]

All of this sets Barth up for what he really wants to argue that this verse is about: the confrontation of the Logos with an entire world caught in an atmosphere of darkness. He writes, "The true point of v. 5 is to make a further statement about the role and significance of the Logos. *The light shines in the darkness. Its revelation means antithesis, conflict, strife. To be the light of men is to stand against a world of enemies.*"[21] The light of the world is alone among humanity, because humanity is caught in the darkness of the world.

Finally, that ἡ σκοτία αὐτὸ οὐ κατέλαβεν means for Barth that the darkness "had no power to appropriate" the light, "to make it its own, to cease to be darkness and itself to become light." A theme is beginning to take form here that ripples throughout the Gospel. Darkness cannot make itself light, nor even make itself capable of *receiving* the light—only those born of God can receive the light (Jn 1:12-13).[22] To put it another way, Barth concludes that, in terms of revelation, the Word creates its own hearers. What confronts humanity is darkness. Even when light pierces the darkness there

---

tion to the πάντα δι' αὐτοῦ, either by explaining that it is an exception, that it has its own genesis, or by explaining that it is included, that evil falls within God's plan for the world. The question of its origin is neither posed nor answered" (Barth, *Witness*, 45).

[19] Barth, *Witness*, 45.

[20] Barth, *Witness*, 46.

[21] Barth, *Witness*, 46, emphasis mine.

[22] Barth, *Witness*, 47.

must also be some receptivity in humanity that corresponds to this light. But this receptivity likewise is an impossibility on the side of humanity alone. Hope begins to emerge, however, with the one we encounter in John 1:6-8, John the Baptist.

John 1:6-8. "There was a man sent from God who was called John. He came for witness, to bear witness to the light, that all might come to faith through him. He was not the light but bore witness to the light" (Barth's translation). Hope begins to emerge with this man John, not because he was the light, but because he bore witness to the light. He bore witness to the light in such a way that those who could not receive the light might come to faith through him.[23] The category of μαρτυρία is profound because of the mediatory imagery it possesses and affords for Barth. There is a turning that takes place in mediation, a change of direction, in μαρτυρία reception becomes reflection (of light).

John sets out clearly what the Baptist's mission is, namely, that others believe through him. It is noteworthy that we see this not only with John the Baptist but also the woman at the well, who upon receiving and believing, goes to the people of her entire town, who then believe on account of her words.[24] The distinction Barth is after is that with witnesses something or someone else is known or believed through them. With Jesus, "the Gospel never says anyone believes 'through' Jesus but always that people believe or do not believe εἰς αὐτὸν or αὐτῷ."[25]

The power of the μαρτυρία imagery is that it contains within itself the necessity of another, of one more foundational, more significant, more "necessary." It contains within itself a notion of dependency. As μαρτυρία, the story of John the Baptist is bound up with the larger narrative of the φῶς ἐρχόμενον εἰς τὸν κόσμον. In this way, Barth reconciles the abrupt interjection of the Baptist in John 1:6 with the larger narrative of the prologue. The introduction of the Baptist is not an interruption to the narrative, but a proper introduction to the what is about to unfold in John 1:9 and following—that is, the light coming into the world.

---

[23]Barth will go on to contend for a similarity of meaning between receiving (παραλαμβάνω) the light and coming to faith.

[24]"This at once sets the Baptist alongside the Samaritan woman, of whom it is said in 4:41f. that many come to believe through her word" (Barth, *Witness*, 51).

[25]Barth, *Witness*, 51.

John 1:9-13.
He was coming into the world as the true light that lightens everyone. He was
in the world, and the world was made by him, and the world knew him not.
He came to his own home and his own people did not receive him. But those
who did receive him, to them he gave the power to become the children of God,
even to those who believed in his name. These were not born of blood, nor of
the will of the flesh, nor of the will of a man, but of God. (Barth's translation)

With John 1:9 we come to one of the most pertinent verses to our topic: Ἦν
τὸ φῶς τὸ ἀληθινὸν, ὃ φωτίζει πάντα ἄνθρωπον, ἐρχόμενον εἰς τὸν κόσμον.
"He was coming into the world as the true light that lightens everyone."
Grammatically and theologically, there are three immediately pressing questions for Barth. The first question is whether it is τὸ φῶς τὸ ἀληθινόν or
πάντα ἄνθρωπον who was coming into the world. Second, what does
ἀληθινός ("true") mean in this context? Third and closely related, what does
it mean to be τὸ φῶς τὸ ἀληθινόν?

As for the first question, Barth makes the case for a reading along the lines
of "the light was coming into the world."[26] In this case, John is making use
of the periphrastic imperfect, which is not foreign to the author's work (cf.
Jn 1:28; 3:23; 10:40).[27] Furthermore, "'coming into the world' is constantly in
this Gospel a function of the light or of Jesus."[28] Therefore, Barth translates,
"The true light, which lights every man, was coming into the world." In this
construction, John 1:9 is a self-contained and complete sentence in itself.

Regarding the second question about the meaning of ἀληθινός, Barth
offers four options for consideration: (1) "genuine," as distinct from false,
imitative, or only apparently corresponding to the concept; (2) close to or

---

[26]Barth acknowledged that there are scholars including Schlatter and E. Schwartz who hold with
what Barth calls the "understanding of older exegesis," a view in which the subject of Jn 1:9 lies
outside of the present verse. It reads along the lines of Luther's translation: "that was the true
light that lights all men that come into this world" (Barth, *Witness*, 59).

[27]"An anarthrous participle can be used with a verb of being (such as εἰμὶ or ὑπάρχω) to form a
finite verbal idea. This participle is called periphrastic because it is a *roundabout* way of saying
what could be expressed by a single verb. As such, it more naturally corresponds to English: ἦν
ἐσθίων means *he was eating*, just as ἤσθιεν does." Daniel B. Wallace, *Greek Grammar Beyond the
Basics: An Exegetical Syntax of the New Testament* (Grand Rapids: Zondervan, 1996), 647. Also,
Harvey Eugene Dana and Julius R. Mantey note, "The periphrastic imperfect is the form [of
periphrastic construction] most common in the New Testament." *A Manual Grammar of the
Greek New Testament* (New York: Macmillan, 1957), 231.

[28]Barth, *Witness*, 60.

coincident with ἀληθής, that is, "related to or filled with the truth," "belonging to the realm of truth," (3) "reliable," "credible;" (4) "true" in the sense of the reality that has only an original and not a copy.[29] By comparison with other passages in John where the term is used, Barth concedes that each of these meanings is present somewhere in the Gospel. In this case, Barth ultimately opts for the fourth possibility.[30] This conclusion is in agreement with Calvin, who writes, "There is no other source or cause of its brightness anywhere. And so he calls Him the true light whose own nature is to be light."[31] Barth adds, "Light in heaven and earth always receives its radiance from elsewhere. But Christ is the light which shines of itself and then fills the whole world with *its* radiance."[32]

Barth then goes on to makes points particularly informative for our discussion. He writes of John 1:9, "Not just an *activity* but an *effect* of light is meant here. It illumines men, it fills them with light, it sets them in the light." From John 1:6-8 to John 1:9 the Evangelist moves from the indirect light of revelation in μαρτυρία to the light of revelation itself. The answer to Barth's third question, then, is that τὸ φῶς τὸ ἀληθινόν is "the *original, uncreated, primary light*, the direct and immediate revelation of life that bears witness to itself."[33]

But what is to be made of the light's illumination of πάντα ἄνθρωπον? Barth quotes J. A. Bengel, "*Quisquis illuminatur, ab hac luce illuminatur*" ("Whosoever is enlightened at all, is enlightened by this Light").[34] Barth explains, "It is in this restrictive sense that we are to take the πάντα, after the analogy of the πάντες of v. 7—that all might come to faith through him.

---

[29]Barth, *Witness*, 60-61.

[30]Barth, *Witness*, 61. Barth's deduction goes as follows: "There can be no question here of opposition to a false or imitation light, for John the Baptist is not regarded as such. The meaning 'related to the truth' is so general that its colorlessness and abstractness make a strange impression in this verse. The sense 'reliable' or 'trustworthy' fits well enough if the thought of the illumination of men by the light is the real point of the statement. But from what we have just said it is not" (Barth, *Witness*, 61). The real point, Barth will argue, is the coming of the Light into the world.

[31]John Calvin, *The Gospel According to St. John 1–10*, trans. T. H. L. Parker, vol. 4 (Grand Rapids: Eerdmans, 1979), 14; Barth, *Witness*, 61.

[32]Barth, *Witness*, 61.

[33]Barth, *Witness*, 61.

[34]Johann Albrecht Bengel, *Gnomon Novi Testamenti: In Quo Ex Nativa Verborum vi Simplicitas, Profunditas, Concinnitas, Salubritas Sensuum Coelestium Indicatur*, 2nd ed., vol. 1 (Tübingen, 1860), 360; Barth, *Witness*, 61.

Everyone who receives light receives it from this source."[35] Τὸ φῶς τὸ ἀληθινόν would not be a faculty of the human mind but a person, and the enlightenment John 1:9 is not a gift granted to humanity at birth but the true light's gracious self-giving in revelation—a gift granted in rebirth. It is a gift that is given not of blood, nor of the will of the flesh, nor of the will of man, but of God. Here in John, and thus also in Barth, we hear the correlation of illumination with imagery of birth and childbearing: "To those who did receive him, to them he gave the power to become the children of God" (Jn 1:12, Barth's translation).

Conversely, the restricting of τὸ φῶς τὸ ἀληθινόν is a function of ὁ λόγος not being at home in ὁ κόσμος. The image is one of hospitality. As ὁ λόγος has come from afar and journeyed to them, so "they ought to receive him willingly and joyfully as one who is at home with them. For they themselves belong originally to him."[36] That they do not know him is "absurd" to Barth. Though the world belongs to him (οἱ ἴδιοι αὐτὸν) it neither knows him nor receives him: "It does not hear and receive the Word in such a way that faith and obedience are found in it."[37] John 1:11 leaves us with the unresolved question, why not?

John 1:12-13 offers an initial answer: the world does not hear and receive *yet*. Those who are born of God do not accomplish this end themselves. Rather, where the light shines and is received—where the divine word is spoken and heard—those who receive and are born of God do so by the ἐξουσία given to them.[38] That there are those who see or hear and believe demonstrates that ultimately the world cannot close itself off to the light and the Word. Light and darkness stand in a "highly unequal if just as highly incomprehensible conflict."[39] Barth concludes, "The divine effected existence of believers replies that the world cannot [close itself to the Word], that the Word is mightier than the world. But only the existence of believers, and

---

[35]Barth, *Witness*, 61.

[36]Barth, *Witness*, 67.

[37]Barth, *Witness*, 68.

[38]"The opposition, the inconceivable fact that the world is closed to the Word and its light, is not a final insight in the framework of the presentation . . . there has also to be said the further and positive thing which comes into the world like a miracle, the inconceivable reality which finally and definitively confounds it, namely, that he gives to some the possibility of becoming the children of God" (Barth, *Witness*, 69).

[39]Barth, *Witness*, 70.

this only as divinely effected, makes this reply."[40] This is the answer to the question implied by John 1:11.

Possibly one of Barth's greatest contributions to this project is the extended reflection he gives to the concepts of γινώσκειν, "to know" (Jn 1:10); λαμβάνειν, "to receive or accept" (Jn 1:11, 12); and πιστεύειν, "to believe" (Jn 1:12). First, λαμβάνειν, both in John and in the rest of the New Testament, "is a regular expression for the willing and responsive acceptance of Jesus, his Word, or his Spirit. It acquires its special emphasis here from the fact that it is parallel to the γινώσκειν of v. 10" (cf. Jn 3:11, 27, 32-33; 5:43; 7:39; 12:49; 13:20).[41] The world that did not know him did not receive him. At the same time, we must understand λαμβάνειν by γινώσκειν.

> The revelation of redemptive life demands that people be open, that they be ready for perception; the light that shines demands an eye that sees, the spoken Word demands receptivity, reason. This *receptive knowing* is what is denoted by λαμβάνειν. To receive the Word is to let it apply to oneself. Thus λαμβάνειν leads from γινώσκειν to πιστεύειν.[42]

For someone to receive (λαμβάνειν) is to "recognize and treat revelation as something that is meant for them and directed to them."[43] The point here is to "appropriate the Word." In this context Barth offers a profoundly relevant breakdown of these concepts vis-à-vis illumination. He writes, "γινώσκειν is enlightenment [*Erleuchtetwerden*], πιστεύειν is brightness [*Hellsein*], and λαμβάνειν is the aptness [*Geeignetsein*] of the subject for both these experiences, which cannot be distinguished chronologically."[44]

This coordination of knowledge, reception, and belief clarifies two aspects of Barth's notion of illumination here. First, as stated, it indicates that for Barth knowledge and faith are chronologically indistinguishable. They may be logically distinguished, but the movement from revealed knowledge to faith cannot be distinguished in time. What can be said is that revealed

---

[40]Barth, *Witness*, 70.

[41]Barth, *Witness*, 71.

[42]Barth, *Witness*, 71, emphasis mine.

[43]To receive is to "recognize and treat revelation as something that is meant for them and directed to them, in which they let themselves be found by it, realizing that they can do no other, that they have already been found by it" (Barth, *Witness*, 71).

[44]Barth, *Witness*, 71.

knowledge is *logically* prior to faith.[45] In this moment there is (1) revelation, (2) illumination, (3) reception, and (4) faith. When one comes to know the divine light in (1) revelation there is (2) illumination of the individual; those who (3) receive this knowledge are those who respond in (4) belief. That there is faith presupposes there is something in which to have faith. In this case, it is a knowledge and understanding of the person of Jesus Christ. Faith is the observable manifestation of illumination. Faith is the brightness of a lamp which testifies to its illumination. Therefore, for Barth in the moment of conversion *faith is indicative of knowledge, yet indistinguishable from the event of coming to know.* For those who receive, the inception of their brightness cannot be distinguished from the event of their illumination, even as the brightness presupposes their illumination.

Second, although Barth situates λαμβάνειν—receiving—between "or comprehensively above" knowledge and faith, he does not open the door for a revelation of knowledge without resulting faith or an illumination without its consequent brightness. Λαμβάνειν does not stand between them as a door which may be locked. Rather, receiving stands between illumination and brightness as a threshold, the entryway of a home. For those who have received, the Word has not only come into the world but has come to them.[46] In their reception, their hospitality to revelation, revelation has found a home—it has "tabernacled" among its own.

The inevitable question that follows is, how? Barth asks it this way, "Although they are in the world and are themselves the world, they do something that the world and others who are in it do not do; they receive the Word as though they were not in the world. . . . How do they come to do it?" The answer comes in John 1:12: ἔδωκεν αὐτοῖς ἐξουσίαν. At this point Barth translates ἐξουσία very generally as "possibility." As they received him, "he gave them the *possibility* τέκνα θεοῦ γενέσθαι. . . . they are put in a position in which they may become God's children."[47] The emphasis here is not on their ability to become children of God, as though it were in their power to

---

[45]McCormack has made infamous use of this distinction with reference to the logical relationship of God's election to the triunity of God. This use of the distinction here, however, is not based on or related to the conclusions that McCormack has drawn regarding God's election and triunity. *Orthodox and Modern: Studies in the Theology of Karl Barth* (Grand Rapids: Baker Academic, 2008), 192.

[46]Barth, *Witness*, 71-72.

[47]Barth, *Witness*, 72, emphasis mine.

be something that no one in all the κόσμος can be (Jn 1:10-11). Rather, the emphasis is on "the fact that the Word *gave* them the possibility of being something—the children of God—and of doing what is in keeping with this—receiving the Word and believing in his name."[48]

To receive him is an event that takes place explicitly as they are given this authority to do so (Jn 1:12).[49] In the language of John's prologue, it is the event of light adopting darkness. There are those in the world who are being given a right to be called children of God, ones who could not claim to be such apart from this ἐξουσία. No one can "take this ἐξουσία to themselves. They must be given it" from the Word, the Son. This right, authority, legitimacy "of the ὅσοι to be children of God is thus enclosed and grounded in the Son."[50] Barth clarifies:

> But let us consider what it means that it is the Word that gives the ὅσοι that ἐξουσία. If the children of God are the λαμβάνοντες or later the πιστεύοντες, and if it is the Word that gives them the right to be God's children, this obviously means that the Word himself is the authority by which the λαμβάνοντες and πιστεύοντες are what they have to be as such. As the Word is spoken to them, they are addressed and called. The Word gives them a new essential character, his own character. Their action becomes a grasping of the Word, their attitude a Yes to it. Their ἐξουσία to be God's children lies in this gift, this self-giving of the Word. They are oriented to it. We see then that the Word creates its own hearers. It is not at all that they are already there as λαμβάνοντες and πιστεύοντες, and for this reason can become God's children. They are not there! σκοτία is there and not the ἐξουσία for this existence. The cosmos is there, ἄνθρωποι are there, *unfaithful* ἴδιοι, who do not understand themselves as such, are there. Into this non-being the light comes.[51]

In this we hear Barth's dictum that "the Word is subject and not object in this action." That is, "the Word convinces, converts, forces and decides . . .

---

[48]Barth, *Witness*, 73. Barth does go on to narrow his translation of *exousia* away from the sense of *dynamis* (power, might strength) and in the direction of *axousis* (authority, legitimation, right). All who are by nature of the world, of the darkness into which the light shines (Jn 1:5) become what they cannot be, children of God, because they are "authorized, legitimated, given a right to be able to do this. Without the corresponding ἐξουσία no one can be a child of God" (Barth, *Witness*, 73).

[49]Barth, *Witness*, 71.

[50]Barth, *Witness*, 73-74.

[51]Barth, *Witness*, 74.

[and so,] *gratitude* is the last and deepest thing with which such people can grasp their existence." Their existence is as those within the self-enclosed circle of revelation "into which one cannot leap from outside."[52] Nevertheless, that they are receivers of the Word is as axiomatic as the givenness of the Word itself.[53] The giving of the Word and the creation of its receivers operate much like the movement of knowledge and belief discussed above—two aspects of a single event.[54] Although one aspect (the giving of the Word) is logically prior, the other (the reception of the Word) cannot be chronologically distinguished. As the Word is given, so the ὅσοι are given the right and authority to be, and are made, τέκνα θεοῦ.[55] Barth summarizes his conclusions eloquently and brings them closely in line with the concepts of this project, illumination and regeneration:

> It's point [v. 13] is that those who receive and believe v. 12 confront their own existence as such as a miracle, a creation of God, from their own standpoint a new birth, the beginning of a new existence. The truth of their own existence, which has been initiated for them by the Word which per se convinces, converts and compels, is a miracle, a creation, a new birth.[56]

John 1:14-18.

And the Word became flesh and dwelt among us, and we beheld his glory, a glory as of an only begotten of his Father, of one who is full of grace and truth. John bears witness to him, and cries and says: This was he of whom I said, he who comes after me surpasses me, for he was above me from the very first. Of his fullness we have all received grace for grace. The law was given by Moses, but grace and truth through Jesus Christ. No one has ever seen God, but the only-begotten, God, who was in the bosom of the Father, he has manifested him. (Barth's translation)

---

[52]Barth, *Witness*, 75.

[53]"There are in the world ὅσοι who receive the Word. John starts with this fact, which is just as axiomatic for him as the givenness of the Word" (Barth, *Witness*, 75).

[54]Barth writes, "It would rather say that πιστεύοντες . . . is one side of the matter that is present in and with the event of ἔλαβον. The other side of the matter is to be expressed in some way with a reference to γινώσκειν" (*Witness*, 78).

[55]"It is not what the ὅσοι are or do, but what is done for them in their relation to the Word. Their right to be God's children is absolutely given to them. They are miraculously born, as v. 13 adds. Can this gift have its presupposition in what they do, in their λαμβάνειν and πιστεύειν, and not the reverse?" (Barth, *Witness*, 79).

[56]Barth, *Witness*, 82-83.

The indivisibility of incarnation and illumination. In John 1:14 illumination and incarnation emerge as defining categories in Barth's reading of John. In Barth's summary of what we know of ὁ λόγος from the prologue, he includes that ὁ λόγος "is the creative Word before all things, and it carries the redemption whose light illumines men even in their darkness." Barth will go on to announce,

> If there is a shining of light, a coming of light into the World, a witness to it; if there can be a giving to real people, living in the world, of ἐξουσία to be God's children; if there can be real people to receive and believe the Word, it is because the Word is not just the divine Word, the Word of the beginning, the superior Word, the epitome of creation and redemption, but because as all these things the Word is also flesh, as all these things the Word is also what we are, how we are, on the way to us, accessible to us. For this reason, his revelation of life is no mere idea but reality.[57]

As mentioned, this is the paradox of immediacy to God being mediated in the Word of God. The beauty of John 1:14 is that alongside of all things *coming* into existence through him, alongside of the *coming* of John, alongside of the be*coming* of those who now have ἐξουσία to be God's children, ὁ λόγος comes as well.

> The divine, creative, redeeming, revealing Word, whose sovereign being and action vv. 1-13 depicted, has left his throne, comes down to the level where creatures are, where the witness is, where the called are, takes his place in their ranks, loses himself as it were among all that and those who might have been the objects of his action, and himself becomes an object. He, the Logos, is there as something or someone else is there.[58]

In his typical word by word fashion, Barth draws out to the fullest his explanation of καὶ ὁ λόγος σὰρξ ἐγένετο. He gives particular attention to the primacy and superiority of ὁ λόγος in relation to σὰρξ.[59] At the same time

---

[57]Barth, *Witness*, 89.

[58]Barth, *Witness*, 87.

[59]"Yet one cannot emphasize too strongly the *superiority* of the Word over the flesh that it assumes, which is obviously Schlatter's concern. The *Word* speaks, the *Word* acts, the *Word* reveals, the *Word* redeems. The *Word* is Jesus, the I that will alone speak for long stretches in the Gospel. Certainly the *incarnate* Word. Hence, not without the flesh but in the flesh, through the flesh, as flesh. Yet the *Word*! One should not ignore the sovereign emphasis that falls on this first member of the equation after all that has preceded. Otherwise one hopelessly destroys what John is seeking to say" (Barth, *Witness*, 91).

he speaks to the necessity of σὰρξ, and the absolute uniqueness, incomparability, and singularity of this ἐγένετο. Of particular relevance is the necessity of σὰρξ. Although the Word is the Word before it assumes flesh, the Word becoming flesh is the Word in its revelation.[60] By σὰρξ, the light of the of the Word becomes visible to the dim eyes of humanity.

> God's Word in the concealment in which it was in the beginning, in which it was with God and was God, God's Word in the form of an angel or finally in the form of a man who by nature stands on the far side of the darkness in which we ourselves stand—all this might be God's Word but it would not be God's Word as his revelation of life to us. As such it could be light in itself but it would not shine for us or come as light into the real world. There could be no witness to it. It could mediate no ἐξουσία. By definition it would not be the object of human λαμβάνειν and πιστεύειν.[61]

But the question remains, why must the Word become flesh in order for us to see its light? Though there is a mixing of metaphors—sight and hearing—Barth understands σὰρξ as the necessary medium of conversation for revelation. For God to embody flesh is for God to speak our language, as it were: "The σὰρξ is a means of dialogue."[62] However, the σὰρξ is only the medium, it is not the content.

> The so-called historical Jesus, abstracted from the action of the Word, is not revelation. The revelatory power and effect of the predicate σὰρξ stands or falls with the action of the subject ὁ λόγος. Revelation is nowhere and never the work of the σὰρξ as such, not even of the σὰρξ of Christ. It is totally the work of the Logos that has become σὰρξ.[63]

John 1:14b reveals the Evangelist's point of reference for revelation. Ἐσκήνωσεν (from σκηνόω) typically translated "dwelt," carries the idea of pitching a tent.[64] Consequently, it brings to mind the Old Testament tabernacle where God made his dwelling "among men." Barth adds,

> What is said afterward about seeing the δόξα of the Logos points us convincingly in the same direction. Δόξα, the manifestation of God's glory, points to

---

60"That the Word became *flesh* is its revelation" (Barth, *Witness*, 90).

61Barth, *Witness*, 90.

62Barth, *Witness*, 93.

63Barth, *Witness*, 92.

64Joseph Henry Thayer et al., *A Greek-English Lexicon to the New Testament* (Boston: Hastings, 1896), 169.

the Hebrew *kabod*, power and dominion, but also the fullness of light, the *shekinah*, which takes its name from its hovering or dwelling or enthroning between the cherubim above the ark of the covenant, and which constitutes the concept of the σκηνή, of the tabernacle of God on earth. When John speaks immediately afterward about this δόξα, we have to assume that in the σκηνοῦν he was thinking very positively of God's solemn taking up of his dwelling among men in this way.[65]

Barth finds expression for the nature of ὁ λόγος σὰρξ ἐγένετο in Hebrews 9, which summarizes the use of the Old Testament tabernacle and its place in the old covenant. Hebrews 9:9 describes the tabernacle of the old covenant as a παραβολή, a symbol or illustration of the greater and more perfect tabernacle in Christ. In this sense, Barth identifies the dwelling of the Logos among us as fulfillment.

But in another way, Barth also understands this dwelling to be a promise. It is the anticipation of the new heaven and the new earth, the new Jerusalem, where God will σκηνώσει—tabernacle, be at home, take up permanent dwelling—among mortals. John writes, "And I heard a loud voice from the throne saying, 'See, the home [ἡ σκηνὴ;] of God is among mortals. He will dwell [σκηνώσει] with them; they will be his peoples, and God himself will be with them'" (Rev 21:3). In this way, this σκηνόω is both fulfillment and promise.

Barth concludes that in terms of fulfillment "to dwell" is the more fitting translation, but in terms of promise "tabernacle" is best. Consequently, Barth lands on "to lodge" as an alternative to best grasp both the fulfillment and yet temporary nature of the σκηνόω. That is to say,

> He has not just pitched his tent on the edge of our sphere of existence but taken up lodging in it. This is what is meant by ὁ λόγος σὰρξ ἐγένετο. But he has not come to dwell here, to be at home here. He has come to lodge and then go back again. The Logos has really come only for lodging. This, too, is what it meant by ὁ λόγος σὰρξ ἐγένετο."[66]

All of this demonstrates the deep connection of incarnation and illumination that is captured in John's prologue. This is the indivisibility of incarnation and illumination. God's light and glory was bound up with God's

---

[65]Barth, *Witness*, 94.
[66]Barth, *Witness*, 94.

dwelling among humans in the Old Testament tabernacle. It is no different as he lodges in the flesh.

As a revelation in σὰρξ, it follows (as we see with Nicodemus, Caiaphas, Pilate, etc.) that there will be those who see but do not perceive. This in Barth's mind is a function of a temporary—fleshly—dwelling, which both reveals and conceals revelation. It is the possibility and the limit of revelation. Of such figures Barth writes, "They saw [*sahen*] his σὰρξ, they saw his σκηνοῦν. They perhaps even saw something 'glorious.' But they did not perceive [*schauten*] him. They did not *know* what they saw. . . . With some it was different. They perceived."[67] This is the paradox at play in many of the narratives of interest here—the question of why some see the σὰρξ and see only flesh, while others perceive ὁ λόγος in the σὰρξ. What brings about the transition from *seeing* the flesh to *perceiving* the Word? John is setting up here in the prologue what will play out throughout the remainder of the Gospel: the drama of people encountering Jesus—darkness being confronted by light—with some only seeing while others perceive.

"We ἐθεασάμεθα the glory of him." Barth builds a case for ἐθεασάμεθα as not simply seeing (*sahen*), but perceiving (*schauen*) or beholding—"seeing in which one grasps the significance of what is seen."[68] This is what constitutes and marks the witness. It does not describe all who have seen him, but only those who are affected by the appearance, the epiphany of ὁ λόγος σὰρξ ἐγένετο. This beholding "cannot be said of all the contemporaries of the ἐνσάρχωσις. For we (in particular) perceived the glory of him who lodged among us (in general)."[69] What is perceived? Here we return to δόξα—glory.

Incarnation as illumination in glory. In defining δόξα, "the different possibilities of meaning in the term, which derive from the Old Testament . . . all meet in the idea of light, of perfect radiance, of total brightness, such as proceeds from God's mighty working and ruling, or simply his presence."[70] Although the Logos is clothed in flesh, his δόξα still shines through. Yet, it

---

[67]Barth, *Witness*, 95. In distinguishing *schauen* from *sehen*, Barth is distinguishing between merely observing the physical form of something and a penetrating grasp of what is embodied within the form—a seeing beyond simply physical vision to processing its significance.

[68]Barth, *Witness*, 96. See discussion of ἐθεασάμεθα for Barth's case for translating as perceiving or beholding over against a simply "seeing" (96-97).

[69]Barth, *Witness*, 96.

[70]Barth, *Witness*, 97.

does not shine as a constant ray of sunlight. That would make revelation a quality of σάρξ itself. Rather, it shines as the strike of lightning—an isolated "event rather than a continuum."[71]

Barth distinguishes δόξα from the φῶς of John 1:4-9 in that δόξα "does not denote God's divine self-manifestation as such but the qualities [or attributes] of God that are at work in it, or may be seen where he reveals himself."[72] That is to say, while φῶς is God's divine self-manifestation, δόξα encompasses the qualities of God that may be seen in that revelation. What is perceived in God's work of revelation and redemption is his δόξα. The qualities or attributes discernible for God's action include but are not limited to those mentioned at the end of John 1:14, χάρις and ἀλήθεια. The glory that was beheld was truth and grace at work in God's self-manifestation in the flesh. Grace and truth are material definitions of the term δόξα. The point of John's addition, "as of the only begotten son" is "to stress what the Father and the Son have in common"—the mutual δόξα of grace and truth.

Illumination and exegesis of the Father. Our final concern of the prologue is the Son's work of exegeting the Father. As no one has seen the Father except the only-begotten Son of God, who makes the Father known, we must inquire into in what sense he makes him known. He is the exegete of the Father in that he is "the communicator, the one with whom we have to do, he who is the *monogenes*, whose information about himself is original, primary, and authentic revelation."[73] He cannot be circumvented. There is no immediacy to God except by him. He exegetes the Father by being in the flesh what he was in the beginning. Though veiled in the flesh, the Logos does not "cease in any way to be totally what he is."[74] As the one true, original, unique, primary, authentic communicator and mediator, he exegetes, or makes the Father known, through his works. In turn, his works manifest the glory held in common between them (Jn 17:22, 24). In gazing on and perceiving the Word in the flesh, we are reading the exegesis of the

---

[71]To make this revealing a quality of σάρξ would mean that revelation and the manifestation of glory is "something that is self-evidently given always and everywhere in and with the σάρξ. It would not do justice to the verb δοξάζειν, which is very common in John, and which indicates that John thinks of the penetration as an isolated, if common, event rather than a continuum, as a concrete happening which strikes like lightning" (Barth, *Witness*, 98).

[72]Barth, *Witness*, 97.

[73]Barth, *Witness*, 131.

[74]Barth, *Witness*, 97.

Father, and those who perceive and believe are given the authority to become children of God.

JOHN 2:23–3:21

We turn now to John 2:23–3:21, the first of several narratives that depict men and women confronted by the Word—darkness confronted by light. At the very outset of his exploration of the Nicodemus pericope, Barth names its meaning: Jesus as revealer pulls people out of the spectator position and into confrontation, into a position where people must make decision about him.[75] Barth leaves no doubt that this is a narrative of encounter, of confrontation. The Logos, the true light that was coming into the world is now coming to humanity, to a particular man, Nicodemus. To set up this encounter, Barth reads John 2:23-25 as the observation to which the Nicodemus passage gives illustration. Nicodemus is one who believed on account of Jesus' signs, but to whom Jesus did not entrust himself.[76]

John 3:1-2.
Now there was a Pharisee named Nicodemus, a leader of the Jews. He came to Jesus by night and said to him, "Rabbi, we know that you are a teacher who has come from God; for no one can do these signs that you do apart from the presence of God."

The language of ἔρχομαι—to *come* to Jesus, as is said of Nicodemus—is provocative for Barth. He understands ἔρχομαι in John's Gospel not as a neutral, superficial process, but almost—though only *almost*—as a synonym for believing in Jesus.[77] This will play a prominent role in Barth's theological exegesis of these encounters with Jesus. To his point, John places "coming to Jesus" alongside of, if not parallel to, believing in Jesus in John 6:35, 37. John places it explicitly under the promise "and whoever comes to me I will never drive away."[78] But in Nicodemus coming to Jesus, it is still a coming to him νυκτός—*by night*. "Night" in John is the darkness that humanity regularly prefers to the light (Jn 3:18). To those who do not believe, the light

---

[75]Barth, *Erklärung*, 211.
[76]Barth, *Erklärung*, 209.
[77]Barth, *Erklärung*, 212.
[78]Barth, *Erklärung*, 212. Εἶπεν αὐτοῖς ὁ Ἰησοῦς · Ἐγώ εἰμι ὁ ἄρτος τῆς ζωῆς · ὁ ἐρχόμενος πρὸς ἐμὲ οὐ μὴ πεινάσῃ, καὶ ὁ πιστεύων εἰς ἐμὲ οὐ μὴ διψήσει πώποτε (Jn 6:35, my translation).

comes in vain because the night returns when no work can be done (Jn 9:4). Barth concludes that Nicodemus's *coming* is a yes, but because it is a coming *by night*, it is a yes enveloped in a no. It is a confession that is swallowed up again by a rejection.[79] In order for belief on the basis of signs to become belief in the light of life, there must first be manifested a πιστεύειν εἰς τὸ ὄνομα αὐτοῦ. But before Nicodemus's belief on the basis of signs could move to a belief in the light of life, his belief is swallowed up again in unbelief.

John 3:3-5.

Jesus answered him, "Very truly, I tell you, no one can see the kingdom of God without being born from above." Nicodemus said to him, "How can anyone be born after having grown old? Can one enter a second time into the mother's womb and be born?" Jesus answered, "Very truly, I tell you, no one can enter the kingdom of God without being born of water and Spirit."

For someone to see the kingdom of God means they also have been born ἄνωθεν. This for Barth is what it looks like for the circle of revelation and faith (*der Ring von Offenbarung und Glauben*) to close itself in John: that one would πιστεύειν εἰς τὸ ὄνομα αὐτοῦ and then Jesus would entrust himself to him or her. That is to say, as with John 1:12, to all who received him, who believed in his name, he closed the circle by giving power to become children of God—to be born ἄνωθεν. Barth attempts to ground his reading of ἄνωθεν as solidly as possible in the immediate context of John 3. To be born ἄνωθεν, anew (*von neuem*, as Barth translates it), is not an event of human existence (as Nicodemus takes it) but an event of divine action. In light of the importance of this term, we will leave its explanation to Barth's own words:

According to the clear delineation of v. 5 ἄνωθεν means: ἐξ ὕδατος καὶ πνεύματος. v. 6 and 8 show that the stress lies on the second term, where it alone returns. The Spirit brings life, gives the life to the children of God, to the same man who does not have this life as such. ἐξ ὕδατος has been understood as a gloss or (according to Calvin) as a paraphrase for the purifying and renewing effect of the Spirit, or as a reference to John's Baptism of repentance and forgiveness of sins, or finally, conscious juxtaposition of the thing communicated to people in the revelation of Christ with the Sacrament of Christian Baptism which denotes this thing. The latter is surely the most

---

[79]Barth, *Erklärung*, 212.

probable in the sense intended by the evangelist. Whereby, indeed, the continuing importance of the Baptist and his witness is also implicitly recognized.
The Spirit creates, the water testifies to the Child of God. Both are set with
their becoming.[80]

The most immediate and least speculative first step toward interpretation is
in the direction of birth from water and Spirit. Barth's conclusion is obviously that the operative word here is πνεῦμα. The birth ἐξ ὕδατος is first a
direct representation of the Spirit's cleansing and renewing work and only
secondarily an allusion to the sacrament of Christian baptism. The Spirit
creates, the water testifies to the child of God. The question remains as to
what kind of life comes as the result of this being born ἄνωθεν. The answer
comes in the next verses.

John 3:6-12.

What is born of the flesh is flesh, and what is born of the Spirit is spirit. Do not
be astonished that I said to you, "You must be born from above." The wind
blows where it chooses, and you hear the sound of it, but you do not know
where it comes from or where it goes. So it is with everyone who is born of the
Spirit. Nicodemus said to him, "How can these things be?" Jesus answered him,
"Are you a teacher of Israel, and yet you do not understand these things? Very
truly, I tell you, we speak of what we know and testify to what we have seen;
yet you do not receive our testimony. If I have told you about earthly things
and you do not believe, how can you believe if I tell you about heavenly things?"

Of first importance for Barth is to communicate that this being born ἄνωθεν
"is an absolutely incomprehensible event, or at most an event whose actuality
is conceivable only in its reality."[81] That is to say, as a divine action, "what
God does in humans is to be seen as possible and true only when and insofar
as *God does it*."[82] As Barth has already said of Nicodemus's encounter with
Jesus, being born ἄνωθεν is an event that cannot be observed at a distance
like a detached spectator. It is conceivable only as one experiences it in their
own life.

This for Barth then gives context for understanding the metaphor of the
wind. As this being born ἄνωθεν is incomprehensible except as it becomes

---

[80]Barth, *Erklärung*, 212, my translation.
[81]Barth, *Erklärung*, 214.
[82]Barth, *Erklärung*, 214.

reality in one's life, so is the case with the wind. Wind is not intelligible in
its "from where? and to where? as a thing standing in a causal and teleological order, to be understood and to be defined, but in the reality of [its]
happening. When God *acts, he* is recognized."[83]

Barth observes a thought-provoking parallel to the headwaiter of the
wedding in John 2, who tastes the wine καὶ οὐκ ᾔδει πόθεν ἐστίν—"and does
not know where it is from." As with the wine, so now with the wind—the
Spirit. The wind comes upon men and women and they know not where it
is from (Jn 3:8). Barth remarks, "Nicodemus' question to his counterpart is
only too appropriate: How can this be? Indeed, How? Only the act of faith
can take the place of the 'how?' That's it."[84] That is to say, the question stands
alongside the act of faith. The implausibility of this being born ἄνωθεν coexists with, even necessarily coexists with, the act of faith, or else it would
not be the act *of faith*.[85] It seems that Barth does not wish to read Jesus'
question to Nicodemus in John 3:10 too harshly. Rather, it is simply to be
understood that this "is the general situation of men in the face of revelation."
As "long as he stands on this side of the *Krisis* . . . 'the teacher of Israel,' the
religious leader, the theological expert as such, does not recognize the overcoming of this 'How?' by faith."[86]

Barth makes much of Jesus' question to Nicodemus, "Are you a teacher
of Israel, and yet you do not understand these things?" How is it that the
collective "we" of John 3:11 understands τὰ ἐπίγεια ("earthly things," Jn 3:12)
and the teacher of Israel does not? This being "born anew" is the new creation of humanity, and the movement of the wind is the work and act of
God.[87] According to Barth's reading of John, Nicodemus cannot understand
this because God himself must be the *ground* of understanding as well as
the possibility and the reality. That is to say,

> Seeing (v. 3) and entering (v. 5) the kingdom of God does not come about by
> man, nor can man even understand how these things can be (v. 9), even if he
> is the teacher of Israel (v. 10), even if it is spoken of and attested to him by men
> as a known and seen reality (v. 11), even if it confronts him in analogy to the

---

[83]Barth, *Erklärung*, 214-25.
[84]Barth, *Erklärung*, 215.
[85]Barth, *Erklärung*, 215.
[86]Barth, *Erklärung*, 215, emphasis mine.
[87]"*Der Neuschöpfung des Menschen als* Gottes *Werk und Tat*" (Barth, *Erklärung*, 215).

earthly possibilities and realities (v. 12). This is about a birth of men from above (vv. 3 and 7), through water and Spirit (vv. 5 and 8), which must be an event in order to be the object of perception, or rather: which only makes itself perceptible because it happens.[88]

This is a faith that exists in humans only as the Spirit births it in them. It is only perceptible as it happens.

John 3:13-16.

No one has ascended into heaven except the one who descended from heaven, the Son of Man. And just as Moses lifted up the serpent in the wilderness, so must the Son of Man be lifted up, that whoever believes in him may have eternal life. 'For God so loved the world that he gave his only Son, so that everyone who believes in him may not perish but may have eternal life.'

In keeping with his wider view of Jesus in John as revealer or revelation, Barth reads John 3:13 most strictly in terms of revelation. Consequently, that which comes down from heaven is knowledge of heavenly things; it comes down by means of the only one who can come down. Barth asserts here that one cannot be a passive observer of this revelation but that revelation occurs as it confronts individuals and calls them into question—as the decision is put to them directly. Barth writes that "one cannot sit and watch the beginning of the new existence of man [i.e., one cannot watch someone being born ἄνωθεν], and subsequently begin with him. Rather, he must himself sit and have been given to see."[89] Only in being set before revelation and having been given sight to see does one determine this new beginning for themselves.

> Revelation in this strict sense, revelation which has exclusively posited itself, which has made itself accessible—because it is God's revelation, because its content is τὰ ἐπουράνια—the begetting of men through the Spirit, Revelation, for which we need not search, because it has found us, . . . such revelation is the revelation of the Son of man, which is at issue in the πιστεύειν εἰς τὸ ὄνομα αὐτοῦ (2:23).[90]

We can begin to hear now how revelation and regeneration are bound up with one another. Revelation making itself perceivable means the begetting

---

[88]Barth, *Erklärung*, 216-17.
[89]Barth, *Erklärung*, 217.
[90]Barth, *Erklärung*, 217.

of human beings through the Spirit. The revelation itself is disclosed in John 3:14, "The serpent in the desert is lifted up, so that it shall be *seen* by the people for their salvation. This ὑψοῦσθαι must befall the son of man (that and only that, in any case, is the point of comparison)." Nevertheless, "As ὑψωθείς, he must encounter men so that he will be revealed as that which he is, as the revealer, so that the vicious circle, in which this is located according to verses 6-12, will be broken."[91] This vicious cycle is that what is born of flesh can only perceive flesh. But when he is seen by the people for their salvation, this ὑψοῦσθαι has accomplished its aim according to John 8:28, "When you have lifted up the Son of Man, then you realize that I am he," and John 12:32, "and I, when I am lifted up from the earth, will draw all people to myself." That he is seen means revelation. That it brings their salvation means regeneration. The exceptional beauty of Barth's reflection here is his articulation of the Son's glorification in the ὑψοῦσθαι. It is readily acknowledged that for John, the moment of Jesus' crucifixion—his being lifted up—is the moment of his glorification. However, Barth takes it a step further to suggest that as we see in the crucifixion-and-resurrection prophecy of John 2, the connection between the death and resurrection of Jesus in John is very close, and "in the term ὑψοῦσθαι he pushes both together into one word." He is lifted up on the cross, and then again, lifted up from the grave. Jesus' glorification comes therefore both in his crucifixion and then also in his resurrection. This is his true and real revelation which grants both faith and the credit of eternal life.[92]

There is a concept that Barth touches on here that he has dealt with quite extensively up to this point, but which we have not yet addressed—that is, the way John makes use of the phrases ἐν αὐτῷ, εἰς αὐτόν, δι' αὐτοῦ, and the related εἰς τὸ ὄνομα αὐτοῦ. So much of what is accomplished on our behalf is said to take place ἐν αὐτῷ. This first comes to the fore in John 1:4, ἐν αὐτῷ ζωὴ ἦν, καὶ ἡ ζωὴ ἦν τὸ φῶς τῶν ἀνθρώπων. There Barth indicates that by this ἐν αὐτῷ, John is witnessing to the reality that this redemptive life was "in him," in the sense that it was "contained and offered in God's Word."[93] It is Barth's conclusion that the emphasis of this verse is precisely on this ἐν

---

[91]Barth, *Erklärung*, 218.
[92]Barth, *Erklärung*, 218.
[93]Barth, *Witness*, 41.

αὐτῷ.[94] In the Logos "objectively and enduringly there stood before them the possibility or opportunity of knowing it [i.e., 'the light of men, the light of revelation which illumined them'], of knowing about it. Whatever the result might be, the light was now here and never absent."[95] So there is this objective aspect of ἐν αὐτῷ in the sense of what is objectively available and revealed in him, but for John there is also a more subjective side, which is seen in John 1:12 in the locution εἰς τὸ ὄνομα αὐτοῦ, "in his name": ὅσοι δὲ ἔλαβον αὐτόν, ἔδωκεν αὐτοῖς ἐξουσίαν τέκνα θεοῦ γενέσθαι, τοῖς πιστεύουσιν εἰς τὸ ὄνομα αὐτοῦ. Barth suggests that the implication is that those who enter into or participate in what is objectively available or revealed ἐν αὐτῷ, those who participate in the presence of this light, this knowledge, this life, are those who believe εἰς τὸ ὄνομα αὐτοῦ. Barth opposes the readings that see in John 1:12 a sequence, transfer, or transaction. Such readings suggest that in exchange for belief, people receive the authority to be God's children. Instead, "logically, the third clause is parallel to the second as well as the first."[96] Therefore, it is not a movement from believing in his name to becoming a child of God. It is a descriptive repetition of sorts, "Those who believe in his name *are* the same as those whom the Word gave ἐξουσία to be God's children."[97] This is evident from Barth's translation ("But those who did receive him, to them he gave the power to become the children of God, even to those who believed in his name") and he finds confirmation of this in John 1:13: "These where not born of blood, nor of the will of flesh, nor of the will of man, but of God."[98] He concludes, "It is not what the ὅσοι are or do, but what is done for them in their relation to the Word. Their right to be God's children is absolutely given to them. They are miraculously born as verse 1:13 adds." Consequently, their λαμβάνειν and πιστεύειν have their presupposition in this gift and not the reverse.[99]

---

[94]"What the author wants to say is that whatever was revelation, the light of life, redemption for men, was only in him—again not directly or immediately from God, from God indeed, but in him, in the same Word that took flesh in Jesus Christ, alongside which there never has been or can be any other Word. In *him* was life, and *this* life was the light of men. The emphasis of the verse—we must not let this be lost—is on the ἐν αὐτῷ. Wherever there was light, it was this light. Apart from him there is only witness to the light (v. 8)" (Barth, *Witness*, 43).

[95]Barth, *Witness*, 41.

[96]Barth, *Witness*, 79.

[97]Barth, *Witness*, 79, emphasis mine.

[98]Barth, *Witness*, 11.

[99]Barth, *Witness*, 79.

The bearing of this is that whether it is in the objective or the subjective movements of the divine action, in each case it is *divine* action. There is that which is made possible and available objectively to all humanity as the true light comes into the world, as the Word becomes flesh and lodges among us. Then there is that which is applied subjectively to the individual. This is the gift of being born of God, the gift of receiving and believing, of being born anew. To speak of subjectivity here is not to speak of the human response or reaction to divine action; it is more to speak of *particularity*. In this sense, *particularity* means divine action upon a specific individual. Regeneration is the implication of revelation when revelation is expressed with particularity.

John 3:17-21.

Indeed, God did not send the Son into the world to condemn the world, but in order that the world might be saved through him. Those who believe in him are not condemned; but those who do not believe are condemned already, because they have not believed in the name of the only Son of God. And this is the judgment, that the light has come into the world, and people loved darkness rather than light because their deeds were evil. For all who do evil hate the light and do not come to the light, so that their deeds may not be exposed. But those who do what is true come to the light, so that it may be clearly seen that their deeds have been done in God.

At the conclusion of the Nicodemus pericope, Barth revisits the programmatic description found in John 2:23-25. Nicodemus is illustrative of the one who believes, but to whom Jesus does not entrust himself. Consequently, now in John 3:17-21, Nicodemus also illustrates the one who believes but whose belief is ultimately revealed and exposed to be *unbelief.*

Nicodemus stands with his questions and objections in the vicious cycle described by John 3:6-12: as one born only of flesh, he can only see earthly flesh. Barth comments, "Which is it? That he came to *Jesus*, or that he came to Jesus *by night*? Has he or has he not acknowledged the one who is to be lifted up?"[100] This for Barth is the decision—*Entschiedung*, the κρίσις, verse 21 —that Nicodemus faces in this encounter. The κρίσις, the dialectic, what Barth calls the double possibility, is that one may be coming to Jesus and yet be coming to him *by night*—that the one who is a believer in the fashion of John

---

[100]Barth, *Erklärung*, 222.

2:23-25 is in fact an unbeliever when confronted with John 3:3-16. Never-theless, "the mission of the Son of God as depicted in vv. 14-16 is completely non-dialectical, quite unambiguously directed to the salvation of the world; it is *life* message and nothing else."[101] Barth wants to contend that for the be-liever, this dialectic has already been undone. In light of the language of John 3:18, "He is not condemned, as little as the Son of God is sent to condemn. This means not only that the decision about him has already been made in that he believes and has eternal life. But also, as such he is the *possibility* of a decision, removed entirely from the realm of a *double* possibility."[102] What confronts Nicodemus in his encounter with Jesus is the κρίσις of his own unbelief, his denial that the decision has already been made about him. That what was perceived as his decision was in reality his own persistence to leave the question open—his question was his objection, his "No."[103] In language well known of Barth, "the Yes of faith does not stand alongside of, but absolutely *above* the No. Yes and No face each other as possibility and impossibility, or as that which God wants in his act of love for the cosmos and as something unwanted which [humanity] *rejects* by means of this act."[104] It is for this no— this unbelieving faith—that Jesus withholds entrusting himself to humans. He waits for what Barth calls their real faith (*wirklichen Glauben*) to confide in them.[105] Barth summarizes the development of the passage this way,

> The communication of eternal life through the sending of the Son brings light
> into the world. This is revelation. Revelation of the love of God for the World,
> but in so doing also revelation of the truth about the uniqueness of the cosmos,
> of man. The revelation revealed that their works are evil. In spite of that, or
> exactly because of that they must be loved, the light must be loved, the ἀλήθεια
> must be actuated [carried out, operated, lived], and precisely that would be
> faith (v. 21). But man loves the darkness rather than the light, which reveals to
> him, that he is darkness. By bringing eternal life to him the darkness is expelled,
> and it makes him a new creation, a child of God begotten through the Spirit.[106]

---

[101]Barth, *Erklärung*, 222.

[102]Barth, *Erklärung*, 222.

[103]"Der Glaube, der sich die Entscheidung noch vorbehält, der noch Fragen und Einwände zu erheben hat, als ob das Nein *neben* dem Ja stünde—und das ist eben der Glaube des Nikodemus und der 2,23 Geschilderten—, dieser Glaube ist *Unglaube*" (Barth, *Erklärung*, 223).

[104]Barth, *Erklärung*.

[105]Barth, *Erklärung*, 223.

[106]Barth, *Erklärung*, 223-24.

The distinction being made here between two types of believers is not that one's works are good and another's are evil. Rather, the distinction comes about as those who come into the light and those who, out of fear of exposure, recoil into darkness.

JOHN 4:1-42

Barth's exegesis of Jesus' encounter with the Samaritan woman offers an exceptional illustration of his theological interpretation, especially with respect to demonstrating a chastened allegorical interpretation. A "chastened" allegorical reading is a reading properly rooted both in the text's literal meaning and in its historical context. Given the length of this pericope and the depth of Barth's exegesis here, this project will only treat the aspects of Barth's engagement that bear directly on illumination.

One of the primary motifs that Barth identifies in this narrative is the slow but progressive pealing back of layers. This is both layers of Jesus' identity and layers of the woman's misunderstanding about who the Messiah would be. Barth articulates compares her progression to the disciples' confessions of Jesus as Messiah at earlier points in the Gospel. Such utterances of the disciples include: "We have found the Messiah" (Jn 1:41); "The one Moses wrote about in the law and about whom the prophets also wrote" (Jn 1:45); "You are the Son of God, the king of Israel" (Jn 1:49). The confession only reaches the level of the disciples' confession when, on the lips of the townspeople, it is declared, καὶ οἴδαμεν ὅτι οὗτός ἐστιν ἀληθῶς ὁ σωτὴρ τοῦ κόσμου ("and we know that this is truly the Savior of the world," Jn 4:42).[107] But the woman herself can only come to the knowledge that he is a prophet (Jn 4:19). She cannot yet arrive at the conclusion that he is the Messiah.[108] For all her effort to comprehend, Jesus' own subtle disclosure, his *verhüllten Messiasbekenntnis* ("veiled Messiah confession"), is required for her to understand. The first of these comes in John 4:10, εἰ ᾔδεις τὴν δωρεὰν τοῦ θεοῦ καὶ τίς ἐστιν ὁ λέγων σοι · δός μοι πεῖν, σὺ ἂν ᾔτησας αὐτὸν καὶ ἔδωκεν ἄν σοι ὕδωρ ζῶν ("If you knew the gift of God, and who it is that is saying to you, 'Give me a drink,' you would have asked him, and he would have given you living water"). This being the first *verhüllten Messiasbekenntnis,* Jesus both

---

[107]Barth, *Erklärung,* 240.
[108]Barth, *Erklärung,* 240.

veils and unveils in relation to John 4:7. Previously Jesus has asked for a drink, as though he were one susceptible to thirst—human—and he now offers a drink as one who gives ὕδωρ ζῶν in the person of the divine gift himself.[109] Although the woman expresses a knowledge of religious history and the current state of the debate (Jn 4:19-20, 25), her recognition of the one speaking to her still requires Jesus' self-disclosure, Ἐγώ εἰμι, ὁ λαλῶν σοι ("I am he, the one who is speaking to you," Jn 4:26).

Although it is not until the conclusion of the narrative that the climactic confession ὁ σωτὴρ τοῦ κόσμου ("the Savior of the world," Jn 4:42) is made, this only comes as the result of Jesus' own comments in John 4:7, 10, 26, which "get the ball rolling." In this way, Jesus' subtle but decisive self-disclosure is present at the beginning, middle, and end of the narrative. Jesus' self-disclosure is present in such a way that "one cannot deny that it initially tended toward (v. 10), then reached its provisional peak in v. 26, and gets its counterpart in v. 42." Consequently, Barth does not find it unreasonable that the Ἐγώ εἰμι ("I am he," Jn 4:26) could be the starting point for explaining the whole. He concludes that evidently the general sense of the text is the demonstration of how Jesus reveals his identity.[110]

Barth explains the crescendo of the episode by interpreting the "true worshipers" (Jn 4:23) in analogy to the true light (Jn 1:9). He writes, "If, as we see, προσκυνεῖν [worship] is equivalent to ἀντλῆσαι ὕδωρ [drawing water], then to continue worshiping on Mount Gerizim and Zion is equivalent to drawing water from Jacob's Well. Consequently, it is revealed that to worship in Spirit and Truth is equivalent to receiving the water that Jesus gives" instead of drawing from the well.[111] When read in this light the entire narrative hangs together. As the Logos is the true light which enlightens everyone, likewise he is the giver of living water which is the source of those who worship in Spirit and in truth.

The person who worships in Spirit and in truth is the one born anew, born not of the will of flesh or of a man, but of God (Jn 1:13). The one who worships in Spirit and in truth is the one born from above (Jn 3:3), the one who has been born of water and Spirit (Jn 3:5), and the one who has received

---

[109]Barth, *Erklärung*, 239.
[110]Barth, *Erklärung*, 240-41.
[111]Barth, *Erklärung*, 247-48.

the true light (Jn 1:9, 12-13).[112] By the πνεῦμα (*Gott in Person*) humans are given a birth, a light, a well of life, that they cannot attain for themselves.[113] In Barth's words, "For humankind, action takes place over against him so that through the begotten flesh, he lives a new life as the child of God through the Holy Spirit, so that his works may be revealed as done in God (3:21), so that he is now an ἀληθινὸς προσκυνητής." Correspondingly, one is ἀληθινὸς προσκυνητής—a "true worshiper"—because one's worship is in ἀλήθεια—"truth." Their worship is in truth because God has made himself recognizable and indeed is recognized by the worshiper. God has become present to humanity both in God's Spirit (πνεῦμα) acting upon humanity to recognize God, as well as in his recognizability (ἀλήθεια) as the light coming into the world. This is the revelation that makes true worship possible. It is no longer the opposition of humanity and revelation as with religious προσκύνησις—drawing water—but the operation of God in humans such that their προσκύνησις is their participation in the reception of revelation— living water as gift.[114]

Barth's theological reading of John's Gospel continues here as we see the way he prioritizes the unity of the text—both the fourth chapter and the entirety of the Fourth Gospel. The light comes into the world, and to those who received him, they were given authority to become children of God (Jn 1); they were born anew, born of the Spirit. Because God loves the world (in the sense of Jn 3:16), illumination culminates as he seeks and finds worshipers who worship in the Spirit and in the truth (Jn 4:24).[115] By his very interpretation, he is building a case for the unity of Scripture's theological witness, and here we see Barth make explicit the intra-divine relationships implicit throughout the narrative of the Gospel so far: the *Father* is seeking worshipers who by his *Spirit* recognize his unveiling of the truth in his *Son*. Worship in Spirit and truth is a gifted—not earned, not self-appointed, not self-justified nor self-sanctified, but gifted—human participation in the divine, as the Spirit gives the truth of the Father to be recognized and received in the Son. For Barth,

---

[112]Barth, *Erklärung*, 248.
[113]Barth, *Erklärung*, 248.
[114]Barth, *Erklärung*, 248-49.
[115]Barth, *Erklärung*, 249.

[This] occurrence of God for men and on men means not merely a divine effect, which man could not enter or escape, but actus purus, in which God is God for his own sake, in which God loves himself from all eternity and to eternity. This is the mystery of conception by the Spirit, the worship in Spirit and in Truth which follows from it (the conception). God and the movement of his own life in itself is the mystery.[116]

Ultimately, this true worship is human participation in the divine life, conceived at the intersection of revelation, regeneration, and illumination.

JOHN 8:12

"Again Jesus spoke to them, saying, 'I am the light of the world. Whoever follows me will never walk in darkness but will have the light of life.'" Barth's lectures conclude with John 8 which means this verse brings us to the last of the texts from *Erklärung* that we will treat here. Nevertheless, it remains one of the most expansive, all-encompassing and yet succinct statements pertaining to Jesus and the language of light in John. The fact that this language of light is coupled with ἐγώ εἰμι as one of John's "I am" statements only intensifies the potency of this proclamation. The context—the second installment of Jesus' great encounter with the Jews at the Feast of Tabernacles—likewise heightens the symbolism and significance. Here the light of the world speaks, shines, as the light situated in darkness.

For Barth, this verse is crucial for understanding the entire Gospel of John because it is "the strongest, most concentrated and at the same time most universal statement of Jesus about himself and his mission that we have in this word before us."[117] What precisely is encapsulated in the content of this statement? Given that Barth has already distinguished this light of the Logos from any nature or property belonging intrinsically to the κόσμος, this light is not a property of creation but an event that happened and happens in it.[118] This means that "light, precisely as an event, as a divine act, is Revelation, opening the truth to men" (1:4). To know him as the light of the world entails on the one hand recognizing that he is the light of life, that is, the life that gives the power to become children of God. It means on the

---

[116]Barth, *Erklärung*, 249.
[117]Barth, *Erklärung*, 358.
[118]Barth, *Erklärung*, 358; see also the above discussion of Barth's exegesis of Jn 1:4.

other hand also "that the intent of the divine act in relation to the world is subjectively his love for it and objectively, the removal of their sin (1:29), the gift of their salvation (3:17, 4:42), the message of life to them (6:33, 6:51)." Thus, "in this expression, φῶς τοῦ κόσμου, revelation, reconciliation and redemption press together into one." Finally, in this expression we encounter again John's profound use of ἐγώ εἰμι ("I am"). Barth contends that of all the ἐγώ εἰμι statements encountered thus far, this one is the most comprehensive— and in the whole Gospel is perhaps surpassed only by John 14:6.[119]

The second half of the verse contains both prerequisite and promise. Recognizing the light of the world in Jesus is the prerequisite with which one will not walk in darkness, and at the same time, it is a promise under which one stands.[120] For the one recognizing Jesus as the light of the world,

> He now loves the light (3:19), he comes to the light at risk to him, to be illuminated (3:20-21, Eph 5:13). He uses the light, since he has recognized that one uses the daylight, so long as one has it (9:4, 11:9, Rom 13:13). He watches so that he does not rush into darkness (12:35). This obedient going-on-guard then actually meets—and that is a second thing, that is the promise—together with the fact that man has the light (the light of life, means it now explicitly and substantially, in remembrance of 1:4). He stumbles not, because he sees the light of the world (11:9). He does not remain in darkness (12:46), but he is (1 John 2:9), he remains (1 John 2:10) in the light. The light is in him (11:10, 12:35; Matt 5:16, 6:23), indeed he was and is a child of the light (12:36; 1 Thess 5:5; Eph 5:9).[121]

Barth observes that John does not make the broader statement, "you are the light of the world," as Matthew has, but that as a child of light, one is "a reflection of the coming redemption. That is the promise of the second section, v. 51 . . . that he will never see death, or with many passages from the third to the sixth chapters: he will have eternal life."[122]

And so the question that confronts the Jewish leaders in this encounter with Jesus is the provocative call, ἀκολουθεῖν μοι ("follow me"). Barth contends that this "ἀκολουθεῖν μοι, as 12:46 shows, cannot be other than πιστεύειν εἰς ἐμέ or ἔρχεσθαι πρός με (7:37) or ἀκούειν τὸν λόγον τὸν ἐμόν

---

[119]Barth, *Erklärung*, 358-59.
[120]Barth, *Erklärung*, 358-59.
[121]Barth, *Erklärung*, 359-60.
[122]Barth, *Erklärung*, 360.

(8:43)." The call is nothing short of offensive to these Jews, but it emphasizes the point: Can these Jews be followers of Jesus; can they recognize him as the light of the world? The answer, Barth concludes, will be no.

This raises provocative questions regarding revelation, illumination, and regeneration. Could one come in direct encounter with, direct confrontation with, the "ἐγώ εἰμι: the actuality of revelation in the person of the revealer," and yet not recognize in him the light of the world? The answer to that question comes down to obedience, "If you hold my teaching, you are really my disciples and then you will know the truth and the truth will set you free" (Jn 8:31-32).

Barth draws the conclusion from the narrative of this encounter that if revelation is indeed revelation, it commands obedience. It commands obedience not in coercion or by threat, not by fear or manipulation. Obedience is the manifestation of received revelation. Obedience is "knowledge in action," which comes as a correlative to knowledge received in revelation. Revelation commands obedience in that an encounter with revelation cannot be mistaken. He writes, "Revelation would not be revelation if it did not demand obedience in this severity and exclusivity. A minimum of tolerance and forbearance would be the denial of revelation. There can only be revelation where the Son speaks and where therefore also the Father's work necessarily takes place."[123] The Jews in this narrative do not recognize Jesus as the light of the world, not because Jesus is not the light of the world, but because of a decision that has been made about them. They have not been drawn by the Father (Jn 6:44). It is not a decision,

> About his religious capacity or incapacity, but about his obedience or disobedience, about the authority that God has or does not have over him. On this knife-edge falls the decision between belief and unbelief. Unbelief is the inability, the inability of disobedience, which is identical with the divine apophasis, indeed rejection. In the lack of ἐξουσία to become God's child (1.12), it shows that one is not one [of God's children].[124]

Barth contends that no one has this capacity for God, not even the believer. Revelation itself establishes this as it comes to him.[125] As this authority is granted, the light of the world is recognized, believed, and obeyed.

---

[123]Barth, *Erklärung*, 384.
[124]Barth, *Erklärung*, 385.
[125]Barth, *Erklärung*, 385.

JOHN 9

In the corpus of Barth's work, there is relatively little exegetical engagement
with the account of the man born blind in John 9. Though he does make
frequent reference to John 9:4 in various contexts throughout *Church Dogmatics*, extended reflection is scarce. The longest of Barth's reflections on John
9 comes in *Church Dogmatics* IV/2. In section sixty-four, titled "The Exaltation of the Son of Man," Barth engages the question of the connection between the works or miracles of Jesus and the faith of those to whom or among
whom they occur.[126] More precisely, it is the question of whether Jesus' works
evoke faith, or if those works are performed among those whose faith is already established. This is the context within which this exegesis occurs.

At the heart of this theological parable of revelation and illumination is a
man who was born blind but who now *cannot deny his capacity to see*. It is
clear that for Barth this man is on a trajectory of awakening. The physical
opening of his eyes initiates the opening of this man's eyes to a recognition
of the Son of Man. The fact of his opened eyes leads inescapably to his confession of being healed and to his confession of the one who has healed him.
"He finally allowed even the very dangerous saying to be wrested from him
that he was necessarily from God."[127]

This man did not yet know his healer, but he was ready to know. In their
second encounter, he does not yet recognize him. The veil has not been fully
removed, the door has not yet been opened, "Who is he, Lord, that I might
believe on him?" That this man has no awareness of who it is that has placed
mud on his face, but slowly and increasing becomes aware, is for Barth a
theological parable of revelation and illumination. It is the gradual removal
of the veil, the inbreaking of the light of the world. Barth will go on to explain, "The act of their faith is only their reaction to the shining of this
light."[128] Barth concludes,

> This door could not be opened from outside. It could be opened only from
> inside, by Jesus Himself. As the Son of Man made himself known to him—"it
> is he that talketh with thee"—he opened the eyes of faith as well as the physical
> eyes. With the irresistible power, it took place that he was awakened and

---

[126]CD IV/2:233.
[127]CD IV/2:237.
[128]CD IV/2:243.

called to faith. He was hurled into that *proskynesis* as though he had been struck by lightning.[129]

In the end, the decisive fact is *"that Jesus Himself spoke of Himself, that of Himself he gave Himself to be known by him through His Word, that as the object of his faith, which he was already, He made himself also the Creator of his faith."*[130]

Although the appearance of this narrative from John 9 is scarce in Barth's corpus, it is not insignificant. Whether it is normative for Barth's wider thoughts on revelation, illumination, and regeneration, or whether it is just strikingly illustrative of his theology, the capacity for this encounter to capture Barth's theology cannot be marginalized. In the next chapter, we will return again to these texts—in particular to the imagery of the blind receiving their sight—as theological parables of Barth's thought.

Conclusion

It goes without saying that the allusions, references, and in-depth theological-exegetical attention given to these Johannine passages throughout the broader corpus of Barth's work, especially in the *Church Dogmatics*, are extensive. Barth returns again and again through the *Church Dogmatics* to the intersections of incarnation and illumination, reconciliation and revelation, life and light.[131] In the following chapter our hope is to tie together some of the looser strands around light and illumination in Barth's theological exegesis of John by bringing them into conversation with Barth's more systematic theological thoughts expressed in the *Church Dogmatics*. In this way, we hope to achieve clearer understanding of Barth's doctrine of illumination and ultimately how it contributes to a more robust doctrine of illumination in itself.

---

[129]*CD* IV/2:237-38.

[130]*CD* IV/2:238, emphasis mine.

[131]See especially *CD* IV/2, §66, "The Sanctification of Man"; *CD* IV/3, §69, "The Glory of the Mediator"; §71, "The Vocation of Man."

SEVEN

Barth's Doctrine of Illumination

U NDOUBTEDLY, a construction of Barth's doctrine of illumination will be strange amidst the contemporary evangelical conversation.[1] This is because much of the contemporary discussion on the doctrine of illumination pertains more narrowly to the Holy Spirit's work in the illumination of Scripture.[2] While Barth's doctrine of illumination has bearing on the illumination of Scripture, this is only because, as we have shown, it first has bearing on the Word of God *himself.* Illumination intersects both with Barth's development of the Word of God in its threefold form (*CD* §4) and with the doctrines of revelation and the Holy Spirit, most specifically relating to the Spirit as the subjective reality and possibility of revelation (*CD* §16). As alluded to in the introduction and in our discussion of Barth's exegesis of John (see chap. 6 above), Barth's doctrine is not simply about illumination of rational faculties but a grasp of the entire person. The product of illumination is faith and obedience, and the ultimate aim is union with Christ (*CD* §71.3). Faith and obedience receive particular attention from

---

[1]It must be acknowledged here that Barth does not provide us with a direct and explicit treatment of the doctrine of illumination. This may be because of his intention to address it in the unfinished portion of his *Church Dogmatics,* "The Doctrine of Redemption," which would focus primarily on the Holy Spirit. It does find expression at other points throughout his massive corpus of work, but nevertheless he has received extensive critique regarding an alleged slighting of the Holy Spirit. Eugene Rogers Jr., "The Eclipse of the Spirit in Karl Barth," in *Conversing with Barth,* ed. Mike Higton and John C. McDowell (Burlington, VT: Ashgate, 2004), 173.

[2]One notable exception here is Michael Seaman's discussion of "initial illumination," which pertains to the work of the Holy Spirit in regeneration—namely, granting an understanding of the gospel and a conviction of its truth. "The Indispensability of the Holy Spirit for Biblical Interpretation: A Proposal for the Concept of Transformative Illumination" (PhD, Southeastern Baptist Theological Seminary, 2010), 68-69.

Barth as the product of illumination. More precisely, Barth calls illumination the subjective work of the Spirit in revelation (*CD* §16). This emphasis on faith and obedience is demonstrated in his lectures on John's Gospel (*Erklärung des Johannes-Evangeliums*) and his *Göttingen Dogmatics* and carries through even to its most mature expression in the *Church Dogmatics*. The intersection of Barth's lectures and the Gospel of John is an exceptional one for developing Barth's thinking on illumination because all these elements pertaining to illumination are present both in the Fourth Gospel and in Barth's theological exegesis of it.[3]

This chapter moves from the previous exploration of Barth's theological exegesis of the relevant Johannine texts to the task of clarifying his dogmatic conclusions. Most significant is the way Barth locates the doctrine of illumination not only in pneumatology but also in Christology and ultimately develops a robust concept of illumination as a fully trinitarian work involving the Father, Son, and Holy Spirit. Barth takes us a long way toward achieving one of this project's objectives, which is to construct a more holistic vision of the doctrine of illumination according to its multifaceted occurrences in Scripture and in the history of theological development. Barth helps us to clarify why we must speak of an economy of divine light.

THE ROOT OF THE DOCTRINE OF ILLUMINATION

In Barth's lectures on the Gospel of John, he references Franz Overbeck's phrase "economy of the Divine light in the world." Overbeck writes that the whole of the Fourth Gospel rests on the basic conception of this economy according to the prologue.[4] This economy that Overbeck speaks of is the inner relationships of various "lights" within the Gospel of John itself, incorporating the work of John the Evangelist, John the Baptist, the light of the Logos, and the ongoing witness of the text itself.

Overbeck writes this in the context of articulating the relationship of John the Baptist to Jesus, and the relationship of Jesus to John the Evangelist. In so doing, Overbeck makes ample use of the category of witness. He writes,

---

[3]Barth, *Erklärung*.

[4]Franz Overbeck, *Das Johannesevangelium: Studien zur Kritik seiner Erforschung* (Tübingen: J. C. B. Mohr, 1911), 416-17; cited in Karl Barth, *Witness to the Word: A Commentary on John 1* (Eugene, OR: Wipf & Stock, 1986), 14.

> As the Baptist is the witness of the Logos, the mediator between him and the world prior to the completion of his epiphany in the world, before the Logos is the point of perfection showing the world by himself the glory of God on earth, so John the apostle is the mediator for the Logos after his departure from the world. . . . He is called John on account of his calling in the Gospel and the inner relationship of this calling to that of the Baptist in the whole economy of divine light in the world according to the basic conception of this economy on which the whole of the Fourth Gospel rests according to the prologue.[5]

The implications of this for the current project are difficult to overstate. First, we see that as the task of this project has been to explore the narratives of illumination as recounted in John's Gospel, the Gospel itself functions as a part of this economy of divine light. It functions as a component of this economy because it witnesses to the Logos's illumination of the world itself. The economy of the divine light in the world originates in (1) this narrative of a witness anticipating the illumination (John the Baptist), (2) illumination itself as the Logos comes into the world, and (3) the ongoing recollection of illumination that has been mediated through the Evangelist and his account of the event.

Second, this finding implies that we are following closely on Barth's own method for developing a doctrine of illumination as it is depicted in the narratives of Scripture. Barth finds the most compelling and normative account of illumination to be the account of the Logos, the light that enlightens people, coming into the world. It is the paradigm by which to envision all other events of illumination. Barth's doctrine is not first and foremost a catalogue and synthesis of all Scriptural texts that reference light and illumination. Rather, it is rooted in this origin story of illumination itself.

Third, the narratives of John that have been explored throughout this project all in some way rest on the basic conception of this economy. In various ways each of these narratives depicts some aspect of illumination and therefore some aspect of this economy of the divine light in the world. It would not be too bold to say that Barth would agree with this conclusion regarding these narratives' depictions of illumination.

And finally, then, this economy of the divine light in the world, as depicted by John's Gospel, demonstrates that human participation in this economy (as

---

[5]Overbeck, *Das Johannesevangelium*, 416-17.

with John the Baptist and John the Evangelist) is essential to its composition and inner workings. The necessity of highlighting each of these implications will become clear as we work thorough a construction of Barth's doctrine of illumination on the basis of his conclusions in his lectures on John.

In moving to a construction of Barth's doctrine of illumination with special attention to his lectures on John, it immediately comes to the forefront that Barth's doctrine is not only pneumatological but christological and trinitarian. To put it explicitly, in Barth's doctrine of illumination the Logos is the objective light that the Spirit shines on us in illumination. This is evident from the outset as Barth articulates an understanding of the unity and distinction of the person and nature of θεός and λόγος in John 1:1-3, and in turn connects with this a Christology of light and life. The prologue of John proclaims that the nature of the Logos is light and life. Barth develops this light (Jn 1:4-5) in terms of a new revelation in Christ. In keeping with Barth's lectures and his theological reflection on revelation and illumination, we begin to articulate his trinitarian framework for illumination by considering the nature of this divine light as embodied in the Logos.

The Nature of the Logos as Light

Without rehearsing all of Barth's reflections on John's first three verses, his conclusions are: (1) the Logos is of the same nature as God; (2) the Logos is a distinct person from the Father in terms of the Trinity; and (3) the Logos, who functioned in the beginning as agent of creation, is now agent of revelation and redemption.[6] In identifying the nature, person, and function of the Logos, Barth works to firmly ground the redemptive and revelatory work of this Logos within the nature, persons, and work of the Triune God.[7] As agent of creation and now agent of redemption, this redemptive life is in him, and this life is the light of humanity. That is to say, the revelation of God is incased within the redemptive work of the Logos. The work of redeeming life is itself revelatory of God's nature. Barth's conclusion that this light is not human reason but the light of revelation has already been thoroughly

---

[6]See the relevant sections of chap. 6 above for further elucidation regarding Barth's conclusions.
[7]Noticeably missing from Barth's discussion here is the person of the Spirit, but this is due to Barth's sticking closely to the text, as the Spirit is absent also from John's discussion in the prologue.

addressed (see chaps. 5–6 above). This conclusion means that this light has its origins in him. Nevertheless, this conclusion raises several questions: Does having its "origins" in God mean that light is an aspect of God's divine nature?[8] Does "light" refer to specific contents of knowledge that are given by the Logos and received by humankind?[9] Is light here an analogy or illustration for revelation? Given the inevitability of such questions, a helpful way forward here is to speak in terms of an ontology of the light.

In chapter six we concluded with Barth that only φῶς as revelation does justice to John's description of the light as coming into the world.[10] This is followed with an identification of this light with a person: Ἐν τῷ κόσμῳ ἦν, καὶ ὁ κόσμος δι' αὐτοῦ ἐγένετο, καὶ ὁ κόσμος αὐτὸν οὐκ ἔγνω (Jn 1:10). Barth concludes that what is meant by this light coming is not merely that light shines from the humanity of Jesus but that this light is the true, primary, and original light. This light is "the primary light of the revelation of life from which all other light derives."[11] But is this light simply the radiance of this revelation, or is it something innate to the nature of the Logos? The answer for Barth is both: "Light in heaven and earth always receives its radiance from elsewhere. But Christ is the light which shines of itself and then fills the whole world with *its* radiance."[12] And, quoting Calvin, he concludes: "There is no other source or cause of its brightness anywhere. And so he calls Him the true light whose own nature is to be light."[13]

It was this primary light of the revelation of life—both in the revealer's nature and in the revelation's radiance—that was coming into the world. By

---

[8]Although Barth does not treat 1 Jn 1:5 in his lectures on John's Gospel, he does give a nod to its ontological significance in *CD* IV/3.2. "Far from being a mere spectator of the light, man becomes and the Christian is a 'child of light' (Jn 12:36, 1 Thess 5:5, Lk 16:8), or 'light in the Lord' (Eph 5:8). He is thus separated from darkness (Jn 8:12; 12:46). *For there is no darkness in God, the original light* (1 Jn 1:5, Jas 1:17). Light and darkness, righteousness and lawlessness, are mutually exclusive (2 Cor 6:14). In the discipleship of Jesus Christ, the divine light shining in the world, it is self-evident that there should be this separation" (510, emphasis mine).

[9]"In making Himself known, God acts on the whole man. Hence the knowledge of God given to man through his illumination is no mere apprehension and understanding of God's being and action, nor as such a kind of intuitive contemplation. It is the claiming not only of his thinking but also of his willing and work, of the whole man, for God. It is his refashioning to be a theatre, witness and instrument of His acts" (*CD* IV/3.2:510).

[10]See the treatment of Barth's exegesis of Jn 1:1-5 in chap 6 above.

[11]Barth, *Witness*, 62.

[12]Barth, *Witness*, 61.

[13]Barth, *Witness*, 61; John Calvin, *The Gospel According to St. John, 1–10*, trans. T. H. L. Parker, vol. 4 (Grand Rapids: Eerdmans, 1979), 14.

virtue of the unity of Father and Son stated at the outset (Jn 1:1-3), this divine light is then a light communicated from the Father through the Son (similar to "life" in Jn 5:26). And at this point Barth's own language provokes the question of ontology: "The *being* of this light in the world is its *coming*." When it comes to Barth, our ears naturally perk up at this line because of its striking resemblance to Barth's theology of the Word of God written—that the Bible *becomes* the Word of God. It also has striking resemblance to Jüngel's well-known title regarding Barth's theology, *God's Being Is in Becoming*. Alan Torrance writes that this description of Barth's theological ontology is accurate because it captures the way in which Barth resisted the possibility of getting behind the back of God, the possibility of constructing, either intentionally or unintentionally, some concept or doctrine of "being" prior to a doctrine of God that is properly based in God's action toward us.[14] It is not a God in development, but a God who "always is and ever will be in the living movement of his eternal Being."[15] Torrance explains, "His becoming is not a becoming on the way toward being or toward a fullness of being, but it is the eternal fullness and the overflowing of his eternal unlimited being. Becoming expresses the dynamic nature of his being. . . . His becoming is his being in movement and his being in movement is his becoming."[16] Barth writes that "the *being* of this light in the world is its *coming*. But its coming in full reality!"[17] In light of T. F. Torrance's exposition of "being in becoming," it might be said that the ontology of the light, the being of this light in the world, has not so much to say about its coming into existence but about the fullness of its expression in the world. Its being is dynamic, in movement, and it communicates eternal fullness and unlimited light. The ontology of the light of the Logos is not that it is coming into being but that the eternal fullness of its being is only now being shed abroad in its full reality, before humanity, in the world. In this way, the uncreated light in the person of the Logos is both his nature and its effect. It is both the nature of who the Logos is and the knowledge of that nature. It is both light as revelation and light as analogy for its brightness in the world

---

[14]Alan Torrance, "The Trinity," in *The Cambridge Companion to Karl Barth*, ed. John Webster (Cambridge: Cambridge University Press, 2000), 84-86.

[15]Thomas F. Torrance, *The Christian Doctrine of God* (Edinburgh: T&T Clark, 1996), 242.

[16]Torrance, *Christian Doctrine of God*, 242.

[17]Barth, *Witness*, 62.

as seen by humankind. This is the correlation of incarnation and illumination in the economy of the divine light in the world. This elucidation of the ontology of this light as both nature and effect alludes to the nature of illumination as participation in the divine light.

ILLUMINATION AND REVELATION

Before progressing any further, we must first address the relationship of illumination and revelation. Admittedly, Barth does not grant us a clear distinction of terms between illumination and revelation in his lectures on John. In fact, at times the language is used almost interchangeably, primarily because the language of light lends itself so naturally both to revelation and to human enlightenment. It is noteworthy, however, that Barth does not refer to Christ himself as illumination, but only as light. If we could make a distinction between revelation and illumination as Barth makes use of them in these lectures, it would be this: *revelation* is the work of the original, uncreated, primary light bearing witness to itself, while *illumination* demarcates the sphere of human participation in this revelation. That is not to say that illumination is purely human response or subjective activity. Revelation is "the original, uncreated, primary light, the direct and immediate revelation of life that bears witness to itself."[18] Illumination is the application of revelation with particularity. This application is the noetic, emotional, and spiritual enveloping of humanity with this revelation. It fills men and women with light and sets them in the light. Revelation is the event of this light's self-disclosure; Φ is the inclusion of humanity in the light of revelation. Illumination demarcates the sphere of all divine and human work in the individual's transformation.[19]

---

[18]"Light in heaven and earth always receives its radiance from elsewhere. But Christ is the light which shines of itself and then fills the whole world with *its* radiance: '*ut non alia sit usquam origo vel causa splendoris. Veram ergo lucem dixit, cui natura proprium est lucere.*' ['There is no other source or cause of its brightness anywhere. And so he calls him the true light whose own nature is to be light.'] Over against the witness περὶ τοῦ φωτός there stood and stands the φῶς τὸ ἀληθινὸν, the original, uncreated, primary light, the direct and immediate revelation of life that bears witness to itself. Of this true light a relative clause tells us, ὃ φωτίζει πάντα ἄνθρωπον. Φωτίζειν is more than φαίνειν (v.5), and the relative clause says more than v. 4b (that the light was the life of men). Not just an activity but an effect of light is meant here. It illumines men, it fills them with light, it sets them in the light. To the extent that they are set in the light at all!" (Barth, *Witness*, 61).

[19]*CD* IV/3:511.

As with John's prologue and Barth's theological interpretation of it, a discussion of the event of illumination begins for Barth in the discussion of the nature of the triune being behind the event of illumination—hence it is not purely human response. We see likewise that Barth will follow this outside of the constraints of the Fourth Gospel as he develops his trinitarian theology at the outset of his *Church Dogmatics*. Furthermore, Barth's doctrine of illumination is not simply or always a function of the economic Trinity, but first has its grounding in the immanent Trinity as *light in himself* (cf. 1 Jn 1:5).[20] What God is to humanity in shining the light of life, he is so antecedently in himself. This trinitarian framework is not unique to Barth's doctrine of illumination, but it is worth recognizing his trinitarian construction, as much of the doctrine of illumination is so frequently relegated to pneumatology alone.[21] As is customary for the doctrine of illumination, Barth focuses it around the Spirit and the Word, but in his case it is more precisely the Spirit and the Word of God revealed (prior to the Word of God written) and therefore located in both pneumatology and Christology.

Pneumatology and Christology

Barth's lectures on John perform a pivotal role in understanding the relationship between illumination and the Word of God. His lectures accomplish this by speaking of illumination with respect to the Word of God *as person* first. However, it leaves open the question of the relationship between pneumatology and Christology in illumination (This is due in part to the fact that it would be foreign to the narratives of John that we have addressed to import the Spirit). In Barth's more constructive theological works (*Göttingen Dogmatics, Church Dogmatics*), he demonstrates a more trinitarian vision of illumination. That the *Göttingen Dogmatics* were produced in a relatively similar era (1924–26) of his theological development means that the Spirit's work in these narratives would not have

---

[20]Barth writes, "We have now to speak of the light of life, of the light which life itself radiates *because it is itself light*. As Jesus Christ lives, He also shines out, not with an alien light which falls upon Him from without and illuminates Him, but with His own light proceeding from Himself. He lives as the source of light whose shining gives light without" (*CD* IV/3:46, emphasis mine). Elsewhere Barth adds, "We are reminded of 1 Jn. 1:5: 'God is light, and in him is no darkness at all.' He is the Holy One who reveals himself, to whom everything is revealed, and who reveals all things in what He does" (*CD* III/3:464).

[21]*GD* I:168.

been far from his mind, even if they are not stated explicitly in his lectures on John.

On a chronological approach to Barth's though, what Barth speaks of as the "subjective possibility of revelation" in the *Göttingen Dogmatics* closely reflects his thoughts on illumination in the lectures on John. The subjective possibility of revelation is defined there as the human receptivity for revelation.[22] Barth writes that the possibility of human reception is indispensable to a complete account of the concept of revelation.[23] In fact, Barth would say that we are not speaking about the revelation of God if it does not conclude in human reception. However, Barth's understanding of revelation makes "possibility" an interesting choice of words here insofar as it suggests a human capacity for reception. Therefore, Barth clarifies that this "possibility of human reception" is both an affirmation of humanity and an indictment of it. It is affirmation in that there is the possibility of human reception of revelation. It is indictment in that Barth insists that this possibility must come from outside of him—the Holy Spirit is this subjective *possibility* of revelation.[24]

That God provides the means for human reception of revelation is necessary for Barth because "there is no organ by which to receive God's revelation. For God himself is the content as well as the subject of revelation."[25] The question of the possibility of revelation is the question of "how we humans who cannot stand before God are the very ones who do stand before God."[26] With this in mind, the woman at the well's question takes on new significance: How is it that you, God, give me, a human, a drink of water? It is because God becomes and does what we cannot have and do; he becomes an organ for the reception of this divine communication.[27] In this way God becomes the subjective possibility of revelation in us by his Holy Spirit. God becomes in us the capacity for "reception, perception and acceptance of revelation."[28]

---

[22]*GD* I:168.
[23]*GD* I:168.
[24]*GD* I:168.
[25]*GD* I:174.
[26]*GD* I:175.
[27]"God will have to bear and fill and make good our human incapacity by the capacity, the sufficiency, the adequacy which can be present only in God himself for God himself" (*GD* I:175).
[28]*GD* 1:176.

Nevertheless, humanity does not simply become a puppet in this process. Humanity really does become a vessel for the content of revelation and therefore for God himself.[29] In the *Göttingen Dogmatics*, Barth refers to this establishment of a real relationship between God and humanity as an "activation of humanity."[30] It is an activation "in which we ourselves will and do and achieve but God does what we ourselves cannot do, positing himself as the beginning, middle and end of this human activity . . . being himself the organ and way and movement in this human activity."[31]

It is helpful at this point to draw in Barth's insistence on the active relationship between humanity and God. This will help us understand how it is that human activity in this relationship is real human activity. It is well known that Barth prefers to speaks in the language of occurrence, happening, event, act, and "at the most general level it means that he thinks primarily in terms of events and relationships rather than monadic or self-contained substances."[32] Barth's theology here, as elsewhere, is formed heavily on the basis of "the sovereignty of grace, the incapacity of the creature, and the miraculous history whereby grace grants what the creature lacks for the sake of love and freedom."[33] Read in light of Barth's emphasis on our active relationship to God and in conjunction with his theological anthropology (which will be developed in the following paragraph), humanity can exist in this relation not simply as an object but as a self-conscious subject because in the *event* of this relationship humanity is not diminished but rather established.

True to Barth's dialectical fashion, this event of God becoming humanity's capacity for the reception of revelation is not an affront or destruction of our humanity but is in fact the establishment of it. This encounter by its very

---

[29]"If, then, there is a being in God in the very activation of our humanity, or, in other words, if there is an activation of our humanity which is from God and in God, then obviously (for how can God fail to know and find himself?) we will stand before God and over against God, in the contradiction to be sure, yet still before and over against God. We will then be vessels (earthen vessels [2 Cor 4:7], but still vessels) for the content of revelation, for God himself. There will then be revelation, that is, the establishment of fellowship between God and us by God's communication to us" (*GD* I:175-76).

[30]*GD* I:179-80.

[31]*GD* I:179-80.

[32]Hunsinger, *How to Read Karl Barth*, 30.

[33]Hunsinger, *How to Read Karl Barth*, 31; see Barth's *Göttingen Dogmatics*, where he outlines four conditions of the subjective possibility of receiving revelation, which align well with Hunsinger's comment here (I:177-80).

nature means judgment. Confronted by God himself there is the most striking and evident judgment. On the negative side it is the judgment that humanity is not God. However, positively speaking, it is the judgment that humanity *is* the covenant partner of God according to his divine good pleasure.[34] Consequently, humanity is what it is by virtue of God's active relationship with it, not by virtue of some static substance in itself. On Barth's account, God is known in his action and relationships, and therefore humanity as the creation of God is best conceived of not as a static substance but as a dependent, active partner with God established by our relationship with God.[35] As a reality grounded in this relationship, the encounter is not a diminution of humanity but a profound confirmation of humanity and of God's love of it in his freedom.[36]

THE CHALLENGE OF A BARTHIAN DOCTRINE OF ILLUMINATION

The apparent challenge of elucidating a Barthian doctrine of illumination is Barth's consistent reference (both in his lectures on John and in *CD* §69.2) to Christ as the "light" or "light of life," while ascribing much of the traditional language around the doctrine of illumination to "the subjective reality and possibility of revelation," which he identifies with the Holy Spirit. To the ears of those engaged in the contemporary discussion of illumination, it may seem as though Barth is being imprecise with these terms and their corresponding theological significance. Is Barth playing fast and loose or is he building toward something specific?

---

[34]*CD* III/2:203.

[35]For more on Barth's theological anthropology and its development in his theology, see *GD* I:72-80; *CD* III/2:136-40.

[36]"With what I have tried to formulate here I have had in mind the miracle of the Holy Spirit who created faith and obedience in us and thus places us before God. He 'creates' them. That is to say, as he creates the world out of nothing, and as he makes a particle of human nature in the body of the virgin the dwelling of the Logos, so he makes a piece of broken humanity into human knowing and doing, with himself in his revelation as the object. As in creation and the incarnation, so here, too, we have a *miracle*, an event which has its only ontic and noetic basis in the freedom and majesty of God" (*GD* I:176). Later, in *CD* I/2, §16.1, Barth will pick this question up again, making the correction that he must first speak of how this relationship, this freedom in humanity for God becomes *real* before he speaks of how it becomes *possible* (Barth only addresses the subjective *possibility* of revelation in the *Göttingen Dogmatics*). The question of the reality of revelation is an objective question regarding how God has made his way to humanity. The question of possibility is the subjective question of humanity's attitude to this movement of God toward it. He writes, "The former is the question of fact, the latter the question of our attitude to it" (*CD* I/2:205).

It is my conclusion that Barth was building beyond a singularly pneumatological doctrine of illumination and toward a robust, fully trinitarian doctrine of illumination—that is, one that is inclusive of the works of the Father, the Son, and the Holy Spirit. In my conclusion, a concise statement of a Barthian doctrine of illumination would go as follows: *divine illumination is human participation in the Son's knowledge of the Father by the power of the Holy Spirit.* Barth's own most complete statement that lends itself to this conclusion is found in his discussion of "The Fulfillment of the Knowledge of God" (*CD* II/1 §25). Having just expounded on the subject of humanity before God, Barth now speaks at length under the subheading, "God before Man." Here he writes,

> If it is true that God stands before man, that He gives himself to be known and is known by man, it is true only because and in the fact that God is the triune God, God the Father, the Son and the Holy Spirit. First of all, and in the heart of the truth in which He stands before us, *God stands before himself;* the Father knows the Son and the Son the Father in the unity of the Holy Spirit. *This occurrence in God Himself is the essence and strength of our knowledge of God.* It is not an occurrence unknown to us; rather it is made known to us through His Word; but it is certainly a hidden occurrence. That is to say, *it is an occurrence in which man as such is not a participant, but in which he becomes a participant through God's revelation and thus in a way inconceivable to himself.*[37]

As an active relationship in which we are made participants, illumination is at once both the *event* of the revelation of God underlying humanity's knowledge and the *event* of humanity's knowledge being established by that revelation.[38]

Lest we fall subject to the typical Barthian criticism of Christomonism by subtly underwriting a christological replacement of the Spirit in illumination, let us be clear in saying that all of illumination still takes place by the power of the Holy Spirit. We are attempting to clarify here that the light that the Spirit is shining on individuals in the Spirit's illumination is no arbitrary notion of "light," or even simply an analogy for dispersing the darkness of our minds, but is the very light of the Word of God himself, rooted in the

---

[37] *CD* II/1:48-49, emphasis mine.
[38] *CD* IV/3:511.

nature of God as light himself. In this way, we are not detracting from the pneumatological role and significance of the Spirit in illumination. Rather, in understanding that the light that shines on us in illumination is the Word of God, we better understand the robustly trinitarian dynamics of illumination and how it is rooted fully in God himself. Barth attaches this conversation to John's language in his prologue (Jn 1:9), where "Jesus is called the true light who, coming into the world, enlightens every man."[39] Barth quotes several passages in John (Jn 1:4; 8:12; 9:5; 12:46), ultimately concluding, "Throughout the Fourth Gospel, to believe in Him and so to have life means to receive and therefore to know this light."[40] Furthermore, this captures well the components of Barth's language around revelation and illumination found in Barth's lectures on John, the *Göttingen Dogmatics*, and elsewhere in the *Church Dogmatics*. It should not at all be surprising that we find such a cogent statement in a section titled "The Fulfillment of the Knowledge of God." After all, I suspect there is broad agreement that this is precisely what illumination is: the fulfillment of God's intended self-communication to humanity.

In both the concise statement provided above and the quotation from Barth, all of the necessary components of a Barthian doctrine as displayed in his lectures on John, the *Göttingen Dogmatics*, and the *Church Dogmatics* are present. As remarked all over John, it is the Son's knowledge of the Father into which we are invited and which we receive (Jn 1:18; 3:31-36; 8:19; 10:14-15; 14:7-11; 15:15). The Son making the Father known to us is a shining of his light on the world. It is an invitation that we then receive by means of the Holy Spirit. This knowledge, then, is not a knowledge possessed, but a knowledge in which we actively participate. It is a participation made available to us by the Holy Spirit.

A second key idea related both to a Barthian doctrine of illumination and to this project more generally is that we must speak of illumination in terms of an economy incorporating both revelation and regeneration. This is because, on Barth's account, illumination is the intersection of regeneration and revelation. More specifically, illumination captures what happens when knowledge is received and new life is conceived. In this, humanity participates

---

[39] *CD* II/1:42.
[40] *CD* II/1:42.

in the Son's knowledge of the Father, which is made possible by the power of the Holy Spirit. The radiance of the Father is communicated via the light in the Son, attracting and compelling humanity to relationship in the power of the Spirit.

ILLUMINATION AND REGENERATION

A profound contribution of Barth's lectures on John is that they offer a glimpse into his understanding of what the movement of this light toward humanity looks like. Within the context of the biblical witness, we are able to glimpse Barth's reflections on the light moving out from itself and into relationship. We are also able to see the light's outworking as it encounters men and women, as it provokes a new birth from above, faith and obedience, and an understanding of the Word as a word addressed *to them*. This brings us to light, illumination, and regeneration.

With few exceptions, the contemporary conversation regarding illumination pertains to coordination of the work of the Spirit with the Word of God *written*—Scripture. However, with the Gospel of John, and consequently Barth's lectures on John, the conversation lends itself more naturally to the Word of God *revealed*—Jesus Christ—and its encounter with humanity.[41] The point here is not to detract from the illumination that takes place as one reads Scripture. The point is to ground those Scriptures theologically. The reason the Spirit illumines our minds as we encounter the words of Scripture is because the Word of God in the Bible is ultimately grounded in the Word of God himself, the second person of the Trinity. This is not a demoting of Scripture in illumination but the establishment of its profound divine foundation. John's prologue narrates for us the moving out of this light from light in itself to light in relationship—in encounter with humanity. Barth's engagement with birth in the first pericope (Jn 1:1-18) focuses on the miracle of regeneration. The miracle of regeneration is the contradiction that the world neither hears nor receives the light, and *nevertheless,* there are children of God (Jn 1:12-13). This being the case, the regenerative component of illumination comes upon men and women from outside

---

[41]Even if this is correct, one might ask where we encounter this revelation now if not in Scripture. The point here is not to say that this illumination pertains only to the Word of God revealed. Rather, this illumination is true of the Word of God written because it is first true of the Word of God revealed.

themselves, both creating the receptivity for their transformation and the transformation itself.[42] The event of regeneration is grounded in the Son, not in the individual. It is also sustained in the Son. More accurately, then, regeneration takes place in the light of the Logos and is sustained so long as one remains in that very light. Regeneration is a divine provision and divine sustenance. The right to be called a child of God, the legitimacy of one as a child of God, resides in this provision and sustenance.[43] But as an event and ongoing existence that is inaugurated and sustained in the Son, it is a participation in an abundant provision that resides outside of the self. It is an effect-in-participation. It is not a deposit in the individual that then becomes self-sufficient and self-sustaining.[44] The participation, therefore, is not only God's movement in the life of humanity but also the event of humanity being drawn into the life of the Father, Son, and Holy Spirit.

The theological concept of vocation becomes relevant at this point as the question becomes, how does it come about that people become children of God in fulfillment of this divine work?[45] It must be said that the nature of human participation in this light is not cooperative or transactional as between God and humanity on the same plane. The nature of this human participation in the light is in freedom.[46] It is a freedom for which humanity has been set free.[47] It is a liberation established on the underlying freedom

---

[42]Barth treats regeneration under sanctification: God's making humankind right with himself. "What is meant by sanctification (*sanctificatio*) might just as well be described by the less common biblical term regeneration (*regeneratio*) or renewal (*renovatio*), or by that of conversion (*conversio*), or by that of penitence (*poenitentia*) which plays so important a role in both the Old and New Testaments, or comprehensively by that of discipleship which is so outstanding especially in the synoptic Gospels" (*CD* IV/2:500).

[43]"Those who receive him, who are given the power to become the children of God, who believe in His name, are not born of blood, or of the will of the flesh, or of the will of man, but of God (Jn 1:12f). Their action is *nourished* by the mystery of the life-giving Spirit by whom the Lord has united these sinful creates to Himself" (*CD* IV/2:529, emphasis mine).

[44]Adam Neder, *Participation in Christ: An Entry into Karl Barth's Church Dogmatics* (Louisville, KY: Westminster John Knox, 2009), 48.

[45]*CD* IV/3:481-680. Here, Barth engages extensively with the concept of vocation, devoting two hundred pages to the topic.

[46]"It comes about as Jesus calls them to discipleship. We can never go beyond this answer. But we can and must put the counter question: how does it come about that they are actually reached by this call in such a way that they render obedience, becoming the disciples of Jesus and doing what they are ordered to do as such? We shall see at once . . . that it is a matter of the freedom which they are given by the one who calls them, by Jesus" (*CD* IV/2:554).

[47]"Jesus Christ is God's command to make use of the freedom which is ours as his children" (Neder, *Participation in Christ*, 54).

of God. Regeneration is liberation, both as birth and as a way of being. Humanity is not forced into this birth or this way of being against its will by an arbitrary divine sovereignty. As Barth will develop in his *Church Dogmatics*, this regeneration is a gracious "awakening and arising from the sleep of death; the sleep from which there can be no awakening except in the power of the mystery and miracle of God."[48] Regeneration is an awakening to a previously inconceivable reality of freedom. It is a reality that is already determined and established for them in the reconciliatory and revelatory work of Christ. It is the receiving of this reality as their own, not because they must, but because they may. It is eyes opening to a light they did not know was shining.

Barth's most sustained engagement with regeneration falls under the heading "The Awakening to Conversion" in the section titled "The Sanctification of Man" (*CD* §66). By the time Barth is addressing this in the fourth volume of the *Church Dogmatics*, the Holy Spirit has found more prominent expression in regeneration and conversion than seen in his lectures on John. (As mentioned earlier, this also has to do with the fact that it would have been foreign to the discussion of John 1 to bring in much about the Spirit there.) Bruce McCormack's assessment of Barth on human participation holds: "Faith, for Barth, is never at any point, a capacity of the creature. It is a response of the creature to a present action of the Holy Spirit; it is never a completed action which would allow the creature to say, 'I have believed.'"[49] This is the crucial concept for our understanding of the divine-human relationship: it is a relationship sustained by the present action of God in the Holy Spirit. The Holy Spirit sustains our participation in God by this ongoing, present action in our life.

This notion of the divine-human relationship captures well the effect-in-participation language used above to describe the dependency of illumination in regeneration. It captures the way in which illumination entails both divine action and human action but in such a way that the human action is always predicated on the *present action* of God. To say that belief is never a completed action goes hand in hand with Barth's conclusion that

---

[48]*CD* IV/2:555.

[49]Bruce McCormack, *Orthodox and Modern: Studies in the Theology of Karl Barth* (Grand Rapids: Baker Academic, 2008), 311.

conversion itself is never a completed action. Rather, one is always in danger of falling asleep once again, and in need of reawakening.[50] Short of sight being given to the blind, there is scarcely a better metaphor than "awakening" for what takes place for the woman at the well.

Finally, regeneration for Barth is best understood as the intersection of illumination and faith. As an event resulting from the present action of God, regeneration is the reception of knowledge as well as the belief in that knowledge. Barth's eloquent deliberation on knowledge as enlightenment, faith as brightness, and reception as the aptness for both of these experiences (knowledge and faith) brings these theological points together beautifully.[51] As previously stated, illumination can be logically but not chronologically distinguished from its brightness. In the same way, in the event of regeneration the experiences of knowledge and faith can be logically but not chronologically distinguished. To be born of God (Jn 1:12-13) and to be born anew (Jn 3:3) are events of illumination. As the full reality of this light moves toward humanity, this light generates knowledge and faith in them by the present action of God.[52] In this event, *knowledge of God is conceived.* It is a living knowledge, birthed as humanity is enveloped in this divine light, and thereby participates in its brilliance. For Barth, this new life of humanity is the decisive work of the event of revelation—the *vivificatio* of humanity.[53] When asked how this liberation is imparted to humans, how they are awakened to repentance, how they find themselves claimed and impelled, how these things are known, how they can be treated as reality, and on what

---

[50]"We cannot, therefore, define Christians simply as those who are awake while the rest sleep, but more cautiously as those who waken up in the sense that they are awakening a first time and then again to their shame and good fortune. They are, in fact, those who constantly stand in need of reawakening and who depend upon the fact that they are continually awakened. They are thus those who, it is to be hoped, continually waken up" (*CD* IV/2:555). Quite naturally, this raises the question of Barth's position on the doctrine of the perseverance of the saints. In light of what Barth says in *CD* II/2, 333, regarding election and *CD* IV/3 regarding awakening, we see that awakening to one's election does not equal one's "status" as either among the elect or reprobate. The basis of election is the election of Jesus Christ, whose election is ours. The basis of our awakening to that election is the present action of God in one's life.

[51]"γινώσκειν is enlightenment [*Erleuchtetwerden*], πιστεύειν is brightness [*Hellsein*], and λαμβάνειν is the aptness [*Geeignetsein*] of the subject for both these experiences, which cannot be distinguished chronologically" (Barth, *Witness*, 71).

[52]"The sleep which he sleeps is the sleep of death, and what is needed is that he should be wakened and waken from death. There is thus required a new and direct act of God himself if there is to be this awakening in which man becomes a disciple, a Christian" (*CD* IV/2:556).

[53]*CD* IV/2:581.

basis we have thought and spoken about the totality of conversion, Barth responds, "The answer is quite simple. We have merely taken seriously what Calvin called the participatio Christi, making it the ultimate foundation of his whole doctrine of sanctification. The actual event which is an event of revelation in virtue of the enlightening work of the Holy Spirit, and as such sets in motion the conversion of man, is the Christ-event."[54] The *vivificatio* of humanity—the regeneration of human beings—is an event of revelation brought to its intended completion through illumination by the Holy Spirit. Illumination is revelation communicated with particularity. This does not imply that the Holy Spirit illumines all. Rather, in so far as one is enlightened, it is by this light. Barth writes that this "*conversio* and *renovatio*, applied to the actual sanctification of man, are nothing less than *regeneratio*. New birth!"[55] This conversion, this renovation, this liberation, this awakening, this regeneration, all has its basis in the *participatio Christi*.

In his work on *participatio Christi* in Barth, Adam Neder explains that one aspect of our participation in Christ is our participation in the history of the life of Jesus Christ. As with justification and sanctification, vocation—of which illumination is a part—is a reality in Jesus Christ on behalf of humanity even before it becomes history in the life of an individual. Barth says it best himself,

> As in the case of his justification and sanctification, his vocation took place before it became an event in his own life, and in a way which is decisive for his situation, existence and history, in the work of God's free grace to him, which in time followed and corresponded to His eternal counsel, in the divine work of reconciliation which was simply effected for him by Jesus Christ without any co-operation or even presence on his part.[56]

The telos of this conversion of humanity to God is union with Christ. It is the culmination or the "goal of vocation" (as *CD* §71.3 is titled). As Jesus Christ *is* the light of the world, all human beings stand in his light "even if with closed or blind eyes."[57] The vocation of a human is, then, awakening to this light. It is "an act of powerful grace and gracious power" in which his

---

[54] *CD* IV/2:581-82.
[55] *CD* IV/2:563.
[56] *CD* IV/3:486.
[57] *CD* IV/2:487.

eyes are opened to the light already shining.[58] It is a shining of this light with particularity.[59] Jesus Christ as the light of the world shines on him, healing his blind eyes by its shining. In vocation, this illumination is making possible "a seeing of which man was previously incapable."[60]

PARTICIPATION AS REPETITION

The key to understanding Barth's notion of participation is, not surprisingly, Christology. It is rooted in the dual movement that takes place in Christ. In Christ condescending to take human nature to himself, all humanity is thereby exalted to God's side. In this exaltation, humanity is placed at the side of God and made capable of living in partnership with God. Keith Johnson explains that Barth's doctrine of participation "provides an account of how the ontological distinction between God and the human remains intact even as the human is united to God through the saving work of Christ and the Spirit."[61] To say that Barth's notion of participation is rooted in Christ's exaltation of humanity to fellowship or ordered partnership with God is to say that it is rooted in Christ's covenantal obedience. Johnson writes, "[Barth's] central presupposition is that Christ's perfect and finished work to unite us to himself through his death and resurrection is ordered toward the goal of creating a human correspondence to God that follows in the pattern of Christ's own obedience to the covenant."[62] Participation, then,

---

[58]*CD* IV/2:497.

[59]"The distinctive element on the event of his vocation, in which Jesus Christ in person meets him as a person and becomes a known and conscious element in his life-history, is that the light, Jesus Christ as the light of the world, illuminates this man. It does not now merely shine for him in general, it now shines for him in such a way that his closed eyes are opened by its shining, or rather his blind eyes are healed by its shining and made to see. This is the process of vocation. Man is called and becomes a Christian as he is illuminated" (*CD* IV/2:508).

[60]"Illumination, however, is a seeing of which man was previously incapable but of which he is now capable. It is thus his advancement to knowledge. That the revelation of God shines on and in him, takes place in such a way that he hears, receives, understands, grasps, and appropriates what is said to him in it, not with new and special organs, but with the same organs of apperception with which he knows other things, yet not in virtue of his own capacity to use them, but in virtue of the missing capacity which he is now given by God's revelation" (CD IV/2:509).

[61]Put differently, participation gives an account for how "human beings adopted as children of God can be included in God's own life even as they do not live this life in the same way God does." Keith L. Johnson, "Karl Barth's Reading of Paul's Union with Christ," in *"In Christ" in Paul: Explorations in Paul's Theology of Union and Participation*, ed. Constantine R. Campbell, Michael J. Thate, and Kevin J. Vanhoozer (Tübingen: Mohr Siebeck, 2014), 454.

[62]Johnson, "Barth's Reading," 461.

is not ontological but deeply covenantal and therefore historical. Johnson explains, "Barth's line of thought here is guided by the basic shape of God's covenantal promise: that God will be our God and we will be his people (cf. Jer. 31:33)."[63] Participation is the means by which humanity is incorporated into the realization of this covenant in history. Because "this promise involves both God and human beings, Barth thinks its fulfillment must take place, not as a state or a singular transaction, but as a history—an ongoing relationship between God and humans in space and time."[64] In being exalted to partnership with God as God intended for his covenant with humanity, the nature of this participation is not "the divination of human nature, but its *determination*."[65] According to Barth's notion of *participatio Christi*,

> Human nature is determined in Christ and by Christ in such a way that it now can exist in "full harmony with the divine essence common to the Father, Son, and Holy Spirit" even while it "remains human." God moves from above to below so that humans can move from below to above and live in partnership with God.[66]

Neder speaks of this participation as a perfect mutual coordination of God with humanity in a definite order.[67] This fellowship (*koinōnia*) or union with Jesus Christ is the goal of vocation. Neder summarizes three specific aspects of this relationship: "(1) It is definitely ordered (i.e., it is a relationship of lordship on one side and service on the other). (2) Jesus Christ and the individual enjoy perfect mutual co-ordination one with the other. (3) Jesus Christ and the individual each retain their particularity and distinction from one another."[68] An aspect of that is to say, it is not a unity of nature, a participation in God's divine nature; rather, it is a participation in the life of God by active relationship. In illumination humanity is awakened to a recognition of the lordship of Christ and therefore to a life of faithfulness and obedience.[69]

---

[63]Johnson, "Barth's Reading," 461.

[64]Johnson, "Barth's Reading," 461, quoting *CD* IV/1:7.

[65]Johnson, "Barth's Reading," 465.

[66]Johnson, "Barth's Reading," 465, quoting *CD* IV/2:72.

[67]Johnson, "Barth's Reading," 458.

[68]Neder, *Participation in Christ*, 77.

[69]Barth, *Erklärung*, 385. "It is not about his religious capacity or incapacity, but about his obedience or disobedience, about the authority that God has or does not have over him. On this knife-edge falls the decision between belief and unbelief. Unbelief is the inability, the inability

It should come as no surprise then, that Barth develops this notion of participation in the context of sanctification (*CD* §66).[70] Sanctification is the realization of our participation in Christ's covenantal obedience.[71] Johnson captures well how this participation is actualized for the individual:

> Believers are caught up in this movement when they are united to Christ and begin to live in harmony with the divine essence in and through him. The beginning of this movement occurs with their faith in Christ. When Christ calls the believer to have faith in him, Barth says, "the history inaugurated *by God becomes man's own subjective history.*" And this call to faith always comes also as a call to obedience.[72]

The nature of this participation then, is not that humanity becomes the divine essence, but that a human being is called and awakened and so begins to live in harmony with the divine essence through him.

This calling and awakening thereby links this sanctification to vocation for Barth, the primary context for his elaboration on illumination. In illumination there is a unity in our being that is grasped in its entirety. It's not that our minds are affected and our passions left to the side. Rather, the disparate faculties of our being are gathered up in the one hand of the illuminating Spirit, turning us to face the radiance of the Son who is reflecting the divine light of the Father. In this light, there stands a recognition of biblical words as the words of God and a conviction of its truth. In this light there stands an acknowledgment of God's glory, Christ's lordship, and the Spirit's animation of one's being as *a being in obedience to God's vocation on their life.*

In articulating a vision of human knowledge of God as human participation in the Son's knowledge of the Father by the power of the Holy Spirit, illumination, then, is one aspect of human participation in that triune life

---

of disobedience, which is identical with the divine apophasis, indeed rejection. In the lack of ἐξουσία to become God's child (1.12), it shows that one is not one [of God's children]."

[70]In fact, Migliore argues that, as with Calvin, *participatio Christi* is the "unifying theme" and "ultimate foundation" for Barth's whole doctrine of sanctification. "Participatio Christi: The Central Theme of Barth's Doctrine of Sanctification," *Zeitschrift für Dialektische Theologie* 18 (2002): 288.

[71]Our obedience is the "concrete realization of our new being in Christ through the power of the Spirit as our being is given a determination that corresponds to Christ's own human life of covenant obedience" (Johnson, "Barth's Reading," 465).

[72]Johnson, "Barth's Reading," 465, quoting *CD* III/2:176, emphasis mine.

more generally. Barth explains, "As Jesus Christ calls us and is heard by us He gives us His Holy Spirit *in order that His own relationship to His Father may be repeated in us*. He then knows us, and we know Him, as the Father knows Him and He the Father. Those who live in this repetition live in the Holy Spirit."[73] This gives logic to the way this participation is not simply an objective pronouncement on humanity in light of Christ's action, but is subjectively realized in the life of the individual by the Holy Spirit. When Barth speaks of human participation in Christ as something precipitated by Christ's reconciling work, we might speak accurately of this participation as *living the repetition* of Christ's life in our own by the Holy Spirit. John Webster argues that there is not a distinguishable objective and subjective moment. The subjective realization of Christ's salvific work is already included within itself in the one grace of Christ's ongoing fulfillment of God's covenant in history.[74] Johnson puts it this way, "in the history of Christ's ongoing fulfillment of God's covenant, the 'objective becomes subjective' as Christ personally guarantees that the consequences of his death and resurrection are realized in the life of the believer through the work of his Holy Spirit."[75] This human participation is Christ's reconciliation of human beings with God repeated in the life of human beings.[76] In summary, the nature of Barth's doctrine of participation is christological, covenantal, and historical. It is the ongoing human partnership with God to which humanity is exalted *in Christ* and which is realized as humans live in the repetition of Christ's covenantal fulfillment by the Holy Spirit. It is "participation-as-partnership."[77]

We conclude with Barth's articulation of this illumination:

> When the process is considered in its formal character as illumination, we are not in any sense dealing with a mere part or beginning in which he becomes a Christian. For what is lacking here when we see it as God's action towards man, as that which comes on man from God? Is not his illumination, and

---

[73]*CD* II/2:780.

[74]John Webster, *Barth's Ethics of Reconciliation* (New York: Cambridge University Press, 1995), 127-28.

[75]"The two aspects of this work stand together in an ordered, narrative relationship that corresponds to the narrative history of the covenant itself" (Johnson, "Barth's Reading," 459).

[76]"Christ reconciles us to God by uniting us to himself through his life, death, and resurrection precisely so we can live *with* him and *in* him as God's partners into eternity" (Johnson, "Barth's Reading," 459).

[77]Johnson, "Barth's Reading," 456.

therefore the revelation of God which underlies his knowledge, and the knowledge established by revelation, the one totality of his temporal and historical experience of the living Jesus Christ? There is no doubt that in time, so far as it is his time, and history, so far as it is his history, this can take the most diverse and widely separate forms. But there is no differentiation or particularity of truly Christian experience in which we are not dealing with the one totality of the vocation of man in his encounter with the living Jesus Christ. Hence there is nothing other or higher or better, e.g., under the title of regeneration or conversion, which has still to follow vocation, which has to deepen and complete it, if it is to be true, effective and valid. There are other angles from which we have to view the one totality of this occurrence if we are to estimate and consider it a right. For the moment we ask formally concerning that which precedes. And we give a full answer to this question when we describe this occurrence in all its possible and actual modifications as the illumination which comes to man from God, which man needs with the same totality at every conceivable turn in the path if he is to be and remain a Christian, but in which he may participate with equal totality. Whether in the divine act or the human experience which makes a man a Christian, there can never be any question of anything more or less or other that his illumination, that the revelation of God which underlies his knowledge and the knowledge established by this revelation. We are guilty of a hopeless cleavage from the speech and thought-forms of the Bible if we try to deny that in the illumination of man there takes place the totality of what makes a man a Christian.[78]

ILLUMINATION AND THE BIBLE

In order to provide a complete treatment of Barth's doctrine of illumination as it intersects with more contemporary conversations, it is necessary to address the question of illumination and the Word of God written—the Bible. In particular, we must discuss the popular question of the relationship between illumination and inspiration. In John, as in Barth's theology, the Word is first and foremost the Logos, the Word of God made flesh, the Word of God revealed. In Barth's trinitarian doctrine of illumination, the illumination of Scripture remains an event between Word and Spirit. This is because the illumination of the Word of God written is derivative of the Holy

---

[78]*CD* IV/3:511.

Spirit's illumination of the Word of God revealed. In this way, the illumination of Scripture falls within the economy of divine light as an event between Word and Spirit.

In Barth's earlier work in the *Göttingen Dogmatics*, he summarizes the relationship between the Word of God as person and the Word of God as text stating, "Only the Word of God himself can bear witness to the Word of God in scripture." This is Barth's summary of Calvin's teaching regarding proof of the authority of Scripture. An aspect of illumination grasping one's whole life is the text exercising authority in the life of the individual. But it is not a matter of Word only, but also of Spirit: "By the Spirit scripture bears witness that it is God's Word." Expanding on this work of the Spirit, he writes, "As we saw in the doctrine of Revelation, the Spirit is God as he turns to us, addresses us, discloses himself to us, opens our eyes and ears, gives us faith and obedience, and intercedes with us. Scripture, corresponding to the incarnation, is itself Logos as the objective possibility of historical communication."[79] Encompassing the witness of the prophets and apostles, God takes up and uses this text to bear witness to himself. Barth concludes that in so doing, "the only competent witness in this matter has spoken, speaks and will speak—the inner testimony of the Spirit."[80]

When it comes to the work of the Spirit in and with the text, Barth does not concede a sharp distinction between the Spirit's prior work in the inspiration of the text and the Spirit's present work in illumination. Rather, "The Holy Spirit is neither a magical quality of some ancient text nor an inner sentiment. The Holy Spirit is God speaking to us, making us his children and servant, giving us mouths and ears and eyes for God's revelation. For he himself is God. . . . We have to say that we must view inspiration as a single timeless—or rather, contemporary—act of God." The Spirit's work in both cases—the biblical authors in inspiration and in us in illumination—is an event. It is an event in the power of the Holy Spirit. In both cases it is a participation in the Word's knowledge of the Father by the power of the Spirit.

---

[79]*GD* I:222.

[80]*GD* I:223. Bernard Ramm writes, "It [the testimony of the Holy Spirit] is the removal of a veil; it is light dissipating darkness. It is illumination granting the powers of spiritual perception. The total inward man now sees revelation as revelation; he intuits truth as truth; he hears Scripture as the truth of God." *The Witness of the Spirit: An Essay on the Contemporary Relevance of the Internal Witness of the Holy Spirit* (Grand Rapids: Eerdmans, 1960), 84-85.

As God provides both the revelation and the capacity to receive it, in the illumination of Scripture "it is an act in which the Spirit speaks to spirit, and spirit receives Spirit." In this way "we are not to distinguish between the light that the Bible sheds and the eye that perceives this light." He paraphrases Calvin: "The same Spirit who has spoken through the mouths of the prophets must find entry into our hearts and persuade us that they rendered faithfully what they had been told to say by God."[81] Finally, Barth gives approval to a statement of the Zurich theologian Heidegger to capture his thoughts:

> The witness of the Holy Spirit is neither a mere persuasion of the mind, which might leave a suspicion of deception (objectivism), nor an irrational movement of the heart such as enthusiasts peddle as divine (subjectivism), but a glowing and shining of the Spirit in our dark hearts which gives us the light of the knowledge of the glory of God in the face of Jesus Christ [2 Cor 4:6], so that, all obstacles are being removed, we are put in a position to see the whole superiority and wealth of the divine Word.[82]

As with Barth's doctrine of illumination more generally, his doctrine of the illumination of Scripture subsists in the present action of God. It is the timeless, continual, contemporary action of God turning to us in his Spirit. It is not a once for all endowment, but an ongoing, renewing occurrence. In God's self-disclosure by witness of the text, God's Spirit continually opens our eyes and ears to see and hear revelation shining and speaking to us. It is not a new word that is given in this illumination, but in the illumination it is a word that is heard anew—it is heard as a word addressed to us. It is both an invitation by God's Word to be awakened and the awakening of us to this Word by God's Spirit.

The product of this is what Nicodemus could not conceive but is conceived by the woman at the well and the man born blind: faith and obedience. As was concluded in the previous chapter, obedience is the knowledge in action that correlates with the knowledge received in revelation. The culmination of faith in the Word and obedience to this Word is union with Christ, *participatio Christi*. This union and participation is not the reward of faith and obedience but the power for the possibility of faith

---

[81]*GD* I:225.
[82]*GD* I:225.

and obedience. This union and participation is the reality in which the awakened one is freed to believe and obey.

CONCLUSION

> In our description of the process of vocation we have seen how this comes about, namely, by his illumination to active knowledge which as such is his awakening. Since this is an act of God, of Jesus Christ and of the Holy Spirit; since it is the active Word of God effectively spoken to him, it is established that his distinction from others is definitely not grounded in himself, nor put in his own hands, let alone made over to him as a possession and as it were placed in his pocket. His distinctiveness stands or falls with the fact that it is freely given him, and that he receives it as a grace with the pure gratitude which advances no claim. . . . We cannot escape the saying that the Christian, as a child of light, is a child of God who is himself light.[83]

A Barthian doctrine of illumination as developed here at least implicitly endorses the notion of an economy of divine light. This is true in that his view of illumination encapsulates the totality of what makes a person a Christian: the revelation of God, human regeneration and vocation in the power of the Holy Spirit, human faith and obedience, and climactically human participation in Christ. Barth's trinitarian doctrine of illumination is expansive and dynamic, encompassing all aspects of the divine light as it shines and confronts his creation. Christ as the light of life coordinates Christ's incarnation with illumination, and his illumination with reconciliation. Christ as the light of life coordinates regeneration with revelation in that illumination is the application of God's revelation with particularity. Illumination is the completion of revelation. In illumination children are born of God (regeneration), and in illumination God's revelation underlies and establishes human knowledge, producing a person's faith and obedience. This is what Barth calls "the dynamic character of illumination."[84] If we accurately define Barth's doctrine of illumination as *human participation in the Son's knowledge of the Father by the power of the Holy Spirit,* we can see clearly how the inspiration and illumination of Scripture fall also within the economy of this illumination for Barth. The Holy Spirit's inspiration of

---

[83]*CD* IV/3:531-32.
[84]*CD* IV/3:513.

Scripture is not first and foremost a statement about the nature of Scripture, but rather a statement about the nature of the Holy Spirit's work in revealing the second person of the Trinity—the Logos. Thus, for Barth, the inspiration and illumination of Scripture are both acts of this work of the Spirit revealing this second person of the Trinity—the contemporary, timeless, continual act of the Spirit's being. In the chapters to follow we will explore what bearing Barth's doctrine has on constructing a more robust and expansive vision for the doctrine of illumination.

PART THREE

A THEOLOGY OF
ILLUMINATION

❖❖❖❖❖❖❖❖❖❖❖❖❖❖❖❖❖❖❖❖❖

EIGHT

John as a Narrative of Illumination

I N MOVING NOW TO THE WORK OF CONSTRUCTING a new pro-
posal for the doctrine of illumination, informed particularly by the work
of Augustine and Barth and their readings of the Gospel of John, the next
and most necessary step is to lay out a Johannine theology for a doctrine of
illumination. This chapter will begin with the method best suited for this
task—biblical theology, a setting forth of the text's theology in its own terms,
concepts, and categories. It will then engage the material in a more systematic theological fashion in preparation for incorporation into the final,
more constructive chapters to follow. In developing this Johannine doctrine
of illumination, a first necessary step is to read the Gospel as a narrative that
unfolds under the thematic setting articulated by the prologue—the drama
of the true light coming into the world. If the entirety of the Gospel is to be
read in light of these programmatic statements of the prologue, it follows
that each encounter in the text is to also be read as an encounter with the
light.[1] Each of these narratives belong to, informs, and is informed by the
larger narrative of the Gospel—the narrative of the true light coming into
the world. We will first give a treatment of illumination as a doctrine rooted
in the doctrine of God itself. Second, we will offer a proposal for illumination as an aspect of the divine mission in the world. Third, we will discuss
the outworking of illumination—faith and obedience. Finally, we conclude

---

[1]This is true of Nicodemus, the woman at the well, the man born blind, Caiaphas, and all of the
rest. D. Moody Smith, *The Theology of the Gospel of John*, New Testament Theology (New York:
Cambridge University Press, 1995), 18; Simon Ross Valentine, "The Johannine Prologue—A
Microcosm of the Gospel," *Evangelical Quarterly* 68, no. 3 (1996): 291-304.

by assessing the adequacy of the role of the Gospel of John within contemporary discussions of illumination. This entails a discussion of primary Johannine texts deployed in doctrines of illumination and how they inform and reinforce the argument of this project.

ILLUMINATION AND THE DOCTRINE OF GOD

In turning to a biblical theology of illumination in the Gospel of John, we begin with the doctrine of God. Whether we begin with John's Gospel or letters, we begin with a God who is light and life.[2] As divine light, God is full of light and there is no darkness in God at all (1 Jn 1:5). God is radiant in truth and glory. In engaging this intersection of the doctrine of God, the Gospel of John, and illumination, we will draw especially on the work of Kevin Vanhoozer. Vanhoozer has written extensively on God as light in his *Remythologizing Theology* and has drawn heavily on the theology of John's Gospel in doing so.

God's nature as light. God as light pertains both to God's holiness and God's glory. God's nature as light means that God is wholly separate from darkness; God's light is the radiance of his holiness. Vanhoozer writes,

> Holiness is more than a moral attribute; it refers first and foremost to the majestic otherness and incomparability of God 'who alone has immortality, who dwells in unapproachable light' (1 Tim. 6:16). . . . Holiness is the excellence of God's own nature and triune life. The "brightness of all his perfections." To say then that "God is light" (1 Jn. 1:5) is to acknowledge God as the "holy other" in both the metaphysical and the moral sense. God's light is the radiant fullness of his communicative activity. God's "holy light" qualifies everything that God does.[3]

Vanhoozer also rightly calls our attention to glory. Both Vanhoozer and C. H. Dodd emphasize this common coordination of "glory" (δόξα) and "light" (φῶς).[4] Implied in Jesus' repeated affirmation of the Father and Son's mutual

---

[2] Jn 1:1-4; 1 Jn 1:1-5. Note: we have already detailed an exegesis of Jn 1:1-4 that accounts for and defends the unity of the Logos with God, and so also his divinity, and John's letters could not be more explicit about the light and life in these verses.

[3] Kevin J. Vanhoozer, *Remythologizing Theology: Divine Action, Passion, and Authorship*, Cambridge Studies in Christian Doctrine 18 (New York: Cambridge University Press, 2010), 248; quoting Brakel, quoted in Richard A. Muller, *Post-Reformation Reformed Dogmatics,* vol. 2: *Holy Scripture: The Cognitive Foundation of Theology,* 2nd ed. (Grand Rapids: Baker Academic, 2003), 499.

[4] Vanhoozer, *Remythologizing Theology,* 250; C. H. Dodd, *The Interpretation of the Fourth Gospel* (New York: Cambridge University Press, 1970), 206.

glorification is a communication of knowledge. There is a communication of knowledge in that, as the Son glorifies the Father (Jn 14:13), he is making the Father's glory known; and in the same way, as the Father glorifies the Son (Jn 8:54), the Father makes the Son's glory known. Vanhoozer writes, "Glorification is 'enlightening' in so far as it is the communicative act of making another's glory known—the publication of a person's excellence, especially through testimony."[5] This mutual enlightening of the Father and Son, and, as we will see, also the Spirit (Jn 16:14) has its origins in the triune life itself.[6] In this respect, this mutual glorification is not a new work, but as Thomas McCall notes on the basis of John 17, this mutual glorification of the Father and Son is a continuation of what was shared before the world began.[7] It is a relationship of mutual glorification, which John 1 suggests existed prior to creation. Herman Bavinck anticipates the systematic theological implications of these observations when he writes, "Implied in the designation 'light' is that God is perfectly conscious of himself, that he knows his entire being to perfection, and that nothing in that being is hidden from his consciousness."[8] This is determinative for Vanhoozer, who writes,

> To speak of God as light, then, is to gain an important insight into the nature of the three person's communicative activity. Each person is a communicative agent in his own right who glorifies—makes known the glory of—the other two. This, then, is the first sense in which we may speak of an "economy of communication": the ordered ways in which Father, Son, and Spirit know one another and make one another known.[9]

This mutual enlightening of each of the other persons in the immanent Trinity is the kind of illuminating communication that the economic Trinity displays in the Gospel of John. As Davies puts it, "It is the speech of God with God, in the immanent Trinity, which is disclosed to us historically and narratively in the incarnation."[10]

---

[5]Vanhoozer, *Remythologizing Theology*, 250.

[6]Vanhoozer, *Remythologizing Theology*, 251.

[7]Thomas H. McCall, "Relational Trinity: Creedal Perspective," in *Two Views on the Doctrine of the Trinity*, ed. Jason S. Sexton and Stanley N. Gundry (Grand Rapids: Zondervan, 2014), 120.

[8]Herman Bavinck, *Reformed Dogmatics,* vol. 2: *God and Creation*, ed. John Bolt, trans. John Vriend (Grand Rapids: Baker Academic, 2003), 191.

[9]Vanhoozer, *Remythologizing Theology*, 249.

[10]Davies, *Theology of Compassion*, 256, cited in Vanhoozer, *Remythologizing Theology*, 251.

In so far as it entails God's holiness, judgment, glory, communicative activity, life, and salvation, *light* is a term that captures the nature of God in God's action toward us as depicted in the Fourth Gospel. Even in judgment, God's action is light, illuminating. For John, God's action is always in the interest of dispersing darkness by the shedding of light.[11] Even the moment of Christ's crucifixion in John is the climactic moment of Christ's glorification. The outcome of this darkest moment of history is foreshadowed from the outset: "The light shines in the darkness and the darkness did not overcome it" (Jn 1:5). The crucifixion is illuminating in that what was intended to be the extinguishing of this light by overwhelming darkness became an opportunity to put on display the incomparably great power and the eternal nature of God. It effected salvation for all humanity, not by circumventing darkness but by conquering it. It is this illumination for which Paul prayed when he asked that our eyes would be enlightened (Eph 1:18).

Divine mission in the world. In addition to understanding the nature of God as light in the Fourth Gospel and John's letters, illumination likewise captures and defines the nature of God's mission in the world. The whole of the Gospel is cast in this light from beginning to end. The prologue begins with the pronouncement of the gospel as the good news of the light shining in the darkness, the true light coming—that is, the Word made flesh, the life that was the light of humanity. This light was judgment, exposing humanity's love of darkness and the wickedness of its deeds (Jn 3:19-20). The light also judged humanity's deed as truth (ἀλήθεια) and demonstrates that what has been done in truth has been done through God (Jn 3:21). John the Baptist was a lamp who burned and gave light by testifying to the Son. However, Jesus' own weightier testimony, the brighter light, is the very work that the Father has given him to finish—this work testifies that the Father sent him (Jn 5:31-38). As the light *of* the world he came to give light *to* the world, in order that those who follow him will never walk in darkness, evil, death, but that they would have the light of life (Jn 8:12). In the light of his day— his presence on earth among humanity prior to crucifixion—Jesus and his

---

[11]"The Light by its shining accordingly creates judgment; in the very act of bringing salvation into the world, it divides the world." George Raymond Beasley-Murray, *John*, 2nd ed., Word Biblical Commentary (Nashville, TN: Thomas Nelson, 1999), 161.

disciples must do the work of the one who sent him (Jn 9:5).[12] This work, based on the context of this statement, is displaying the work of God in human life by healing and rescuing them from the darkness of blindness and giving them sight, vision, the benefits of luminary reception. In this way, he was the light of the world while he was in the world (Jn 9:5).[13] Those who recognize this light (of the world) and walk in it will not stumble (Jn 11:9-10). These are the ones who put their trust (πιστεύω—believe) in the light and become children of light (Jn 12:36). Therefore, climactically, when one believes (πιστεύω) in Jesus, one does not only believe in Jesus but also in the one who sent him (Jn 12:44). When someone looks at Jesus, they see the Father, the one who sent him (Jn 12:45). Jesus reflects the radiance and glory of the Father by coming into the world as a light. His divine mission in the world is to come into the world as a light, so that no one who believes in him should stay in darkness (ἐγὼ φῶς εἰς τὸν κόσμον ἐλήλυθα, ἵνα πᾶς ὁ πιστεύων εἰς ἐμὲ ἐν τῇ σκοτίᾳ μὴ μείνῃ, Jn 12:46). Especially noteworthy for our argument is the ἵνα clause in Jn 12:46 (constituting a purpose statement) which indicates that this illumination, this liberation from darkness, is the reason he came into the world as light. In this way "the illumination is not presented as primarily intellectual (as in some of the Hermetic tractates) but as the direct bestowal of life or salvation (and thus it is comparable with the gift of living water [4.10; 7.37f] and of the bread of life [6.27])."[14] For John, *illumination is an aspect of the divine mission in the world*. Not merely the liberation from intellectual darkness, but from the darkness of evil deeds (Jn 3:19), hate for our brothers and sisters (1 Jn 2:9-11), blindness from both sin

---

[12]"That Jesus now says he is the light of the world (v. 5) recalls 8:12. It is rather curious that this saying seems to put a limit on the period in which Jesus is the light of the world, as if that is something he would be only during the period of his earthly ministry. Something similar maybe said of Jesus' statement in 11:9–10. Yet in the context of the gospel as a whole, such statements can hardly mean that Jesus' function as light of the world will be terminated with his death and exaltation. Probably, the import of the time constraint really applies to Jesus' hearers, his opponents—their opportunity to believe and confess—rather than to Jesus (12:35-36). There is an urgency about recognizing who he is. Yet Jesus' own ministry is under a time constraint: he must get his work on earth done before his hour of departure arrives (v. 4). He must be about his mission with dispatch." D. Moody Smith, *John*, Abingdon New Testament Commentaries (Nashville, TN: Abingdon, 1999), 192.

[13]Nevertheless, at the same time, for those who believe that they see all too well, the true light is devastatingly blinding to them. C. K. Barrett, *The Gospel According to St. John: An Introduction with Commentary and Notes on the Greek Text*, 2nd ed. (Philadelphia: Westminster, 1978), 354.

[14]Barrett, *John*, 354.

and self-righteousness, and finally the darkness of death. Stevens concludes, "His bringing life and light to men on his mission to earth was grounded in the larger and deeper truth that he had always been illumining the minds of men. All through the Old Testament period of revelation the true light of the Logos was shining (Jn 1:9-10). This fact again, was based on the essential nature of the Logos, who was with God in the beginning, and was God."[15] But the Logos's divine mission does not end with John 12. For John, the hour for which the Logos came was the hour of his glorification, and this hour of glorification is inextricably bound up with and identical to the hour of his crucifixion—the light of day will give way to the glory of his hour.[16]

The hour of his glorification at the crucifixion is the hour for which the Logos was sent (Jn 2:4; 7:30; 8:20; 12:23-28; 13:1; 16:32; 17:1). The hour of his crucifixion is the illuminating supernova of the Logos's glory. The twelfth hour of the day will be the brightest (Jn 11:9). The night will fall (Jn 9:4; 11:10) when no work can be done and men who walk, will stumble because they do not have the light. But the night will not last. "Early on the first day of the week, Mary Magdalene went to the tomb" (Jn 20:1). The light had shone in the darkness, but the darkness has not overcome it. Darkness will again be dispersed.

This motif of the Son having been sent by the Father is ubiquitous in John, occurring at least seventeen times (Jn 3:17, 34-36; 5:36-40; 6:29, 57; 7:29; 8:42; 10:36; 11:42; 17:3, 8, 18, 21, 23, 25; 20:21). In this regard, Andrew Walls's work on missiology and Christology is especially helpful and insightful within the context of illumination as divine mission in the world. In particular, Walls speaks to the correspondence between the divine nature and the nature of this mission. Walls contends that Christology is itself missiological. He writes, "Christian faith rests on a divine act of translation: 'the word became flesh, and dwelt among us' (Jn 1:14)."[17] The Logos's incarnation is itself inherently missiological—it is the mission of God. This Logos who

---

[15]George Barker Stevens, *The Johannine Theology: Study of the Doctrinal Contents of the Gospel and Epistles of the Apostle John* (New York: Charles Scribner's Sons, 1895), 3-4.

[16]Michael Gourgues, "The Superimposition of Symbolic Time and Real Time in the Gospel of John: The Symbolism of Light as Time Marker," *Proceedings of the Irish Biblical Association* 31 (2008): 64.

[17]Andrew F. Walls, *The Missionary Movement in Christian History: Studies in Transmission of Faith* (New York: T&T Clark, 1996), 26.

was in the beginning with God, and through whom all things have been made—in him was life, and this life was the light of people. Now, through this divine act of translation, this light shines among people. As already quoted of Stevens, "His bringing of life and light to men on his mission to earth was grounded in the larger and deeper truth that he has always been illumining the minds of men."[18] He goes on to say, "What God has done in revelation and redemption it was according to his nature to do. If God has loved the world, it is because he is love. If God has enlightened the world, it is because he is light."[19] In this way the mission of God in the world to illumine people is grounded in God's nature as light, as 1 John will summarize (1 Jn 1:1-5). In giving light in John's Gospel, God gives himself. It is not only self-revelation but "self-impartation."[20] Stevens writes, "God is perfect and self-imparting holiness. As light, he blesses men, banishes from their lives the darkness of sin, and makes them participants in his own purity."[21] Consequently, by his light we participate in a purity that is not our own, but his; his holiness, his glory, his life and light.

COMING TO SEE THE LIGHT AND WALKING IN IT: REGENERATION, FAITH, AND OBEDIENCE IN JOHANNINE THEOLOGY

The coordination of faith and obedience pervades the entirety of John's Gospel and letters (e.g., Jn 3:36; 8:31-38; 12:45-46; 15:14; 1 Jn 2:3-6; 3:22-24; 4:21; 5:2-3; 2 Jn 4-6; 3 Jn 3-4). It might be said that faith and obedience encapsulate the entirety of the Christian life. To believe Christ and to trust his commands are inseparable concepts in John.[22] There is no clearer depiction of illumination as the life of faith and obedience than John's own prescription—walk in the light (Jn 8:12; 12:35-36; 1 Jn 1:7). Illumination is awakening to the glory of his kingship and to the light of his priestly holiness and prophetic judgment. In speaking of illumination as an aspect of the divine mission in the world, the

---

[18]Stevens, *Johannine Theology*, 3. This is not a conclusive statement that all people throughout time have been illumined in the regenerative sense; we are speaking of a sort of general illumination. Rather, Johann Bengel's comment clarifies the issue: "Whosoever is enlightened at all, is enlightened by this Light" (*Gnomon Novi Testamenti*, 1:360).

[19]Stevens, *Johannine Theology*, 4.

[20]Stevens, *Johannine Theology*, 61.

[21]Stevens, *Johannine Theology*, 61.

[22]R. Alan Culpepper, *The Gospel and Letters of John* (Nashville, TN: Abingdon, 1998), 98. "For John, believing is not a static response; it is a way of life."

life that was in him, which is the light of humanity, animates all of the Christian life from regeneration to resurrection to eternal life.

The life of faith for John first entails the generation of God's children (Jn 1:12-13). These children are born not of blood or of the will of the flesh or the will of man, but of God. Their generation is not a birth but a rebirth. It is a birth from above, a birth to light and not to darkness.[23] "Darkness symbolizes the old sinful life, 'light' the new spiritual life."[24] The life of the Logos was both in the beginning with the creation of humanity, and now also in the incarnation with the re-creation of humanity. In re-creation light shines in the darkness, and to all who receive this light is given what must be given to become children of God—ἐξουσία.[25]

In Jesus' encounter with Nicodemus we witness the faith of a man who believes the signs of God in front of his eyes, but who has not believed that Jesus is the Son of God. He sees the signs of the Son but not his nature. Jesus explains why: he has not been born anew, again, from above (Jn 3:3). This regeneration demands a reorganization, a regermination of the mind in order to grasp the things of the Spirit. A faith to which Jesus entrusts himself (Jn 2:24) entails this regermination of the mind. This kind of faith entails the obedience to do the truth. It is the obedience of those who come to the light, not because of what they have done, but because what has been done in them has been done by God (Jn 3:21).

The woman at the well's sudden illumination to faith entailed the immediate reaction to engage in evangelism. Her obedience in this instance was animated by the Word of God, not demanded by it. She is illumined by the one that we come to find out is the light of the world. Her resolute action following illumination illustrates the clarity granted when light shines on a dark path. The repeated admonition to walk in the light, to walk and to work

---

[23]"Faith in himself and appropriation of the light which he has brought to men are spoken of (verses 18-21) as the *conditions* of the divine approval" (Stevens, *Johannine Theology*, 164).

[24]Stevens, *Johannine Theology*, 132.

[25]Brown reports that Dodd, "characterizes 'power' as a most misleading translation. However, to make of this a semi-judicial pronouncement whereby the Word gave men the *right* to become God's sons is to introduce an element strange to Johannine thought: sonship is based on divine begetting, not on any claim on man's part. Bultmann, p. 36, and Boismard, pp. 42-43, are probably correct in seeing the Greek as an awkward attempt to render the idea behind the Semitic expression, 'he gave [*nathan*] them to become children.'" *The Gospel According to John*, Anchor Bible Commentary (Garden City, NY: Doubleday, 1966), 10-11.

while it is day, is at the very least the demonstration that in the pure light of the Logos, obedience is not a choice between paths. In the pure light of the Logos, obedience follows the only illumined path that lies before us. It is when night falls that we begin to thrash arms about in the dark feeling our way for some sense of a clearing.

The coordination of faith and obedience is inseparable in John because faith is the "condition of the new spiritual birth" and faith "stands organically related to the abiding fellowship with Christ, which constitutes the Christian life."[26] Obedience for John, especially according to John 15, is easily captured in this phrase "abiding fellowship with Christ." For this reason, the faith of regeneration by illumination

> is neither a subjective play of feeling nor a speculative conviction or assent; it is a personal relation. It carries man out of himself, and commits him to another. It is self-renouncing trust, repose of soul in Jesus Christ. It involves, therefore, an experience which tests and proves the external grounds on which it reposes, and which gives to the soul an assured certainty of their validity.[27]

It is more than subjective but not void of experience. It is more than assent but not void of assurance. It is personal relation. It is participation: "union with Christ is a result of faith."[28]

Two Johannine metaphors capture the nature of this participation and its correlation with obedience: eating/drinking and abiding. For the former (as in Jn 6), we take into ourselves all that Christ is: "To eat his flesh and drink his blood is to make Christ wholly ours, to participate spiritually in his life."[29] Nourishment by his teaching and refreshment by his Spirit, enliven and animate us to walk in his light. John Lightfoot writes, "To partake of the messiah is to partake of himself, his pure nature, his righteousness, his spirit; and to live and grow and receive nourishment from that participation of him."[30] When Christ is taken fully into the self, obedience is animated by participation in that divine life which we partake. Christ is multiplied in our

---

[26]Stevens, *Johannine Theology*, 234.

[27]Stevens, *Johannine Theology*, 239.

[28]Stevens, *Johannine Theology*, 229.

[29]Stevens, *Johannine Theology*, 163.

[30]John Lightfoot, *Horæ Hebraicæ et Talmudicæ; Hebrew and Talmudical Exercitations upon the Gospels, the Acts, Some Chapters of St. Paul's Epistle to the Romans, and the First Epistle to the Corinthians* (Oxford: University Press, 1859), 3:307-9, cited in Stevens, *Johannine Theology*, 163.

partaking of him, not diminished. The radiance of the light of the world is magnified as we walk in it, not extinguished.

Conversely, our light and life grow dim when we do not abide in him (Jn 15). The brightness of human light demands our union with the light of the Logos for its intensification. As a branch severed from its vine cannot sustain its own life, a lamp on its own soon grows dim and dies. Abiding in Christ, union with him, is our life source and our light source. By it we walk, by it we obey, by it we remain. If we return to illumination as divine mission in the world, we see again an antithesis between light and darkness with respect to where we abide: "I have come as light into the world, so that everyone who believes in me should not *remain* [μένω] in the darkness" (Jn 12:46). That is to say, those who remain in the vine (Jn 15:5-8), who remain in his love (Jn 16:9-17) remain in the light. Those who remain in the light are those who bear much fruit, who keep his commands, who love one another (Jn 15:5, 9-10, 16; 1 Jn 2:7-11). The fruit of this illumination is obedience, but for those who do not remain in his vine, his love, his light; darkness is all that remains (Jn 12:46).

The issue this project takes with contemporary constructions of the doctrine of illumination is that, in their exegesis of relevant biblical texts, they include engagement with only seven texts from the Gospel and letters of John at most (Jn 14:15-17, 25-26; 15:26; 16:7-15, 1 Jn 2:20, 27; 5:20). Surprisingly, there is very little if any engagement with the prologue (especially Jn 1:4-9), Jesus' declaration to be the light of the world (Jn 8:12; 9:4-5), or Jesus' self-reference as light/daylight (Jn 11:9-10; 12:35-36, 46) in these constructions. Consequently, a hope of this project is to rouse us from our dogmatic slumber and to awaken us again to the implications of the text's own witness to the christological and indeed even trinitarian work of divine illumination.

The issue is not significant disagreement with the conclusions of these contemporary constructions; rather, it is a matter of completeness. Raymond Brown has written that everything the Evangelist says of the Holy Spirit is spoken elsewhere in John of Jesus himself.[31] This must raise questions as to whether the doctrine of illumination is complete if the only work that is spoken of is that of the Holy Spirit. Therefore, in an effort to address this

---

[31]Raymond E. Brown, "The Paraclete in the Fourth Gospel," *New Testament Studies* 13, no. 2 (1967): 126.

material and articulate this argument as directly, succinctly, and palatably as possible, the remaining portion of this chapter will reflect the form of other contemporary constructions of the doctrine of illumination by addressing the relevant verses in isolation and in order.

John 14:26. "But the Advocate, the Holy Spirit, whom the Father will send in my name, will teach you everything, and remind you of all that I have said to you." In terms of constructing a doctrine of illumination, the primary content harvested from this text is the role of the Spirit in teaching (διδάσκω) and reminding (ὑπομιμνῄσκω). It is contended that the content communicated in this teaching is not a new revelation but a calling to attention and a generating of understanding for what has already been revealed in Christ.[32] The notion of the Spirit as teacher or executor of understanding is basic to all doctrines of illumination. Drawing on Grudem, Seaman writes, "The product of the Holy Spirit's teaching and illuminating activity in the life of the believer is understanding."[33]

The question for our purposes is not whether the Spirit constructs its own teaching or if its teaching simply "reveals the truth of the Word of God in order to garner understanding in the heart and mind of the believer."[34] This is all well and good. The question is whether Christ too is a teacher of his Word who communicates understanding of that word, conviction of its truth, and remembrance of its content.

It is interesting to note that so much of what the Spirit is and does in relation to the Son, the Son is and does in relation to the Father. That is to say, the Holy Spirit's work of illumination is not some new work but "continues the earthly ministry begun by the Son."[35] In taking the verse phrase by phrase, we see that Jesus and the Spirit are sent by the Father (Jn 14:26; 3:17).

---

[32]John Calvin, *The Gospel According to John 11–21 and the First Epistle of John*, trans. T. H. L. Parker, Calvin's Commentaries (Edinburgh: Oliver and Boyd, 1959), 88; Wayne A. Grudem, *Systematic Theology: An Introduction to Biblical Doctrine* (Grand Rapids: Zondervan, 2000), 645; Leon Morris, *New Testament Theology* (Grand Rapids: Zondervan, 1986), 260.

[33]Michael Seaman, "The Indispensability of the Holy Spirit for Biblical Interpretation: A Proposal for the Concept of Transformative Illumination" (PhD, Southeastern Baptist Theological Seminary, 2010), 121. Wayne Grudem writes, "The illuminating work of the Holy Spirit is seen in the fact that he enables us to understand: 'We have received not the spirit of the world, but the Spirit which is from God, *that we might understand* the gifts bestowed on us by God (1 Cor 2:12)'" (*Systematic Theology*, 645).

[34]Seaman, "Indispensability," 122.

[35]D. Crump, "Re-Examining the Johannine Trinity: Perichoresis or Deification?" *Scottish Journal of Theology* 59, no. 4 (2006): 406.

We see that the Father will send the Spirit in Jesus' name, as the Son was sent in the Father's name (Jn 14:26; 5:43), the Spirit speaks and teaches about the Son, as also the Son speaks and teaches about the Father (Jn 6:59; 7:14, 18). We see that the Spirit will "remind" (ὑπομιμνήσκω) the disciples of everything Jesus has said to them (Jn 14:26), and at the same time, the resurrected, *glorified* Christ reminds (μιμνήσκομαι) his disciples of what he has said, and in fact leads them to believe the truth of the (Old Testament) Scriptures and of his own words (Jn 2:22; 12:16).[36] Furthermore, he reminds his disciples of crucial teachings pertaining to his crucifixion, resurrection, ascension, and return (Jn 14:28-29; 16:19-28). In fact, in John 16:29-30, it is evident that Jesus reminds the disciples of a teaching in such a way that they are now confident that Jesus knows all things. On the basis of Jesus' reminder, they are now convinced of the truth that he came from God. In his teaching—a reminder of prior teaching, though with parables and figures of speech—Christ has surely revealed "the truth of the Word of God in order to garner understanding in the heart and mind of the believer" as Seaman spoke of the Spirit's work.[37] Given the witness of John 14:15-17, there is not simply a striking similarity in Johannine theology but an identification between the work and life of the Son and the work and life of the Spirit: the Spirit was "*another* paraclete" implying that Jesus himself was the first, "an observation that gains credence from 1 John 2:1."[38]

John 15:26. "When the Advocate comes, whom I will send to you from the Father, the Spirit of truth who comes from the Father, he will testify on my behalf." In turning to John 15:26, the Paraclete is now sent from the Father at the behest of the Son. This Spirit of truth who comes from the Father will testify on Christ's behalf. Zuber writes of this verse, "In sum, the witness of the Spirit is not to add to Christ, but to take the given of Christ's self-disclosure (5:36 τὰ ἔργα; 5:47 τοῖς ῥήμασιν) and testify to its veracity."[39]

---

[36]Μιμνήσκομαι and ὑπομιμνήσκω share the same root (μιμνήσκω). Ὑπομιμνήσκω carries a more active connotation (2 Tim 2:14, Titus 3:1, 2 Pet 1:12, 3 Jn 1:10, Jude 1:5), although this is not exclusively the case given Lk 22:61, where it is used in a very similar sense to Jn 2:22; 12:16. See William F. Arndt, Walter Bauer, and Frederick W. Danker [BDAG], *A Greek-English Lexicon of the New Testament and Other Early Christian Literature*, 3rd ed. (Chicago: University of Chicago Press, 2000), 652, 1039.

[37]Seaman, "Indispensability," 122.

[38]Brown, "Paraclete," 127.

[39]Kevin D. Zuber, "What Is Illumination?: A Study in Evangelical Theology Seeking a Biblically

In John 15:26, the thought is that "the testimony of the Spirit in the church perpetuates the testimony of Jesus himself to the truth, so that the hostile, persecuting world never ceases to be confronted with the truth of God."[40] The obvious irony here in referring to Jesus' own testimony to the truth is that it is a testimony to himself *as the truth* (Jn 14:6). And Jesus' witness was not only to himself as truth but to himself as the light of the world (Jn 8:12-14, "But even if I testify on my own behalf, my testimony is valid"). It is contended that the language of witness in illumination is not the revelation of "new truths" but witness to "the things of Christ."[41] Even still, Christ's other witness is the Father (Jn 8:18) until, of course, we are introduced to the Paraclete's witness. Given the text's juridical context, Christ's testimony to himself is no less valid than that of others *to him*. Rather, it is the foundation on which all other witnesses have their validity. That is to say, Christ's work testifies that the Father has sent him (Jn 5:36), that he is who he has claimed to be (Jn 8:28), that he is who the Scripture testified he would be (Jn 5:39), and who Moses testified he would be (Jn 5:46). The Spirit's witness to Christ is thus a continuation, a prolongation, of Christ's own witness to himself into the future church (Jn 15:27).[42] Francis Beare writes,

> the mission of the Paraclete is as it were the extension or prolongation under changed conditions of the mission of Jesus on earth. The father sends him in the name of Christ, that is to say, he is not sent to reveal the name of some other Saviour, nor to supplant the historical mission of Jesus, but to complete and give full effect to the revelation that Jesus has brought. *The light by which the Spirit illumines our inward being is still the light that shone in the face of Jesus Christ.*[43]

In John 14:26, the work of the Spirit is linked back to the light that shone in Christ. In John 15:26-27, the work of the Spirit is linked to the mission of the church—the vocation to participate in the economy of divine light in the world. According to Overbeck, this economy incorporated the

---

Grounded Definition of the Illuminating Work of the Holy Spirit" (PhD diss., Trinity Evangelical Divinity School, 1996), 169.

[40]Francis Beare, "Spirit of Life and Truth: The Doctrine of the Holy Spirit in the Fourth Gospel," *Toronto Journal of Theology* 3, no. 1 (1987): 117.

[41]Charles Hodge, "The Witness of the Holy Spirit to the Bible," *Princeton Theological Review* 11, no. 1 (1913): 48.

[42]Barrett, *John*, 482.

[43]Beare, "Spirit of Life," 116, emphasis mine.

Evangelist and the Baptist and now also the lamp that shines in the historical mission of the church.[44]

John 16:12-15.

I have much more to say to you, more than you can now bear. But when he, the Spirit of truth, comes, he will guide you into all the truth. He will not speak on his own; he will speak only what he hears, and he will tell you what is yet to come. He will glorify me because it is from me that he will receive what he will make known to you. All that belongs to the Father is mine. That is why I said the Spirit will receive from me what he will make known to you.

Much has been made of the argument that the Spirit in John is none other than the Spirit of Jesus himself.[45] This New Testament concept is only further affirmed here in John 16 as the Spirit of truth comes to guide us into all truth—Jesus—who is himself the way and the truth.[46] Craig Keener writes that in turning to the illumination of the disciples, "The primary task here is Christological, revealing the message of Jesus."[47] Again, there is agreement with Seaman in his observations that the Spirit ὁδηγήσει his disciples into all truth. The Spirit guides them by the light of Christ's own life. To guide them would be to "assist someone in acquiring information and knowledge."[48] That is to say, "This illuminating work of the Spirit paves the way for a deeper understanding and fuller comprehension of the things of God viz. the Word of God."[49] The emphasis here "is on the term 'all': the truth has been made known by Jesus, to the disciples, but their grasp of it has been limited."[50] Seaman concludes his observations by quoting Ingle, "As Jesus had guided his disciples and others into the correct understanding

---

[44]Beare, "Spirit of Life," 117. "We might remark that in previous passages the operations of the Spirit have been linked with the historical work of Jesus. Here they are linked and all but identified with the concrete historical mission of the church." Franz Overbeck, *Das Johannesevangelium: Studien zur Kritik seiner Erforschung* (Tübingen: J. C. B. Mohr, 1911), 416-17.

[45]Crump, "Re-Examining the Johannine Trinity," 406; Brown, "Paraclete," 127. Brown writes, "If the Paraclete is 'another Paraclete,' this seems to imply that Jesus was the first Paraclete, an observation that gains credence from I John ii. I. If the Paraclete is the Spirit of Truth, Jesus is the truth (xiv.6). If the Paraclete is the Holy Spirit, Jesus is the Holy One of God (vi. 69). These observations, combined with those about Jesus' sending of the Paraclete, show that John shared the general New Testament picture of the Holy Spirit as the Spirit of Jesus" (127).

[46]Brown, "Paraclete," 127.

[47]Craig S. Keener, *The Gospel of John: A Commentary* (Peabody, MA: Hendrickson, 2003), 1035.

[48]Seaman, "Indispensability," 124.

[49]Seaman, "Indispensability," 124.

[50]Beasley-Murray, *John*, 283.

of scripture (Matt 5:1-7:29; 15:16-17; Mk 7:18; Lk 24:27, 32, 45), so will the Spirit guide them when he comes."[51] He will lead them to "comprehend the depths and heights of the revelation as yet unperceived by them," a comprehension of the "full revelation of God's character in Christ."[52] In this way, the Spirit's work in illumination is again the continuation of Christ's enlightening/illumining work in the incarnation.

Seaman also addresses the derived authority of the Spirit in that the Spirit does not communicate a new revelation, but conducts himself as "the ambassador of the Trinitarian Godhead who reflects and illumines the truth that is found in Jesus."[53] Nevertheless, even as the Spirit speaks only what he hears, his work is not unlike that of Christ who makes known to his disciples what he has learned from the Father (Jn 15:15). On the basis of the fact that the community can both trust that Jesus speaks on behalf of the Father, and that "the Spirit Jesus sent speaks for Jesus," Keener suggests, "this would imply that disciples of later generations could experience the same relationship with Jesus his first disciples did, an intimacy modeled by Jesus in his relationship with the Father (1:2, 18; 14-15)."[54] One might say that, by virtue of the Spirit's presence and communication, later generations of disciples may participate in the Son's knowledge of the Father.

This conclusion is confirmed in John 16:14-15. If glorifying is the work of *making known* another's glory, there is an aspect of the Spirit's illuminating work that is further expounded here. In fact, the connection could not be made any more clearly that Christ himself does in John 16:14. The Spirit's very act of taking what is Christ's and disclosing it to his disciples is glorifying him.[55] The glorification of Jesus by the Spirit may relate to a continuing exposition of his character. Schlier writes, "The Spirit illumines the work of Jesus in his glory."[56] There is what Köstenberger calls a "Trinitarian collaboration" being described in John 16:14-15 in which the things of the

---

[51]Jeff Ingle, "A Historical and Scriptural Survey of the Doctrine of Illumination with Application to Hermeneutics" (ThM thesis, Grace Theological Seminary, 1987), 63.

[52]Beasley-Murray, *John*, 283; Keener, *John*, 1038.

[53]Seaman, "Indispensability," 124.

[54]Keener, *John*, 1038.

[55]Keener, *John*, 1041.

[56]Heinrich Schlier, "Zum Begriff des Geistes nach dem Johannesevangelium," in *Besinnung auf das Neue Testament*, Aufsätze und Vorträge II (Freiburg: Herder, 1964), 269; quoted in Keener, *John*, 1041.

Father, being possessed and embodied by the Son (Jn 1:14), are being made known to disciples by the Spirit.[57] This making known the things of the unseen God (Jn 1:18) by the Word/Son, who is himself God and in closest relationship with the Father, is the work of glorification. Glorification of the Father by the Son opens up knowledge of the Father "and creates the entrance into it for the believers."[58] If we do not ignore this crucial component and context to Jesus' comments on the Spirit in John 16:13, we see again how contemporary doctrines of illumination have not gone far enough. We see in full light of John 16:13-15 that there is a trinitarian collaboration in illumination. In this collaboration, the Spirit guides people into the one who is the truth and the Spirit glorifies the Son by making known the Son's knowledge and intimacy with the Father.

1 John. The theological engagement with the letters of John as it pertains to illumination is both interesting and perplexing. The primary textual witnesses treated in doctrinal constructions of illumination are 1 John 2:20, 27 and to a lesser extent 1 John 5:20. The verses in 1 John 2 pertain to an anointing, presumably of the Holy Spirit, by which the true children of God have knowledge (οἴδατε πάντες, 1 Jn 2:20), which teaches them about all things (διδάσκει ὑμᾶς περὶ πάντων), and by which they remain in him (μένετε ἐν αὐτῷ, 1 Jn 2:27). Zuber argues that it is an anointing of the Holy Spirit by Christ, the Holy One.[59] Seaman, on the other hand, contends that the holy one *is* the Holy Spirit.[60] But the absence of a direct mention of the Spirit aside, the whole context of the passage nevertheless pertains to those who have left the fold on account of never having really belonged in the first place; they did not belong because they did not "remain with us" (μεμενήκεισαν ἂν μεθ' ἡμῶν, 1 Jn 2:19). But those who have an anointing know and acknowledge the truth of the Son and therefore have the Father also (1 Jn 2:20, 23). If they let what they have heard from the beginning remain (μένω), then they in turn will remain in the Son and the Father. This anointing precludes the need for a teacher, as the anointing itself is the teacher, and just as the anointing has

[57]Andreas J. Köstenberger, *A Theology of John's Gospel and Letters* (Grand Rapids: Zondervan, 2009), 245.

[58]Felix Porsch, *Pneuma und Wort: Ein Exegetischer Beitrag zur Pneumatologie des Johannesevangeliums* (Frankfurt am Main: J. Knecht, 1974), 300.

[59]Zuber, *What Is Illumination?* 99.

[60]Seaman, "Indispensability," 141-42.

taught, abide in him (1 Jn 2:27). If we conclude with the majority opinion that the Spirit is the anointing spoken of here, then the Spirit again is benefactor of knowledge and teacher who enables those who acknowledge the Son in order to remain in him (1 Jn 2:20).[61]

What is especially surprising regarding the witness of 1 John is Seaman's treatment of 1 John 5:20, "And we know that the Son of God has come and has given us understanding so that we may know him who is true; and we are in him who is true, in his Son Jesus Christ. He is the true God and eternal life." Seaman argues that this verse "informs the doctrine of progressive illumination," with which we can agree. However, we part ways when Seaman makes the giving of understanding (καὶ δέδωκεν ἡμῖν διάνοιαν) a work of the Holy Spirit. This is exegetically and therefore categorically incorrect in this text. Incontestably, ὁ υἱὸς τοῦ θεοῦ is the subject of δέδωκεν ἡμῖν διάνοιαν and is therefore the agent of illumination in this text.[62] What we have here is a witness to the work of the Spirit (1 Jn 2:20-27) and the Son (1 Jn 5:20) in illumination, both of whom enable the children of God to remain/abide or "be in" (ἐσμὲν ἐν) him (the Father and Son).

1 John 1:5-10; 2:7-11. What is inadmissible is the neglect of 1 John 1:5 in this conversation. The fact that "God is light" in our doctrine of God is scarcely carried into the discussion of God's work of enlightening people is a serious methodological and theological error. Its absence is a glaring void. How can we sever the light of illumination by the Holy Spirit from the light in the nature of God himself, much less the light of the Logos as articulated by John? That God is light permeates all aspects of his being, his glory, his self-communication. It is the work of the true light of the Logos coming into the world and the prolongation of the Logos's work by the Holy Spirit as teacher and guide in all truth. God is light, Christ is illumining, the Holy Spirit is illumination.[63] The Holy Spirit's work in progressive illumination

---

[61]Seaman, "Indispensability," 140-42.

[62]Seaman also makes the argument that διάνοιαν refers to the faculty of thinking or reasoning, rather than understanding itself, and therefore the believer has "not received all wisdom and all knowledge, but the capability of apprehending wisdom and knowledge" (Seaman, "Indispensability," 143). It is possible that he is arguing that the Holy Spirit comes along and grants that wisdom and knowledge in illumination, but he cites his source incorrectly; διάνοιαν does have that connotation, but BDAG does not list its use in this verse under that connotation. Rather, BDAG lists it specifically under the connotation of simply "insight" or "understanding" (234).

[63]In light of his actualistic theology, Barth develops his doctrine of the Trinity in terms of God's

might fit nicely within an understanding of an economy of illumination in which the work of the Spirit is the opening up of truth and the granting of an entrance into it.[64] The message we have heard is that God is light. It has been heard by the Spirit from the Son (Jn 16:13). It is the knowledge and possession of the Son's because all that belongs to the Father belongs to the Son also (Jn 16:15). The disciple hears and receives this by the anointing of the Spirit (1 Jn 2:20), and they abide in the Father and Son by this same anointing. What we see here in the Johannine epistles is the encapsulation of a trinitarian account of illumination.

Within the broader economy of divine light, 1 John 1 and 1 John 2 demonstrate also the ethical dimension of illumination. The economy of divine light entails not only the restoration of cognitive fellowship with God but also the restoration of loving fellowship with humanity in the community of faith. For John, knowledge is inherently performative: to simultaneously know the light of God and walk in darkness is simply irreconcilable. Rather, loving fellowship with humanity is walking in this light, and walking in the light demonstrates knowledge of and intimacy with the divine light itself (1 Jn 1:7; 2:10; 4:20-21). In the economy of light, "walking in the light" is embodied as an indivisible Johannine triad: love of God, love of neighbor, obedience of divine commands (1 Jn 2:9-11; 4:20–5:3). Though each may be spoken of in distinction from the other two, none are fully complete without the others. Love of God and love of neighbor are both cognitive and affective. Obedience of divine commands corresponds to love of God. Though the commands might be carried out for reasons besides love of God, such reasons will eventually be brought into the light and judged as such. To love God, love neighbor, and obey divine commands is to know the divine light intimately and to walk in the sphere of its shining.

---

action toward us, which is captured in the concept of revelation: "God's Word is God Himself in His revelation. For God reveals Himself as the Lord and according to Scripture this signifies for the concept of revelation that God Himself in unimpaired unity yet also in unimpaired distinction is Revealer, Revelation, and Revealedness" (*CD* I/1:295-96). That is to say, Barth seeks to articulate revelation in terms of its subject, God, and so "the first thing we have to realize is that this subject, God, the Revealer, is identical with His act in revelation and also identical with its effect" (*CD* I/1:298-99). To speak, then, of God as the subject of illumination is to understand God, the light, as identical with his illumination and also with its effect in human beings.
[64]Porsch, *Pneuma und Wort*, 300.

EXCURSUS
The Economy of Illumination in the Broader Canon

In order to offer a fully fleshed out dogmatic account of illumination, it is essential that we speak to the broader canon's witness to this economy of illumination. Though a sustained engagement with the entire canon is beyond the scope of this work, we can and must address some of the key texts pertaining to illumination. The great arc of Scripture begins with a God who is the initial Creator and giver of light, a gift that reflects his nature in creation as a God who shines light into the darkness. The Scriptures build toward the climactic moment of the incarnation of the light of the world, along with this light being extinguished in his death before he is resurrected to new radiance for all the world to see his glory. This light is then taken out into the world as the Spirit communicates it through the church, culminating in a coming kingdom of God, a new Jerusalem, a bright city that needs no sun because God himself gives it light (Rev 21:23; 22:5). In this way, all of God's illuminating work originates in and is oriented toward the revelation of God's great glory.

As we engage in each of these texts, it is important to keep in mind that our intent here is not the replacement of the Spirit's work in illumination with Christ's, but a fuller fleshing out of how the entire Godhead participates in communicating his divine light into the dark places of creation, not the least of which is our minds. We do that first by grounding all of God's work of illumination in God's own nature as light. This then moves outward as God puts his own light on display in the second person of the Trinity, the Son, the Word of God made flesh, Jesus Christ. Finally, this light is applied to our hearts and minds as the power of the Spirit enables us as individuals to participate in the Word's knowledge of the Father. This Word's knowledge comes to us in the form of the Scriptures, which the Spirit opens our hearts and minds to receive. This Word is a light which we cannot receive apart from the great grace of God in his Spirit's illuminating work.

Genesis and Psalms. "God said, "Let there be light"; and there was light. And God saw that the light was good; and God separated the light from the darkness" (Gen 1:3-4) God is the original giver of light. God's first work in all of creation is illumination. All other giving of God's light originates from this one, explosive, seminal moment of God giving light to creation. It is in God's nature to give light, and this light has no origin other than God himself.

The psalter offers us a host of verses that invite God to grant us understanding (Ps 119:33), open our eyes (Ps 119:18), and teach us (Ps 119:34), but many of these verses speak more generally of calling on YHWH for this enlightenment. Psalm 119:105 does declare, "Your *word* is a lamp unto my feet, a light for my path," speaking of YHWH's decrees, not the words of Scripture themselves. It is not inappropriate that we now apply them to the Scriptures, but this "word" refers initially to God's self-expression, not a written text. This self-expression of God has its culmination in Jesus Christ, the Word become flesh, whose life the whole of Scripture anticipates in the Old Testament and remembers in the New. At the very least, there is resonance with the claim that the light the Holy Spirit shines on us is not some theoretical or even metaphorical light with origin outside the Godhead but the light of the Word of God himself. The light originates in the nature of God made objectively present in the Word and applied subjectively in our lives by the Holy Spirit. In this way, God proceeds through the Son and the Spirit in the collaborative, unified work of illumination while each person of the Trinity exercises a distinct role in the execution of this work itself.

Ephesians 1:19-20. Ephesians gives us one of the most explicit expressions of God's enlightening work, in this case by the Spirit of wisdom and revelation (Eph 1:19-20).[65] Pheme Perkins notes, "Verse 18 describes the result of this wisdom as 'the eyes of your heart enlightened.'"[66] Perkins goes on to explain that "although the OT regularly uses 'heart' for the seat of human understanding (Ps 10:11; Prov 2:2), the phrase 'eyes of your heart' has no biblical antecedents." In searching for Jewish context for this phrase, Proverbs 20:27 does speak of the human spirit as "the lamp of the Lord" searching our inmost parts, and we see "Jewish texts refer to the darkened or clouded eyes as equivalent to a depraved will."[67] Matthew 6:22-23 "refers

---

[65]It is important to note that πνεῦμα is anartharous here and thus could also be read as "a spirit."

[66]Pheme Perkins, *The Letter to the Ephesians,* in *New Interpreters Bible Commentary,* vol. 10 (Nashville, TN: Abingdon, 2000), 381.

[67]Perkins, *Ephesians,* 381.

to an eye that is healthy and one that is evil or diseased," a saying that "refers to the inner light required for ethical discernment."[68] Paul also speaks in Ephesians 4:18 of Gentiles who do not know God as "darkened in their understanding," a darkening that is correlated with a hardening of the heart. The outcome of this is a way of life that is inconsistent with the "life of God." Perkins concludes, "Ephesians treats the darkness-to-light image as a reference to the moral conversion associated with turning to God."[69] In this way, those who put their faith in Christ are enlightened to live a life for the praise of his glory (Eph 1:13) receiving the seal of the Holy Spirit and an inheritance with all the saints (Eph 1:13-14, 18). Francis Foulkes writes,

> The Old Testament gave hope for the future in terms of the coming of light into a world in darkness and as the opening of the eyes of the blind (e.g. Isa. 9:2; 35:5; 42:6; 49:6; 60:1–2, 19). When Christ came his presence was described as the dawning of a new day, the breaking in of the light of God (Matt. 4:16; Luke 1:79; John 1:9; 8:12; 2 Cor. 4:6). Apart from him, or in rejection of him, the eyes of people's hearts are closed, and they are in the darkness of sin and ignorance and despair (5:8; cf. Matt. 13:15; Rom. 1:21); but those who receive him into their lives find their eyes . . . *enlightened* and made able to see (cf. Matt. 13:16–17; Acts 26:18; Heb. 6:4; 10:32).[70]

Their enlightenment is to "walk in the light," as we might say according to our Johannine conclusions, and we learn here that the power at work in those who believe is none other than that which God exerted in Christ when he raised him from the dead (Eph 1:19-20). The power to see the light does not come from somewhere inside of humans but is dependent on the work and power of God, which raises a person from the utter lifelessness of death. We are made to see this light by the power of God and made able to walk in it by his ongoing power at work in us through his Holy Spirit. It is faith and obedience sustained by the present action of God.

1 Corinthians 2:6-16. One of the most pertinent biblical texts to the doctrine of illumination is 1 Corinthians 2:6-16. In particular the passage speaks to the "secret and hidden wisdom of God" (1 Cor 2:7 ESV), "things God has revealed to us through the Spirit" (1 Cor 2:10 ESV). Consequently, "no one

---

[68]Perkins, *Ephesians*, 382.
[69]Perkins, *Ephesians*, 381.
[70]Francis Foulkes, *The Letter of Paul to the Ephesians: An Introduction and Commentary*, vol. 10, Tyndale New Testament Commentaries (Downers Grove, IL: InterVarsity Press, 1989), 68.

comprehends the thoughts of God except the Spirit of God" (1 Cor 2:11 ESV), and now "we have received the Spirit who is from God, that we might understand the things freely given us by God" (1 Cor 2:12 ESV). These "words are not taught by human wisdom, but taught by the Spirit, interpreting spiritual truths to those who are spiritual" (1 Cor 2:13 ESV). "The natural person does not accept the things of the Spirit of God, for they are folly to him, and he is not able to understand them because they are spiritually discerned" (1 Cor 2:14 ESV). In every way this passage points to the importance and necessity of the Holy Spirit for us to understand the wisdom of God. In fact, as Anthony Thiselton points out, this passage "points in the direction of Barth's maxim, 'God is known through God alone.'"[71] We do not take anything away from the bearing of the role and responsibility of the Holy Spirit in illumination as indicated by this passage. However, it must be asked what the "content" of this secret and hidden "wisdom of God" is. According to v. 16 the Spirit has been given so that we might understand "the mind of the LORD," that is, the mind of God the Father (confirmed by Paul's reference to Isa 40:13 LXX). The answer to the rhetorical question, "Who has known the mind of the LORD?" is, of course, Christ alone knows God's mind and can open it up to us. The Spirit's role is to make present in our minds the image of the Father that is present in the mind of him who alone understands his Father's mind. Christ, then, is the content of the Spirit's revelation (1 Cor 2:10), education, and interpretation (1 Cor 2:12-13). Paul has just informed us (1 Cor 1) that Christ is this wisdom of God (1 Cor 1:24), indeed, the manifold wisdom of God (Eph 3:7-13). It is Christ, the Word of God, who is the personification of the wisdom of God, who is taught and interpreted for those who have received the Spirit of God.

2 Corinthians 4:4-6. In Paul's second letter to the Corinthians the metaphors of light and darkness, sight and blindness, are especially prominent once again. Paul writes, "The god of this age has blinded the minds of unbelievers, so that they cannot see the light of the gospel that displays the glory of Christ, who is the image of God" (2 Cor 4:4 NIV). The god of this age—Satan—has been about the work of closing people's eyes, veiling the light which Paul describes here as the light of the Gospel. To say that

---

[71] Anthony C. Thiselton, *The First Epistle to the Corinthians: A Commentary on the Greek Text* (Grand Rapids: Eerdmans, 2000), 285.

'the god of this age has blinded the minds of unbelievers" is a metaphorical use of τυφλόω, and "means 'deprive of (spiritual) sight,' 'prevent from
understanding.'"[72] Murray Harris writes, "It is the understanding of the
truth and the attractiveness of the Gospel that are effectively blocked by
the devil."[73] This *light*, φωτισμός, as an astronomical term, "refers to refracted luminosity, the radiance of the moon as a reflection of the sun's
light." However, "more generally, the term means 'illumination,' 'light,' 'enlightenment'" and might be translated woodenly, "the light that comes
from the gospel."[74] This light refracted by the Gospel is none other than
the glory of Christ. The gospel shines light, we might say, because it "contains and proclaims the glory of the Messiah."[75] In this way, because the
gospel proclaims Christ's glory, it creates illumination.[76] Finally, Paul's affirmation that Christ is εἰκὼν τοῦ θεοῦ is the affirmation that "Christ both
shares and expresses God's nature." Moreover, "given passages such as
Phil. 2:6, Col. 1:19, 2:9, we may safely assume that for Paul εἰκὼν here, as in
Col. 1:15, signifies that Christ is an exact representation as well as a visible
expression of God."[77]

Harris himself acknowledges the resonance with Johannine theology
here: "Similarly, in Johannine theology, Jesus Christ as λόγος both inherently participates in deity (John 1:1) and reveals the Father's person (John
1:14-18)."[78] A. Feuillet also argues that "if interpreted in light of *Wisdom* 7:25-
26, the title 'image of God' appears to be practically equivalent to the Johannine *Logos*."[79] In drawing this together with Paul's comments in his first
letter to the Corinthians, we might say that the light by which the Spirit illumines is none other than the divine light of God displayed in Christ. In

---

[72]Murray J. Harris, *The Second Epistle to the Corinthians: A Commentary on the Greek Text*, New
International Greek Testament Commentary (Grand Rapids: Eerdmans, 2005), 328.
[73]Harris, *Second Epistle to the Corinthians*, 328.
[74]Harris, *Second Epistle to the Corinthians*, 330.
[75]Alfred Plummer, *A Critical and Exegetical Commentary on the Second Epistle of St. Paul to the
Corinthians*, International Critical Commentary (New York: Scribner, 1915), 117.
[76]Harris, *Second Epistle to the Corinthians*, 330. "It is Christ's own glory that is proclaimed in the
gospel, and it is the gospel that creates illumination."
[77]Harris, *Second Epistle to the Corinthians*, 331.
[78]Murray J. Harris, *Jesus as God: The New Testament Use of Theos in Reference to Jesus* (Grand
Rapids: Baker, 1992), 54-71.
[79]A. Feuillet, "The Christ Image of God According to St. Paul (2 Cor. 4:4)," *Bible Today* 1 (1965):
1413. Feuillet's reference is to the apocryphal book of *"Wisdom of Solomon."*

fact, after Paul clarifies in 2 Corinthians 4:5 that it is not himself that he preaches, but Jesus Christ as Lord, he says just that.

Paul writes, "For God, who said, 'Let light shine out of darkness,' made his light shine in our hearts to give us the light of the knowledge of God's glory displayed in the face of Christ" (2 Cor 4:6 NIV). As we have argued through this project, Paul here also takes illumination all the way back to the beginning, to God's originating gift of light to the world in creation (Gen 1:3). All illumination is grounded in God's nature as light and God's grace to give light as gift to the world. This light has no other source than in God himself. Paul is depicting the redemption of the human heart in terms of God's creation of the human world: as in creation God pours forth light to disperse the darkness, so in conversion God floods the darkened human heart with divine light.[80] Harris observes, "Paul's thought moves from the physical creation (λάμψει) to the spiritual re-creation (ἔλαμψεν), from nature to grace. The God of redemption is none other than the God of creation."[81] As Augustine so eloquently put it, "Let the one who created you, recreate you."

Finally, God has given us this light, illumined our hearts, "to give us the light of the knowledge of God's glory displayed in the face of Christ." Interestingly enough, Harris observes that the cognate verb φωτίζω almost always has a divine agent expressed or implied (10 out of 11 occurrences).[82] One such occurrence is John 1:9, where we first encounter the illumination of the Logos, the true light coming into the world, which enlightens everyone. The divine light who gave light in creation now also enlightens by the light of the Logos. In the Logos, the Word made flesh, we have seen his glory, glory as of the only Son of the Father, full of grace and truth. No one has seen God, the only God, but the one who is at the Father's side, he has made him known. It's as if the author is saying that God has given this light so that human beings may know the glory of God, which is put on display in Jesus Christ. Which author? Both. We hear Paul and the Johannine Evangelist speaking with one voice here: the light by which the Spirit illumines is none other than the divine light of God displayed in Jesus Christ.

---

[80]Harris, *Second Epistle to the Corinthians*, 335.
[81]Harris, *Second Epistle to the Corinthians*, 335.
[82]The only occurrence that describes human action in φωτίζω is Eph 3:9.

Revelation 21:23-25. As with God's work of giving light in the generation of creation, so in creation's culmination in the new kingdom the new Jerusalem is a city that "has no need of sun or moon to shine on it, for the glory of God gives it light, and its lamp is the lamb" (Rev 21:23 ESV; cf. Rev 22:5). Not only do we see once again that God is the source of light but that Christ, the lamb of God, is the means by which this light is made objectively present. He is the lamp, the illuminating light on display. Moreover, the author tells us, *"By its light will the nations walk* and the kings of the earth will bring their glory into it, and its gates will never be shut by day— *and there will be no night there"* (Rev 21:24-25 ESV). That is to say, a defining characteristic of God's coming kingdom that is distinct from our present reality is the inescapability of God's ever-present light. It will penetrate our lives day and night in an ongoing, ever-present, illuminating experience of the light of life enlightening our lives.

Conclusion. The doctrine of illumination that we see in the Johannine literature is an economy incorporating the divine light of the Father, the enlightening of the Logos, and the enlightened effect on disciples by the work of the Spirit. This Johannine economy of illumination entails the revelation of God in Christ, the glory of the Father and Son, the judgment of the world, and the regeneration to faith and obedience in humankind. Those who come to see the light of Christ do so by virtue of the Son's divine mission in the world. Jesus renders sensible and accessible the divine light of God. Faith and obedience are the visible manifestation in life of the rebirth that has taken place by the Spirit. In this birth men and women are made children of God, united with Christ, participating in what is shared between the Father and the Son. People are made to understand truth and made to know and acknowledge the Father and Son's shared glory. It is an existence made possible by the Spirit (1 Jn 4:13). In this economy, "light" captures the nature of God and God's action toward us as articulated by the Gospel and letters of John. The Holy Spirit enacts the effects of illumination in order that humanity may participate in the Son's knowledge of the Father. In the light of life men and women are awakened and reborn to an acknowledgment of and obedience to the Word, and a knowledge of the divine light himself.

NINE

Coming to See the Light
and Walking in It

W E NOW COME TO THE CULMINATION of our task—the construction of a dogmatic account of illumination. The task of this
chapter is to expound on our brief definition of illumination as human participation in the light of the divine life. In more trinitarian language, illumination is participation in the Son's knowledge of the Father by the power of
the Holy Spirit. Participation in this knowledge is implicit in the faith and
obedience of the participant. This participation is implicit in faith and obedience, not the consequence, the outworking, or the reward of this participation. In this way, illumination is not only an effect, nor is it simply something that happens to us. Illumination is a communion within the triune life
in which we are made active participants.

A primary objective of this project thus far has been to articulate a dogmatic account of illumination that works to locate this doctrine within the
larger economy of God's work in the world, especially as it is witnessed to
in the Johannine literature. The task of the present chapter is to weave together the various threads of the project, stemming from the reflections on
both Augustine and Barth, their methods and demonstrations of theological
interpretation in the Johannine literature, and the concluding thoughts on
their doctrines of illumination. These strands will be woven in with those
drawn from the survey of John's witness to illumination as articulated in the
previous chapter. In doing so, this chapter will articulate a dogmatic account
of illumination that is situated within the triune economy and an account

of this illumination as it bears on the life of the illumined. In light of our proposed definition, this chapter will clarify the inner workings of this doctrinal statement including the nature of this participation, the doctrine's location within the triune economy, its relationship to revelation and regeneration, and the bearing of this participation on the life, faith, and obedience of the individual.

The common threads that run the full course of this project include: illumination as the initiation of human participation in the divine life, participation as the means of our ongoing illumination, Christ as illuminating light (not only in John's prologue but in Augustine as agent of illumination and in Barth as light of life), the trinitarian aspects of illumination—divine light, light of the Logos, and the Spirit of illumination—and the necessity of speaking of illumination as an economy both as it pertains to the external works of the triune persons and because of its dogmatic intersection with revelation and regeneration. All of these threads come together here as essential elements for constructing a doctrine of illumination.

A couple of comments are necessary by way of introduction. First, as it pertains to methodology, the pattern of development to this point has been to articulate Augustine's and Barth's methods of theological interpretation in John respectively, to engage their interpretations, and then to draw out the dogmatic implications of those interpretations as they come to bear on the doctrine of illumination. In keeping with this methodology in which the Fourth Gospel has been primary, the focus will remain on the theological interpretation of John and its implications for illumination. This will remain the focal point more so than either Augustine or Barth or the potential for reconciling their work. Though these will be addressed in so far as it is necessary to advance the case of this project, the intent instead is to continue to employ Augustine and Barth—elements of the Christian traditions—in aiding us to read Scripture well as it pertains to the doctrine of illumination. This is a hallmark of what has come to be known as the discipline of the theological interpretation of Scripture and will be adhered to here as well.[1]

---

[1]Citing Calvin's title for book four of the *Institutes*, Kevin J. Vanhoozer writes, "Tradition, like the church itself, is in Calvin's words an 'external means or aid by which God invites us into the society of Christ and holds us therein.'" He adds, "The reformation was not a matter of Scripture versus tradition but of reclaiming the ancient tradition as a correct interpretation of Scripture versus later distortions of that tradition. The Reformers regarded the early church councils by

Inevitably at points the text will demand that we make choices between the two, or demand an account of how the text makes room for both their readings, but the desire is more to get at what Scripture teaches on illumination than what either Augustine or Barth teach and how they can be reconciled.

Second, in the course of constructing a dogmatic account of illumination, it is necessary to give a definition of "dogmatic account" in the first place. In short, the work of dogmatics is the work of locating a doctrine within the triune economy.[2] Given that God's work in the economy pertains to God's work *ad extra*, John Webster speaks accurately of dogmatics as "well-instructed material conceptions of the modes and instruments of God's dealings with his intelligent creatures."[3] To "locate" a doctrine within this triune economy is to offer a coherent "schematic" and "analytical" articulation of Scriptures' witness to the doctrine's place with respect to each of the divine person's work and mutual relations, and its place in God's salvific activity in free relationship to his creatures.[4] If we are to give a dogmatic account of illumination, then, it must first locate the doctrine of illumination within the economy of God's work in the world. This dogmatic account must be faithful both to the biblical witness and to the whole history of the ecclesial witness (in so far as faithfulness to this second witness is possible and desirable). It has been of highest value to be biblically faithful (hence the attentive listening to the witness of John) and to be historically faithful to the witness of the church. In seeking faithfulness to the ecclesial witness, we have therefore reached back beyond the Reformation

---

and large as true because they agreed with Scripture, not because they had authority in and of themselves." *The Drama of Doctrine: A Canonical-Linguistic Approach to Christian Theology* (Louisville, KY: Westminster John Knox, 2005), 160, 233. See also Francis Watson, *Text, Church and World: Biblical Interpretation in Theological Perspective* (Grand Rapids: Eerdmans, 1994), 241; Todd Billings, *The Word of God for the People of God: An Entryway to the Theological Interpretation of Scripture* (Grand Rapids: Eerdmans, 2010), 149-94. See also what Matthew Levering does with Aquinas in *Participatory Biblical Exegesis: A Theology of Biblical Interpretation* (Notre Dame, IN: University of Notre Dame Press, 2008).

[2]John Webster, *God Without Measure: Working Papers in Christian Theology* (London: T&T Clark, 2015), 1:128.

[3]John Webster, "The Domain of the Word," in *The Domain of the Word: Scripture and Theological Reason* (New York: T&T Clark, 2012), 9.

[4]"Dogmatics is the schematic and analytical presentation of the matter of the gospel" (Webster, "Biblical Reasoning," in *Domain of the Word*, 131). See also, Karl Rahner, *The Trinity*, trans. Joseph Donceel (New York: Crossroad, 1997), 3-5.

and post-Reformation witness to retrieve the seminal work of Augustine as it pertains to properly locating this doctrine within the triune economy. In summation, then, the dogmatic account presented here will gather in a systematic way what has been dispersed throughout the Johannine witness (and its interpreters) regarding the theological place of illumination with respect to the work and mutual relations of the divine persons and its place in God's salvific activity toward us as his creatures.[5]

ECONOMY

The first major constructive contribution of this chapter is to articulate the necessity of speaking of illumination in terms of an economy. This includes developing the concept of an economy of divine light as it pertains both to the Trinity and to the dogmatic loci with which illumination intersects. In order to locate this doctrine within the triune economy, we must first clarify the way in which we are making use of the language of economy.

The primary way we are speaking of an economy is as it relates to the economy of salvation: the place of illumination in God's plan of salvation and in "God's management and dispensation of grace."[6] To give an account of the economy of divine light is to give an account of the whole of the divine light's being, actions, and effects as it pertains to the inner-trinitarian relations, God in relationship to humanity, and other doctrines with which it intersects (regeneration, revelation). This language of economy applied to light and illumination is drawn from Franz Overbeck's work on John, *Das Johannesevangelium*. There he describes the inner relationships of various "lights" within the Gospel of John. These "lights" incorporate the work of John the Evangelist, John the Baptist, the Logos, and the ongoing witness which is the text itself. The inner workings of these various lights comprise what Overbeck calls the "economy of divine light in the world."[7]

---

[5]Webster explains that a dogmatic account "is 'systematic,' not in the sense that it offers a rigidly formalized set of deductions from a master concept, but in the low-level sense of gathering together what is dispersed through the temporal economy to which the prophets and apostles direct reason's gaze" (Webster, "Biblical Reasoning," 131).

[6]Rahner, *Trinity*, 1.

[7]Franz Overbeck, *Das Johannesevangelium: Studien zur Kritik seiner Erforschung* (Tübingen: J. C. B. Mohr, 1911), 416-17.

This language of economy is substantiated also by John Owen in a reference to a "denomination" of illumination that encompasses the many dynamics of illumination (regeneration, revelation, etc.).[8] And now, most recently, Kevin Vanhoozer has taken up the language of an economy of light/illumination in reference to the inner and outer workings of the Trinity in communicating the divine light in the world.[9] The utility of speaking of an economy as it pertains to illumination is that it provides the grammar for answering the question: How do we give an account of illumination in its multiplicity of dogmatic implications and in all of its dogmatic intersections?

The language of an economy in a theological context often pertains to the *economic* Trinity and how the dogmatic locus under discussion is developed in light of the triune economy. Without a doubt, there is intersection here also between the present construction of the doctrine of illumination and the triune economy. Therefore, this too will be a significant matter of exposition, though more so insofar as it aids in articulating the economy of divine light than a development of the immanent Trinity. In so far as it relates to the immanent Trinity, what we are working out is the biblical witness that God is light (1 Jn 1:5) and that God exchanges light in himself (i.e., the mutual glorification referenced in John 17).

Economy as **oikonomia.** As we have seen, in its dogmatic implications the economy of light touches on everything from the nature of God as light (1 Jn 1:5) and God's action toward humanity in the Logos as light to the world (Jn 8:12; 9:4-5), to the light that shines in the darkness making judgment and

---

[8]John Owen, *Pneumatologia* (Grand Rapids: Sovereign Grace, 1971), 157.

[9]Kevin J. Vanhoozer, "The Spirit of Light After the Age of Enlightenment: Reforming/Renewing Pneumatic Hermeneutics via the Economy of Illumination," in *Spirit of God: Christian Renewal in the Community of Faith*, ed. Jeffrey W. Barbeau and Beth Felker Jones (Downers Grove, IL: IVP Academic, 2015), 149-67; Kevin J. Vanhoozer and Daniel J. Treier, *Theology and the Mirror of Scripture: A Mere Evangelical Account* (Downers Grove, IL: IVP Academic, 2015). In further support for the use of the language of "economy" to order the complex notion of illumination, Bernard Ramm writes, "To sum up at this point: if the Spirit witnesses in truth, if he grants the illumination which accompanies revelation, then when that truth and that revelation become written, the Spirit works with the written Word. *Our investigation of the scriptural references concerning the witness of the Spirit revealed that this was no narrow doctrine, but a very complex one. However, it is a tightly-knit complex. Perhaps it is best to call it one truth with many facets. The* testimonium *must be grasped as a unity in, complexity, and a complexity in unity.*" *The Witness of the Spirit: An Essay on the Contemporary Relevance of the Internal Witness of the Holy Spirit* (Grand Rapids: Eerdmans, 1960), 66-67, emphasis mine.

convicting of sin (Jn 3). In an effort to give an account of this whole, we also take on the question of its intersection with regeneration and revelation as effectual and progressive aspects of our participation in Christ, the light of the world. That is not to say that illumination is the dogmatic location encompassing all that regeneration and revelation are. Rather, regeneration and revelation intersect in this household of illumination, so their treatment is demanded in our dogmatic account also. As "God's external works are communicative," it follows that God's acts toward humanity, which are both regenerative and revelatory, are also self-interpreting.[10] That is to say, God's external works are not simply actions left open for misperception and confusion, but in themselves grant understanding of themselves in the life and mind of the one these actions encounter. This is to speak of illumination as the subjective application of revelation—the completion of revelation without which revelation would not be revelation.[11]

Triune economy. Locating the doctrine of illumination within the triune economy demands, at the very least, an account of the unity and plurality in this triunity. In this regard the work of Thomas McCall is instructive. As it pertains to their diversity, McCall is right when he writes, "The divine persons are *distinct in action* in the economy of creation and redemption."[12] His clarification of this is even more helpful as he explains that this coactivity is not analogous to human coactivity in the sense of "teammates," but rather is deeply unified as "divine activity . . . 'originates in the Father, proceeds through the Son and is completed in the Holy Spirit.'"[13] McCall writes that it is so unified, in fact, "that there is a sense in which it should be

---

[10]"God's external works are communicative. The reconciling and perfecting missions which the Son and the Holy Spirit undertake at the Father's behest are both regenerative and revelatory, because the relation of the triune God to the world is that of a self-interpreting agent" (Webster, "Domain," 7).

[11]"As God reconciles, he makes created intellect come newly alive by his instruction and enlightenment. Like every work of divine grace, revelation is effective; it generates actual knowledge, not just its possibility. Revelation is not merely an offer or initial manifestation which requires completion by a self-originating human act; rather, the scope of revelation includes the generation of acts of intelligence, the moving of creatures to the operation of their given powers" (Webster, "Preface" in *Domain of the Word*, ix; see also Barth, *GD* I:168).

[12]Thomas H. McCall, "Relational Trinity: Creedal Perspective," in *Two Views on the Doctrine of the Trinity*, ed. Jason S. Sexton and Stanley N. Gundry (Grand Rapids: Zondervan, 2014), 231.

[13]McCall, "Relational Trinity," 120, quoting Khaled Anatolios, *Retrieving Nicaea: The Development and Meaning of Trinitarian Doctrine* (Grand Rapids: Baker Academic, 2011), 231.

understood as one action."[14] As is McCall's aim in this essay, he is helpful in articulating both the distinction of divine persons and their unity as they operate, for our purposes, in the economic Trinity.

At the same time, however, McCall goes on to clarify the notion of divine appropriations. That is to say, simply because we assert with the tradition that the works of the triune persons are never divided, it does not thereby necessarily entail "that the agency of the divine persons in the economy is not genuinely distinct."[15] Rather, we can speak of the *Son's agency* in a certain work while simultaneously speaking of the Father and Spirit's agreement in the action and their coactivity in it.[16] McCall's work here in elaborating the nature of the relationships as they operate in the economy bear directly on our work as we articulate a robustly trinitarian doctrine of illumination. For in this way, to speak of the Holy Spirit's illumination is to speak of a coactivity in the triune economy that originates in the divine light of the Father, proceeds through the illuming Son, and is completed in the illumination of the Holy Spirit. The agency of the Spirit in illuminating the hearts and minds of human beings is the agency of one of the divine persons but also the agreement and colaboring of the other two in this activity as well.

Kevin Vanhoozer clarifies how the triune economy works in its communicative activity regarding light. It is God's nature as light and the divine persons' mutual glorification that grant entry into understanding the economy of communication. If the economy of communication entails "the ordered ways in which the Father, Son and Holy Spirit know one another and make one another known," then to speak of locating illumination in the triune economy is to comprehend the ordered ways in which the Father, Son and Holy Spirit "light" one another and effect that illumination in the world.[17]

---

[14]McCall, "Relational Trinity," 120-21.

[15]McCall, "Relational Trinity," 121.

[16]McCall's example here is Maximus the Confessor, who argues that the Father and the Spirit "themselves did not become incarnate, but the Father approved and the Spirit cooperated when the Son himself effected his Incarnation" ("Relational Trinity," 121).

[17]Kevin J. Vanhoozer, *Remythologizing Theology: Divine Action, Passion, and Authorship*, Cambridge Studies in Christian Doctrine 18 (New York: Cambridge University Press, 2010), 249. R. R. Reno writes, "The light comes into the world, and the darkness is whatever remains outside its fulfillment. This separation is not a necessity forced upon God by human sinfulness. . . . Thus, the first act of separation should be understood as the triumph of love that God intends from the beginning. There was nothing, and nothing cannot participate in the light of the Word that was in the beginning and that shines toward its fulfillment, calling into existence all that is, all

To speak of this communication of light, Vanhoozer asserts, "is to evoke the entire economy of revelation and redemption which, like the primordial separation of light from darkness, features a dividing line that cuts through the whole drama of salvation."[18] Consequently, in the work of locating illumination within the triune economy, we inevitably encounter the triune economy as it pertains to revelation and redemption. This leads to a second way in which we will speak of economy as it pertains to illumination—the economy that attempts to give an account of all aspects of illumination in its intersection with other dogmatic loci.

The concept of the triune economy as it will be deployed in this dogmatic account of illumination roots the economic activity of God, his divine missions, within "the excellence of God's own nature and triune life."[19] The illumination of humanity is the bathing of creation in a brilliance of light that shines from God's illuminating life in itself. John Webster articulates this vision of the economy exceptionally well in *The Domain of the Word*:

> The divine economy is grounded in the immanent perfection of the Holy Trinity. God's dealings with creatures, in which he makes it possible for them to know and love him, are a second, derivative reality. In more directly dogmatic language, the economy is the field of the divine missions: The Father's sending of the Son and the Spirit to gather creatures into fellowship with himself and to uphold them on their way to completion. But this outpouring of love in the divine missions is the external face of the inner divine processions, that is, of the perfect internal relations of the triune persons, the fountain from which the external works of God flow.[20]

Several elements of this definition are key. First, Webster succinctly articulates a grounding of the divine economy in the immanent Trinity, which the present dogmatic account of illumination hopes to reflect. Second, the divine economy is thereby a *derived* reality based in the grander reality that

---

for the sake of the divine plan. God brings things into existence. They shine with being, and this creates a boundary between that which is and what which is not." *Genesis*, Brazos Theological Commentary on the Bible (Grand Rapids: Brazos, 2010), 46-48.

[18]Vanhoozer, *Remythologizing Theology*, 247; see also, Reno, *Genesis*, 47.

[19]Vanhoozer, *Remythologizing Theology*, 248. Vanhoozer uses this language to describe God's holiness, which falls under God's nature as light. Nevertheless, it captures well the brilliance of God's illuminating life in itself.

[20]Webster, "Biblical Reasoning," 117.

is the life of God itself. Third, as we indicated in the previous chapter on the Johannine literature, illumination as an external work of God is captured well when we speak of it as a mission of God in the world. Paul Fiddes writes, "The 'missions' of God in the world are already 'processions' within God's eternal being."[21] That is to say, as we have made the case throughout this project, the illumination of humanity as an economic activity of God is grounded in and derivative of God's being as light in God's self. The activity of God in the mission to illumine the world is the outworking and external face of the inner divine processions. Fourth, the Father sends the Son and the Spirit for the purpose of gathering creatures into fellowship with himself. This gathering of creatures into fellowship with himself is both the means and the end of our illumination. His creatures are illumined as they are gathered into—participate in—fellowship with the divine life. Fifth and finally, as the perfect internal relations of the triune persons are the fountain from which the external works of God flow, this same life is the fountain of light from which divine illumination flows.[22] The light of this life is the light in which one participates as she comes to see the light of Christ, as she is born anew and from above to believe and do the truth. In speaking of an economy of divine light, we are speaking of a communication of light that flows out of God's own nature in God's self. It is a light shared within God's own life, and it is shared with creatures in the derived reality of God's creation. This illumination of humanity by God's external work is a mission of God in his world. This external work *is* the life of the Logos coming into the world, which is also the light of all humanity. In the sending of his Son and of the Spirit who teaches, reminds, and executes understanding and conviction, the economic activity of God draws people into relationship. This activity invites participation in the life from which this illumination flows. In this outpouring of love, humanity is invited to participate in the light of the perfect internal relations of the triune persons. People are upheld in that

---

[21] Paul S. Fiddes, *Participating in God: A Pastoral Doctrine of the Trinity* (Louisville, KY: Westminster John Knox, 2000), 6.

[22] "In the Beginning was the Word, and the Word was with God, and the Word was God. From where the dew has sprinkled upon you, you will come to the fountain; from where the ray has been sent to your shadow-filled heart by a winding and oblique path, you will see the naked light itself; and to see and endure [it] you are being cleansed." Augustine, *Tractates on the Gospel of John 28–54*, Fathers of the Church 88 (Washington, DC: Catholic University of America Press, 1993), 35.9.1.

participation and fellowship by the power of the Holy Spirit.[23] The effect of this illumination is both knowledge and life—two aspects of one effect that cannot be divorced from one another. Knowledge and ethics can be distinguished logically. However, if illumined knowledge is the restoration of cognitive fellowship with God (à la Webster), then "if we say we have fellowship with him while we walk in darkness, we lie and do not practice the truth (1 Jn 1:6 ESV)."[24] In this way, John indicates that ethics is *living* knowledge.[25] John continues in his first epistle, "Whoever says 'I know him' but does not keep his commandments is a liar, and the truth is not in him" (1 Jn 2:4 ESV). Therefore, those who participate in the Son's knowledge of the Father by the power of the Holy Spirit abide in the light "so that it may be clearly seen that his works have been carried out in God" (Jn 3:21 ESV). It is to the nature and consequences of this participation that we now direct our attention.

PARTICIPATION

The "what" of illumination, or its "benefits," receive the lion's share of attention in dogmatic accounts of illumination. What receives far less attention is the "how," or the means. A hope here is to remedy this. The means of illumination proposed here is, not surprisingly, *participation*. If we are to speak of an illumination that takes place by means of our participation in the light of the divine life, it is necessary to address what precisely the nature of this participation is.

Earlier chapters developed Augustine's and Barth's individual constructions of participation. For Augustine's part, we follow the dynamic nature of his proposal for participation. The participation is "dynamic" with respect to the change and progress it produces in human lives. Darren Sarisky writes, "Humans are mutable beings, who can change as time passes, and they ought to progress in their participation in God as their lives unfold." This participation functions within the domain of soteriology: by means of salvation,

---

[23]Webster, "Biblical Reasoning," 117.

[24]John Webster, "Illumination," *Journal of Reformed Theology* 5 (2011): 329. The Spirit's "illuminating gift restores cognitive fellowship between God and lost creatures."

[25]This is akin to Vanhoozer's language of "performing doctrine," Hauerwas's notion of "theological ethics," and Barth's theological ethics demonstrated in the ethical conclusion to each volume of the *Church Dogmatics*.

human beings participate by grace in who God is by nature.[26] By participating in God's nature through grace, humans will progress in their embodiment of that character, virtue, and holiness.

As for Barth, we will go a long way toward appropriating his notion of participation here. However, one point of dissent demands discussion first—namely, we part ways at Barth's tendency to universalize human participation in God. Barth contends that all humanity is elevated to the side of God in Christ's taking humanity to himself, that all are made recipients of grace in Christ, that all humanity is made obedient members of the covenant and that all consequently participate in Christ's covenantal fulfilment in history. Barth is not wrong in saying that this is the objective reality of things in Christ. Barth is wrong, however, in how he articulates the relationship of the objective reality to its subjective execution. Barth contends that the subjective execution of this objective reality is not a second moment or work but two aspects of one work. Barth concludes, then, that to split the grace of God in Christ into an objective grace in Christ's atoning work and a subjective grace in a human being's free acceptance and realization of that possibility is to empty the objective grace of Christ of all its power.[27] This, however, leaves open the question near to the heart of this work: How it is that some participate in the light of the divine life and so come to shine themselves as they walk in it, and others do not?

We contend that the one grace of God is not compromised and the objective grace of Christ in his atoning work is not weakened if that grace entails the Spirit uniting an individual to the one who is full of grace and truth. It is the one work of salvation even if its aspects are separated in space and time. What Barth cannot stomach is the notion that Christ's work to establish an objective reality for all humanity might only be a *possibility* until

---

[26]Darren Sarisky, "Augustine and Participation: Some Reflections on His Exegesis of Romans," in *"In Christ" in Paul: Explorations in Paul's Theology of Union and Participation*, ed. Constantine R. Campbell, Michael J. Thate, and Kevin J. Vanhoozer (Tübingen: Mohr Siebeck, 2014), 364.

[27]"If it is a matter of the grace of the one God and the one Christ, there can be only one grace. We cannot, therefore, split it up into an objective grace which is not as such strong and effective for man but simply comes before him as a possibility, and a subjective grace which, occasioned and prepared by the former, is the corresponding reality as it actually comes to man. But the grace of the one God and the one Christ, and therefore the objective grace which never comes to man except from God, must always be understood as the one complete grace, which is subjectively strong and effective in its divine objectivity, the grace which does actually reconcile man with God" (CD IV/1:87-88).

authorized by the individual to become a reality by means of their repentance and belief. Nevertheless, we might question Barth on his own grounds. If God's reconciliation with humanity is bound up with his revelation, and his revelation is not revelation apart from its subjective realization in humankind, we are left with two possibilities. Either, on the one hand, God's revelation is not revelation at all because the objective reality has not been realized subjectively for all, or God's reconciliation is an objective reality in Christ and a possibility for human beings that is made a reality for some in the power of the Holy Spirit. Despite being the famed forerunner of the renewal of trinitarian thought, Barth seems unwilling here to acknowledge that the one grace of God is not "divided" when two persons of the one triunity are at work in its communication. Rather, we contend, as stated earlier, that the one grace of God "originates in the Father, proceeds through the Son and is completed in the Holy Spirit."[28] In this regard, John Webster speaks in terms of a "correspondence" between the redemptive work of Christ and the "further mission" of the Spirit in the regeneration and restoration of his creatures.[29] In this way, the work of salvation in the triune economy is so unified that it should be understood as one single action.[30]

We now turn to clarify the precise nature of the participation that we are applying to the concept of divine illumination. Participation itself has been a theological topic of significant scholarly attention of late, which means there are ample resources for elaborating the vision of participation that we may draw on to give a more robust account of participation in the divine light.

First, we must acknowledge that as participation in the light of the divine life, this participation is necessarily *eschatological*. The teleological end of this participation is to experience the brilliance of God at the consummation of all things. In the new Jerusalem, "the city does not need the sun or the moon to shine on it, for the glory of God gives it light, and the Lamb is its

---

[28] Anatolios, *Retrieving Nicaea*, 231.

[29] "Corresponding to the perfect and wholly sufficient work of the Son in the redemption of fallen creatures, there is a further mission of God in their regeneration and restoration to intelligent, consensual, affective and active fellowship with God. This is the mission of the Holy Spirit, by whose grace it comes about that there is a company of creatures in whom redemption is brought to full realisation in the renewal of creaturely nature" (Webster, "Illumination," 328-29).

[30] Here we apply our development of the triune economy to the particular issue of the nature of participation, and in particular, the way in which the divine persons might be *distinct* in action even as they are never *divided* in action (McCall, "Relational Trinity," 120-21).

lamp" (Rev 21:23). The new Jerusalem is a bright city illumined by God's own light. All understanding of this participation in the divine light depends on arriving at this end. For now, participation in the light of divine life is the inbreaking of the kingdom of light, which is already but not yet, and the inauguration of the new creation in the life of individuals.[31] The light that shines in the face of Christ, the words of the text, and the witness of the church all anticipate the consummation of the divine radiance in itself (2 Cor 4:4-6).

Second, as extensively developed in conversation with Barth, and in light of its eschatological end, this participation is deeply *covenantal* and *historical*. In agreement with Barth's doctrine of participation, we maintain that human beings are made faithful partners of God as the divine nature condescends in Christ and human nature is exalted to the side of God.[32] In this exaltation, humanity is made capable of being the partner of God and is made the faithful covenant partner that God intended for relationship with his people. In light of our dissent with Barth, however, this partnership with God is a reality in a human being as it is completed in the power of the Holy Spirit. It is an objective reality proceeding through Christ and completed in the lives of men and women.

Third, humanity is made this faithful partner by means of *identification* and *incorporation*.[33] This participation entails our identification with Christ's covenantal obedience. Paul captures this language well in his letter to the Colossians wherein he states that we have died; that we have been raised with Christ; that our life is now hidden with Christ in God; and that when Christ, who is our life, appears, we will be with him also in glory (Col 3:1-3). This participation entails our identification with Christ's life, death, resurrection, and *glorification*. By participation in the light of divine life, we will eschatologically participate in his glorification also. There is incorporation in the sense that not only are we identified with Christ's fulfilment of the covenant but we are incorporated into the future fulfilment of this covenant

[31]Hans Burger, *Being in Christ: A Biblical and Systematic Investigation in a Reformed Perspective* (Eugene, OR: Wipf & Stock, 2009), 35.

[32]Keith L. Johnson, "Karl Barth's Reading of Paul's Union with Christ," in *"In Christ" in Paul: Explorations in Paul's Theology of Union and Participation*, ed. Constantine R. Campbell, Michael J. Thate, and Kevin J. Vanhoozer (Tübingen: Mohr Siebeck, 2014), 461.

[33]Constantine R. Campbell, *Paul and Union with Christ: An Exegetical and Theological Study* (Grand Rapids: Zondervan, 2012).

as God's partners. As identification looks both backward to Christ's fulfilment and forward to future glory, incorporation looks primarily forward
to our incorporation into Christ's body and our involvement in the ongoing
realization of the covenant in history.[34]

Fourth, one of the most profound contributions of Barth's vision of participation in Christ is the language of *repetition*. Repetition captures how it is
that the Spirit involves us in the divine life. In this union, "he gives us His Holy
Spirit *in order that His own relationship to His Father may be repeated in us*."[35]
It is not that we become the divine life—and especially not the divine nature.
But rather, in the power of the Holy Spirit, we repeat the way of the divine life
in our own. In our incorporation into the ongoing realization of the covenant,
we repeat in our own lives the light and life, the knowledge and character, the
brilliance and abundance, the justice and love that is all possessed by divine
nature in God himself. It is affirmed by Augustine's notion of dynamic participation in that we participate by grace in what God is by nature.

Fifth, following Barth again, this participation entails our *determination*.
Johnson writes, "Christ becomes truly human so that *we* might become truly
human partners of God. This does not mean the divinization of human
nature but its *determination*."[36] What Johnson means is that "human nature
is determined in Christ and by Christ in such a way that it now can exist in
'full harmony with the divine essence common to the Father, Son and Holy
Spirit.' Even while it 'remains human.'"[37] This capacity *to exist* in full harmony
with the divine essence is determined of human nature by this participation
in Christ. This existence in full harmony with the divine essence is what
makes possible our repetition of the divine life. By living in harmony with
it, it is the grounds from which our reflection of that life and light has its
launch point.

---

[34]Constantine Campbell uses the language of both identification and incorporation (*Paul and Union*, 413). However, in our definition, we only follow him on his deployment of incorporation as pertaining to incorporation into the body of Christ. As it relates to identification, we follow more closely a Barthian notion of *identifying with* Christ's covenantal obedience more so than its shaping of identity. This aspect falls more under what I will call "repetition."

[35]"As Jesus Christ calls us and is heard by us He gives us His Holy Spirit *in order that His own relationship to His Father may be repeated in us*. He then knows us, and we know Him, as the Father knows Him and He the Father. Those who live in this repetition live in the Holy Spirit" (*CD* II/2:780, emphasis mine).

[36]Johnson, "Barth's Reading," 466.

[37]Johnson, "Barth's Reading," 466, quoting *CD* IV/2:528.

Sixth, it follows from this repetition and determination that this participation is active. It is an *active* relationship sustained by the present *action* of God. It is an ongoing, renewing occurrence. This active relationship is sanctification—the ongoing "actualization of Christ's saving work here and now as we hear Christ's call and respond."[38] The one grace of God finds its completion in the work of God's Spirit to realize Christ's saving work here and now. Sanctification is the active outworking of the divine light as we see his light shining and walk in it.

Seventh, this participation is *communicative*—it communicates knowledge about God with the aim of drawing us into communion with God.[39] Kevin Vanhoozer observes,

> *Communication* means "to make common," and is especially appropriate for describing the inner-Trinitarian activity in which Father, Son, and Spirit share their light, life, and love, amongst themselves (*in se*) and with the church (*ad extra*). Inasmuch as the Spirit enables believers to share in the Son's light, life, and love—which is to say, his fellowship with the Father—then we could say that being in Christ means being "communicants" in this triune fellowship.[40]

Within the context of a conversation on light and illumination, the notion of communicating knowledge is especially relevant. However, what Vanhoozer is communicating here is the sense in which the knowledge is communicated with a greater end in mind: communion, intimacy. Vanhoozer captures this fullness of this communication and communion component by speaking of the useful term *commune*: "To commune (verb) is to communicate intimately with another person. A commune (noun) is a group of people who live together in community, sharing privileges, possessions, and responsibilities."[41] This participation in the light of divine life is both God's intimate communication of himself with his creatures, and the intimate community of God with his people in active relationship.

---

[38]Johnson, "Barth's Reading," 465.

[39]Kevin J. Vanhoozer, "From 'Blessed in Christ' to 'Being in Christ': The State of Union and the Place of Participation in Paul's Discourse, New Testament Exegesis, and Systematic Theology Today," in *"In Christ" in Paul: Explorations in Paul's Theology of Union and Participation*, ed. Constantine R. Campbell, Michael J. Thate, and Kevin J. Vanhoozer (Tübingen: Mohr Siebeck, 2014), 27-28.

[40]Vanhoozer, "Being in Christ," 27.

[41]Vanhoozer, "Being in Christ," 28.

Eighth, it follows naturally, then, in speaking of divine communion, to say that this participation is undoubtedly *trinitarian*. In this regard we follow Hans Burger in stressing "union and the economic Trinity: the Spirit enables the church to participate in the Son and thus in the Son's fellowship with the Father."[42] This notion of union and the economic Trinity is at the core of our basic definition of illumination as human participation in the Son's knowledge of the Father in the power of the Holy Spirit.

Ninth, the contemporary discussion surrounding participation uses the language of participation and being "in Christ" interchangeably. This raises the interesting question of location: Where are we when we are "in Christ?" Quoting Stanley Porter, Vanhoozer clarifies, "Believers are not in Christ spatially the way coins are in a piggy bank, but rather *spherically*, that is, 'in the sphere of Christ's control.'"[43] To participate in the light of divine life, then, is to exist within the sphere or domain of the divine light's shining. It is walking in the light as he is in the light. It is coming into the light so that it may be seen that what has been done has been done in, by, with, and under the authority of God (Jn 3:21; 1 Jn 1:7).

Tenth and finally, this participation that we have in Christ is *mystical* and *ethical*.[44] The "communion we have with Christ is in heaven." It is with the divine light. And yet "it is lived out—communicated—on earth" and thus ethical.[45] The ethical dynamic of participation is that we become lamps that shine a light on earth, which have been lit by union with another, who is in heaven. In the most profound sense, the mystical and the ethical culminate in the notion of the Christian as witness. What is done on earth is the repetition of what we see and experience in this mystical union with the one in heaven. Not coincidentally, John the Baptist is our example par excellence. He was a witness, a lamp that burned and gave light which the religious leaders of his day enjoyed for a while. Nevertheless, his witness was to a reality far greater than they could see and receive.

In summary, then, the nature of human participation in the light of divine life is eschatological, covenantal, and historical. It entails identification with

---

[42]Vanhoozer, "Being in Christ," 26.
[43]Vanhoozer, "Being in Christ," 28.
[44]Vanhoozer, "Being in Christ," 29.
[45]Vanhoozer, "Being in Christ," 29.

Christ and incorporation into his body. It is the repetition of the divine life
in our own and demands the determination of our existence to be such
partners with God in his divine life. It is an active relationship sustained by
the present action of God, and in this relationship there is communication
aimed at deeper communion still with the triune community of divine
persons. To participate in the divine light is to live within the sphere of
Christ's control, for his light to shine on us and assess us and purify us of all
unrighteousness. In this sphere of divine light, we live a mystical communion
with the divine light in heaven, even as we toil and labor as lamps in the
world. The question to which we must now turn is, how do Christ and the
Spirit act together to draw humanity into this participation?

Travis Ables's *Incarnational Realism: Trinity and Spirit in Augustine and
Barth* is especially helpful in this regard, particularly in explaining how the Spirit
participates in the *same* work, in a *different* way.[46] God's self-communication is
illustrative of this. If human knowledge of God is made possible by the incarnation, its successful communication is accomplished—realized—by the
Spirit's performance of conforming our lives to that knowledge. In this sense,
knowledge of God, like pneumatology, is not just a body of ideas and information—that is, a doctrine—it is action. The Spirit's participation in God's
self-communication is both the work of making God known and the work of
conforming our lives to that knowledge.

This is where we gain purchase on all that has been stated thus far. If, as we
have attested, illumination is human participation in the Son's knowledge of the
Father by the power of the Holy Spirit, Ables grants us the theological grammar
necessary for speaking of the Son and the Spirit working toward the same end
(the shining and reception of divine light) but in distinctly unique ways. The
Word revealed and the Word written shine a light—are illuminating—and the
effect of this illumination is the Spirit conforming our lives to what is revealed
in the light. In this way, the Spirit not only grants us understanding of this Word
and a conviction of its truth but produces a way of life *in us* that reflects this light
in our faith and obedience. To be enlightened is to walk and live in that light too.

The power of the Holy Spirit, by which humanity participates in the Son's
knowledge of the Father, is what continually redirects humanity's focus

---

[46]Travis E. Ables, *Incarnational Realism: Trinity and the Spirit in Augustine and Barth*, T&T Clark
Studies in Systematic Theology (New York: T&T Clark, 2013).

toward this fellowship's eschatological end. The Holy Spirit is active in this work by recalling for humanity its place in the covenant. It is Christ's identity to which the Spirit actualizes our identification, and it is Christ's body into which the Spirit incorporates us for the covenant's future fulfillment in us. It is the Spirit performing the *Son's* relationship to the Father in us when we repeat that relationship in our lives, and it is the determination of humanity in Christ's work that is lived out as the Spirit enacts in us a partnership with God. It is the Spirit that actualizes our illumination in sanctification by the ongoing performance of the nature of Christ in us (i.e., the fruit of Christ's Spirit). The Spirit performs the knowledge of Christ communicated to us in this communion by our action on earth (ethical). Finally, the Spirit performs our mystical relationship with one who is in heaven. In this way, the Son's knowledge of the Father in which humanity participates is not simply a knowledge of the truth which the Logos communicates; it is also a doing of the truth (Jn 3:21) animated by the performance of that knowledge *in us* by the Spirit. It is *revelatory regeneration and regenerative revelation.* Richard Averbeck gets this exactly right. To rephrase a statement of his with the language of the current project: the light of the Word written intends to make something happen in the heart of the reader that will bring about the appropriate response in the reader's life—the arena in which the Holy Spirit performs illumination.[47]

The knowledge is not simply noetic because it is not simply a body of ideas and information. This knowledge is action; it is a way of life. It is in this way that illumination bears not only on the mind but also the heart, and encompasses all of one's life.[48] As God's nature as light pertains to God's holiness, the radiance of all his perfections, so it pertains also to our holiness. All those who do the truth come to the light so that what has been done may be seen as done in God.[49] Coming to the light is both a reception of truth and its performance. It is seeing by the light and sharing it (Jn 4); it is seeing by the light and walking in it.

---

[47]Richard E. Averbeck, "God, People and the Bible: The Relationship Between Illumination and Biblical Scholarship," in *Who's Afraid of the Holy Spirit?*, ed. Daniel B. Wallace and M. James Sawyer (Dallas: Biblical Studies Press, 2005), 150.

[48]*CD* IV/3:519.

[49]This does not imply that we never sin, but that what obedience we do perform, and what holiness we do possess, is done and possessed in God (cf. 1 Jn 1:5-10).

ILLUMINATION

"For God, who said, 'Let light shine out of darkness,' has shone in our hearts
to give the light of the knowledge of the glory of God in the face of Jesus
Christ" (2 Cor 4:6 ESV). It must be said from the outset that illumination
begins in creation, in God's nature to give light (1 Jn 1:5). In fact, God's in-
augural creative act was the illumination of creation. R. R. Reno advises that
in referring to the light of this first day, "We should direct our thoughts
toward the light of divine wisdom, the light of the Word already implied 'in
the beginning,'" not just to light as a physical reality.[50] That God begins with
"let there be light," "it is as if he were saying, 'let there be the illumination and
divinization of creation that I have planned from the beginning . . .' the light
of the first day refers to both the eternal divine purpose and to the scriptures
themselves, which tell of the outworking of the divine plan. For it is written:
'in thy light do we see light' (Ps 36:9)."[51] It is as though God always intended
that we would see by his light. This elaboration that God's giving of light in
creation is not only a physical light but a directing to the light of divine
wisdom and the light of the Word gives theological context for the illumination of humankind by that same Word. The illumination of God's creation
anticipates the narrower work of God in enlightening his children.

In John Webster's exceptional article, "Illumination," he, too, grounds the
economic work of divine illumination in the person and nature of God: "Missions follow processions; the character of the work is determined by the nature
of the one who works."[52] The work of illumination is intrinsically grounded in
the "Holy Spirit who is in himself infinite divine wisdom, light and radiance."[53]
According to Webster, out of this nature as infinite divine wisdom, light,
and radiance, the special mission of the Holy Spirit is accomplished in
making humanity the "creaturely coordinate" to this divine radiance. This

---

[50]Reno, *Genesis*, 46.

[51]Reno, *Genesis* 46. Some may see this tendency to overreach as the main problem with the theological interpretation of Scripture. However, the point is not to say that it does not in the first
place refer to the creation of natural light but that in first referring to that, it has wide-ranging
implications for all the rest of God's creation. See, for example, Barth on Gen 1:3-5, where he
elaborates on the implications of the creation of natural light, and by virtue of that, natural
darkness and its implications for all the other days of creation and then human existence (CD
III/1:117-19).

[52]Webster, "Illumination," 329.

[53]Webster, "Illumination," 330.

complements well our contention that this participation in divine light entails God's creatures being exalted to partnership with God. Webster clarifies what this participation-as-partnership is as it pertains to the reality of divine illumination. First, in the work of illumination God orders rational creatures such that God is the primary mover of all human intellectual faculties. "Divine illumination sets created intellect in motion."[54] Second, this illumination entails a self-declaration of God that provokes human recognition of the divine. "This recognition is the creaturely movement corresponding to the divine work of illumination."[55] Third, in illumination God gives humans the necessary capacity to receive, understand, grasp, and appropriate what is said to them in God's revelation as it shines on them. As developed by Barth, this capacity is not humanity's but is encased within the revelation itself—God's granting both the knowledge and the capacity to know it. In this way, "It is in *God's light* that creatures see light; but in God's light creatures really do *see* (Ps. 36.9)."[56] Fourth, illumination is the Spirit's movement of the human intellect to understand, impart, and interpret, "so that there arises a reception of the 'thoughts of God' (1 Cor 2:11), spiritual understanding and discernment."[57] Fifth, this illumination is pedagogical—that is to say, "Creatures are not only taught, but are trained to use their cognitive capacities, repaired by God, to proceed towards understanding of divine truth." This ordering of rational creatures means that God not only teaches but trains human intellect to teach itself. This is an especially significant point for our purposes because this pedagogical aspect of illumination "is what distinguishes 'illuminated' reading from 'pneumatic' reading, in which the natural properties of text and reader are suspended. Illumination engages and redirects a range of human rational powers, advancing them to proper objects and ends as it conducts us out of darkness into intellectual day."[58]

Webster's contribution to the conversation might best be captured in the concept of "renewal"—namely, renewal in the knowledge of God. However, the real significance of his work is that though he addresses the cognitive

---

[54]Webster, "Illumination," 333. On this initial point, Webster draws from the thought of Aquinas on the ordering of the human intellect.

[55]Webster, "Illumination," 333.

[56]Webster, "Illumination," 333.

[57]Webster, "Illumination," 336.

[58]Webster, "Illumination," 338.

component of illumination as it is traditionally construed, he is able to do so in such a way as to communicate the indivisibility of the knowledge of God and its relational ramifications. A prime example here is that although this illumination may be spoken of as a renewal of human knowledge of God, the purpose is not the renewal of knowledge in itself but the restoration of cognitive fellowship with God.[59] This illumination restores that cognitive fellowship by overcoming the depravity of our nature, which resists "acquiring knowledge of God's mind," and imparting the "principles and habits which enable us to complete the circle of revelation by meekness, reverence and deference in seeking the knowledge of God from Holy Scripture."[60] In line with the present work, Webster, too, recognizes illumination as the intersection of revelation and regeneration: "Illumination is subjective revelation in its reconciling and regenerative effectiveness."[61]

Our primary point of disagreement with Webster, however, is that he, too, remains within the cognitive realm and does not venture into the indivisibly affective aspect of illumination. The vision of illumination that is proposed here entails a grasping of the entire person, including the heart. Averbeck writes, "The text of scripture intends to make something happen in the heart of the reader that will bring about the appropriate response in the reader's life. This is, in fact, the arena in which the Holy Spirit's work of illumination takes place."[62] What we can draw from Webster's contribution and apply to this affective aspect of illumination is the *renewal* of humanity's emotional faculties. Dwight Hole makes the case in his 1976 thesis "The Relation of Illumination to Emotion" that if humanity is affected in every aspect of their nature by the Fall, then humanity's emotions require renewal in salvation as well.[63] In the

---

[59]Webster, "Illumination," 329.

[60]Webster, "Illumination," 338.

[61]"God's work of redemption and regeneration includes a fresh publication and receiving of the knowledge of God, that is, both a fresh iteration of the divine splendour to darkened sinners, and the reestablishment of a productive creaturely subject of revelation" (Webster, "Illumination," 338).

[62]Averbeck, "God, People and the Bible," 150.

[63]Dwight Hole argues from a self-declared Calvinist view of human depravity. Nevertheless, his argument stands with softer views of humanity's fallenness as well. He writes, "That man is a unity and his spirituality is a tint or shade that covers all aspects of his life militates that his affections must be brought into conformity with Christ. That man is depraved in all his nature suggests that his emotions need renewal." "The Relation of Illumination to Emotion" (master's thesis, Western Conservative Baptist Seminary, 1976), 49-50.

Spirit's work of reforming human loves toward love of God, "the Bible is the chief tool of the Spirit to influence man."[64] Therefore, "it is only logical that he would use scripture to influence the emotions of man" in his work of illumination.[65] The illuminated reading of Scripture, which entails the conviction of its truth and the engendering of a love of this Word, inevitably involves this emotional component. As the one who lights in love, the Spirit renews a cognitive fellowship that is necessarily an emotional fellowship as well.[66]

Triune illumination. It has been a primary objective here to articulate the whole triune economy of divine light, not simply illumination as a doctrine located within pneumatology alone. Moreover, since the Reformation, illumination has pertained to the successful application of revelation by means of the Holy Spirit to the mind or heart of the believer. The aim here has been to provide a trinitarian thickening of the doctrine in which this communication is not only the work of the Spirit but of the whole triune economy. In fact, this confession of the church and its Scriptures: God is light (1 Jn 1:5). The Son is "eternally begotten of the Father, God from God, light from light."[67] In locating the place of illumination within the triune economy and within its economy of dogmatic intersections with revelation and regeneration, the triune economy is God's self-revelation to humankind in which humanity is remade to recognize, acknowledge, and thereby participate in knowledge of God by the Holy Spirit. As this participation in knowledge is specifically and economically by participation in the Son's knowledge of the Father by the Holy Spirit, it is not simply the communication of revelation but its execution as illumination. In such an encounter, the triune life executes its activity as the divine light of the Father proceeds through the illuminating and enlightening of the Son and finds its completion in the illumination of the Holy Spirit.

Nicaea elected to speak of the unity of divine nature between Father and Son as analogous to light and its brightness. This is indicative of the indivisibility of Father and Son in the work of illumination. That the Son is the brightness and

---

[64]Hole, "Relation of Illumination," 49.

[65]Hole, "Relation of Illumination," 49.

[66]This language is drawn from the title of chap. 5 of Vanhoozer's *Remythologizing Theology*, "God in Three Persons: The One Who Lights and Lives in Love" (241).

[67]Valerie R. Hotchkiss and Jaroslav Pelikan, *Creeds and Confessions of Faith in the Christian Tradition* (New Haven: Yale University Press, 2003), 1:159.

the Father the light demonstrates that, while distinguishable as two, they are one and the same substance.[68] He is the radiance of the Father's glory and the sum total of the divine perfections.[69] As the Word of God through whom all things came into being, and "light from light," "he is 'the father's very own self-illuminative and creative activity, without whom He neither creates anything nor is known.'"[70] We are given the light of the knowledge and glory of God in the face of Christ. Athanasius continues, "Whatever works the Son accomplishes are the Father's works, for the Son is the manifestation (εἶδος) of the father's divinity, which accomplished the works. Indeed, the Father achieves nothing except through the Son, Who is the Godhead regarded as active in the work of divinizing and illuminating."[71]

Among the vast array of influences that the retrieval of Augustine's doctrine exercises in this project, the most profound of these is the accent he places on the nature and language of God as divine light. In witnessing to the significance of this theological dogma, Augustine stirs us to reconsider the implications of Scripture's declaration that God is light for what it means that God illumines his people. When this is brought to bear on Barth's contribution, we see the light brought by Christ in terms of revelation.[72] The giving of light in revelation is grounded in God's broader nature to give light.[73] In turn this illumination awakens and takes hold of humans, liberates them, claims them, renews them, and impels them into the light of life. All of this takes place and is sustained by the present action of God. The theological interpretation of John in the previous chapter identified that there was a mutual glorification of the Father, Son, and Holy Spirit in which each makes the glory of the others known.[74] In this mutual glorification there is the revelation that God, both in God's nature and God's action, is light (1 Jn 1:5). There is a radiance, a dynamism, and a fullness of expression of God's nature as divine light that cannot be captured in static language. For this reason

---

[68]J. N. D. Kelly, *Early Christian Doctrines* (New York: Harper & Row, 1959), 245.

[69]Hebrews 1:3 ESV. The language of this sentence is drawn from Kevin Vanhoozer in email correspondence.

[70]Kelly, *Early Christian Doctrines*, 247.

[71]Kelly, *Early Christian Doctrines*, 247.

[72]This is in opposition to the interpretation of Jn 1:4, 9 in which the light of the Logos is that which is granted in creation—the light of human reason.

[73]This is one point at which where we run up against the limits of Barth's contribution to our project.

[74]See also, Vanhoozer, *Remythologizing Theology*, 250.

Barth writes, "the being of this light in the world is its coming." Only such dynamic language can capture the ongoing, overwhelming, unlimited luminescence of the light of illuminating life. This is the light of divine life in which humanity participates by the enlightening power of the Holy Spirit.[75] This is the light of the divine life in which there is no darkness.

CONCLUSION

This expansive vision for a dogmatic account of illumination is an attempt at broadening what it means to speak of the divine light encountering his creatures. It intends to do so as the witness of the biblical text requires it. Although the predominant engagement has been with the witness of the Johannine literature, the broader canon has much to say that reiterates the conclusions of this argument. In broadening beyond the Gospel and letters of John, the diverse witness of the Old and New Testaments only further reinforces the necessity of speaking in terms of an economy of divine light.

In chapter eight we identified the grounding of regeneration in participation in Christ. We conclude here by taking that doctrine to its fullest explication: regeneration is initiated as humans begin to participate in the divine light of this Logos. Within the economy of divine light, then, it is clear that this new life of humanity is the decisive work of the event of revelation—it is the *vivificatio* of humanity.[76] In this regenerative revelation and revelatory regeneration, liberation is imparted to men and women. It is the means by which they are awakened to repentance, the reason they find themselves claimed and impelled, the reason for their embodied knowledge of God. It is nothing short of the total conversion of humanity. This is all possible on the basis of the *participatio Christi*. In fact, it is the ultimate foundation of the whole doctrine of sanctification.[77] The event of Christ sanctifying human existence by his abiding in human flesh and the giving of himself in flesh and blood "is an event of revelation in virtue of the enlightening work of the Holy Spirit, and sets in motion the conversion of man."[78]

---

[75]*CD* IV/2:581-82.

[76]*CD* IV/2:581.

[77]*CD* IV/2:581-82. Barth makes this claim of Calvin.

[78]*CD* IV/2:581-82. For an excellent treatment of the order of salvation, see Demarest, *Cross and Salvation*, 36-44.

All of that is to say, this *vivification* of humanity, the regeneration of human beings, is an event of revelation accomplished through illumination by the Holy Spirit. As we have said, illumination is revelation communicated with particularity. The legitimacy of its reality as illumination is granted by the present action of God and Spirit-enabled human participation in Christ. Barth writes that this "*conversio* and *renovatio*, applied to the actual sanctification of man, are nothing less than *regeneratio*. New birth!"[79] This conversion, this renovation, this liberation, this awakening, this regeneration—all have their basis in the *participatio Christi*. In this participation in Christ, we see and know God by his own light.

---

[79]CD IV/2:563.

TEN

The Human Experience
of Illumination

MUCH OF THE PRESENT WORK has been occupied with understanding illumination as a divine action: the work of God and the way we participate in it. We now turn to address a second matter: illumination as human reception. In so doing, we will bring illumination into conversation with two related yet unresolved challenges in contemporary theology. These challenges pertain to understanding the human experience of illumination. If illumination is the work of God in which we participate, the question at hand is this: What is the experience of illumination as we read Scripture and encounter Christ?

THE EVENT OF ILLUMINATION IN THE READING OF SCRIPTURE

This project has engaged at length the theological interpretation of Scripture (TIS) as exemplified by two of the most prominent influencers of the contemporary movement—Augustine and Barth.[1] The aim now is to articulate how illumination as participation in the Son's knowledge of the Father by the power of the Holy Spirit pertains to our encounter with Christ in Scripture. Even as we have drawn conclusions about illumination from the theological exegesis of Augustine and Barth, it is clear from their work that illumination

---

[1]Daniel J. Treier describes Augustine's *De doctrina Christiana* as the "most influential [work] on premodern hermeneutics," which he closely identifies with the theological interpretation of Scripture, and then taps Karl Barth as "the forerunner of its recovery." *Introducing Theological Interpretation of Scripture: Recovering a Christian Practice* (Grand Rapids: Baker Academic, 2008), 11, 137.

was also involved in their very acts of reading Scripture itself. Barth is a profound example of this. In expounding the concept of *Nachdenken* for interpreting Scripture, he speaks extensively about the way the objective of interpretation is to encounter the subject matter of the text itself—the self-revelation of God in Jesus Christ.[2] That is to say, the work of interpretation is not fully complete apart from its culmination in illumination.

As we have argued, illumination is a way of life in which we participate. Faith and obedience are the observable and embodied manifestation of this illumined way of life. This faith and obedience intersect with interpretation in the economy of divine light. It is "walking in the light" (Jn 11:9-10; 12:35-36; 1 Jn 1:5-10; 2:9-11). The demonstration of this illumination as one comes before the biblical text is one's anticipation and transformation. It is anticipatory in that by faith we approach the text with hearts expecting that God will speak. It is transformative in that it provokes the conforming of one's life to the words spoken in the text—that is, obedience. In the economy of divine light, the text is heard as divine communication and received as instructive for one's way of life. This is where Lydia Shumacher's contribution to Augustine's theory of knowledge shines: engaging Augustine's theory theologically rather than philosophically awakens us again to the reality that illumination is not first and foremost about theories of cognition. Augustine's theory of illumination is about the conformity of human lives—including their minds—to the image of God as they were originally created.[3]

This is why "Augustine assumes from the very first lines that John's Gospel is necessarily speaking to him and to his listeners."[4] It is why Augustine instructed his parishioners, "Lift up your hearts."[5] It is a readying of ourselves to hear the word. It is a disposition toward the text which for Augustine is not a work but a way of being. It is a being in humility and prayer. This is why for Barth all of the historical-critical and grammatical-linguistic work is only preparation for interpretation. It is why Barth writes that the

---

[2]Karl Barth, *The Epistle to the Romans*, trans. Edwyn Clement Hoskyns (London: Oxford University Press, 1933), 7. See also Richard E. Burnett's excellent discussion of *Nachdenken* in *Karl Barth's Theological Exegesis: The Hermeneutical Principles of the Römerbrief Period* (Tübingen: Mohr Siebeck, 2001), 58-59.

[3]Lydia Schumacher, *Divine Illumination: The History and Future of Augustine's Theory of Knowledge*, Challenges in Contemporary Theology (Malden, MA: Wiley-Blackwell, 2011), 17.

[4]Barth, *Erklärung*, 4-5.

[5]Augustine, *Tractates on the Gospel of John 1–10*, 1.7-9.

Gospel demands to be read in faith, or it isn't the Gospel we are reading at all.[6] It is not because we set aside all of the critical, historical, grammatical, and religious investigative findings in a simplistic way. Rather, after having established what stands in the text by these means, in illumination, "The walls which separate the sixteenth century from the first become transparent! . . . The conversation between the original record and the reader moves around the subject matter, until a distinction between yesterday and today becomes impossible."[7] As Barth considered this with regard to Calvin, so too in our day illumination overcomes this barrier as well.

In illumination we think the thoughts of Scripture as truth; it is truth taking the reader captive.[8] In this event the Word of God as word of truth comes to people and establishes fellowship with them, inviting them into participation.[9] And, finally, the event of illumination is a confrontation not only with humanity in general but individuals in particular. In it men and women are addressed by God. It is "a word that is spoken to us from the very first in the name of God."[10] As these words of Scripture are the participation of human words in God's words, the event of illumination is the participation of human beings in the triune communicative activity of God. As God has made these words his own, by these encounters in Scripture God makes these humans his own as children of God.[11] The manifestation of this

---

[6]"If the Gospel, John's Gospel, is not directed to us in the name of God and does not presuppose and demand our faith—then what else can we say of it but that it is a fantasy no matter how truly it might be before us on paper in what is probably its earliest text? It if is simply the monument of no more than a historical entity—no matter what else it may be, it is not the Gospel, it is not John's Gospel. The true Gospel of John that we have to study can be only the Gospel of John that comes to us" (Barth, *Erklärung*, 4).

[7]Barth, *Romans*, 7-8. Barth had been accused by none other than Harnack himself of establishing a "pneumatic" school of interpretation. The danger Harnack identifies was the way in which this might legitimize all sorts of interpretations and threaten the objectivity of interpretation. Barth's answer, however, resides in the accountability of the authority of the church. The objectivity of reading Scripture in the freedom of the Holy Spirit is secured by reading under authority of the church (*GD* I:228, 232; see also chap. 5 above).

[8]"I might make the general observation that in the prologue, too, there is a concern to make clear to readers of the Gospel that they are in a specific situation in relation to it, that they are in some sense from the very first its prisoners. A word, no *the* Word has spoken which in principle, as the Word of the Creator, precedes and is superior to all that is (vv. 1-3)." Barth, *Erklärung*, 13; ET: Karl Barth *Witness to the Word: A Commentary on John 1* (Eugene: OR: Wipf & Stock, 1986), 12.

[9]*GD* I:254.

[10]Barth, *Erklärung*, 6; *Witness*, 4-5.

[11]"The image of Christian readers of Scripture participating in the triune drama has several distinct virtues. It reminds us that knowledge of God is not simply a matter of mental assent, but

encounter in the life of the disciple is faith and obedience. The light of illumination animates our lives (Jn 3:21), and we come to the light so that it may be seen that what has been done has been done in God.

The way in which Kevin Vanhoozer appropriates the grammar of "middle voice" accounts for this type of action well. Quoting Philippe Eberhard, Vanhoozer notes that in a "middle voice" phenomenon, the subject is "neither wholly active nor wholly passive." Rather, "in the middle voice, as opposed to the active, the subject is within the action which happens to him or her and of which he or she is subject."[12] This participation and walking in the light is both a "happening" and a "doing." The shift is "away from agency towards the notion of location" of action. That is to say, this participation in divine life and walking in the light "happens and I am its subject."[13] I am the location in which this divine action takes place.

Illumination occurs when the light of the objective Word of God is impressed on the heart and mind of the human being by the Holy Spirit. Illumination is a Spirit-sustained existence of participation in the glorious light of the divine life. With respect to the written Word of God, then, this Spirit-sustained way of being informs how we obtain "meaning" from the text. It is obtained in encounter with the Lord of the text *in the text*. "Walking in the light" is therefore a form of life that functions as a fruitful means for understanding the biblical text.

The Event of Illumination in Human Experience

One of the more intransigent questions we face anytime we speak of an encounter between God and humanity is the question of religious experience. A significant point of contention in theological dialogues—especially as it pertains to revelation, theological prolegomena, and theological epistemology—is the role and contribution of human religious experience. This found exceptionally clear expression in George Lindbeck's *The Nature of*

---

of active participation in a world in which the triune God is active in saving, judging and redeeming." Todd Billings, *The Word of God for the People of God: An Entryway to the Theological Interpretation of Scripture* (Grand Rapids: Eerdmans, 2010), 201.

[12]Kevin J. Vanhoozer, "Discourse on Matter: Hermeneutics and the 'Miracle' of Understanding," *International Journal of Systematic Theology* 7, no. 1 (2005): 19.

[13]Vanhoozer, "Discourse on Matter," 20.

Doctrine, which categorized a major model of religious doctrinal construction under the descriptive heading "experiential expressivism."[14]
Lindbeck listed the following four theses as characteristic of this model:

> (1) Different religions are diverse expressions or objectifications of a common
> core experience. It is this experience which identifies them as religions. (2)
> The experience, while conscious, may be unknown on the level of self-con-
> scious reflection. (3) It is present in all human beings. (4) In most religions,
> the experience is the source and norm of objectification: it is by reference to
> the experience that their adequacy or lack of adequacy is to be judged."[15]

Ultimately, because of experience's subjectivity and susceptibility to psycho-
analysis, it was dismissed as a negative and problematic criterion for theological construction.

However, experience is an inescapable aspect of our existence as theological beings. Consequently, as we have attempted to articulate the doctrine
of illumination in the triune economy, it follows that a closely related conversation is the nature of illumination in human experience. Our goal here
is to address and account for the human experience of illumination without
derailing into all the pitfalls and sinkholes that line the road of such a
venture.

In *Church Dogmatics* Barth makes the following statement as he begins
a subsection on "The Word of God and Experience": "Man does not exist
abstractly but concretely, i.e., in experiences, in determinations of his existence by objects, by things outside him and distinct from him."[16] With respect to this, there is the question of illumination as a work in the triune
economy, and then there is the question of illumination as an event in the
course of human experience. Barth's statement acknowledges the component of human experience in illumination and that the human life is constituted and determined by an ongoing series of such experiences. What we
have seen in John's Gospel have been experiences, encounters with the Word
of God, that constituted and determined the individuals' existences from
that point in the narrative forward.

---

[14]George A. Lindbeck, *The Nature of Doctrine: Religion and Theology in a Postliberal Age* (Louisville, KY: Westminster John Knox, 1984).
[15]Lindbeck, *Nature of Doctrine*, 31-32.
[16]*CD* I/1:198.

The objects and events that a person encounters inform their self-understanding and their relationship to the world. It is also the case, then, that "if knowledge of God's Word can become possible for humanity, this must mean that they can have experiences of God's Word."[17] One objective of this work has been to articulate precisely what is happening in the event of illumination—in the aha moment when one has an encounter with the Word of God and is utterly and inexplicably transformed by the experience. Though we will offer some corrective adjustments in drawing on Barth's section titled "The Word of God and Experience," his work there nonetheless captures well what this project hopes to assert about the doctrine of illumination in human experience.

DETERMINATION

Barth's articulation of the human experience of the Word of God revolves around two key concepts—determination (*bestimmtheit*) and acknowledgment (*Anerkennung*).[18] The question of determination pertains to the extent to which one's existence is based in one's self (the decisions one makes, the abilities one exercises, the impact of one's personality, etc.) and the extent to which all external factors (social class, geographical location, medical history, family background, culture, etc.) have the ability to determine one's life. The same can be asked of the Word of God. To ask in what way the experience of God's Word determines one's life is to ask in what way one's life is grounded in and constituted by the experience of God's Word. In what ways has the experience of God's Word shaped us ethically, intellectually, emotionally, spiritually, relationally, vocationally, and eschatologically.[19] In the previous chapter we used "determination" to describe one aspect of the nature of participation. That description of determination in illumination captures the nature of this determination-in-participation.

---

[17]*CD* I/1:198-99.

[18]For Barth, "*Menschliche Existenz heißt menschliche Selbst-bestimmung*" ("Human existence means human self-determination") (*CD* I/1:204). When Barth speaks of "determination" he is referring to how much and in what way one's existence is constituted by the concept in question (i.e., religion, gender, occupation, etc.).

[19]It bears recognizing that we have encountered all of these under the rubric of illumination at some point in this project.

However, before we get too far ahead of ourselves, if we hope to have any purchase on the language of "experience" beyond and apart from Friedrich Schleiermacher's legacy, we must first clarify our distance from him. To have an "experience" of the Word of God must entail some concept of "religious consciousness," even if we find ourselves uncomfortable with that terminology. For the sake of clarity, we will use it here but without defining it in the individualistic sense of a religious consciousness that nineteenth century thinkers assumed existed universally or could be possessed individually. Rather, "experience" entails a religious consciousness that humans can have but only because "the Word of God can become the ground and object of man's consciousness."[20] In the language of this study, it is an "enlightened" consciousness that can be possessed as we participate in the light of the divine life and as it is sustained by the present action of God but not otherwise. Here the agent of enlightenment is not autonomous human reason but the Holy Spirit. Drawing on John Owen, Webster observes, "The Spirit works not by circumventing but by arousing and actuating human intelligence: 'It is the fondest thing in the world to imagine that the Holy Ghost doth any way teach us but in and by our own reasons and understandings.'"[21] Therefore, following Barth, we distance ourselves from Schleiermacher in that the consciousness of God remains rooted in the Word and Spirit and never in the person, while also maintaining the possibility of "being affected" (Schleiermacher) or "being determined" (Barth) by God's Word.

In addition to this distinction between our thought and that of Schleiermacher, we also assert that the effect on one's existence caused by the experience of God's Word "is not to be confused with a determination man can give his own existence."[22] In other words, even though an experience of the Word of God can only ever occur within the context of one's ongoing self-determination, it is not then the case that the human being has the ability to fabricate or even initiate an experience of the Word of God.[23] As a result,

---

[20] *CD* I/1:199.

[21] John Webster, "Illumination," *Journal of Reformed Theology* 5 (2011): 337; John Owen, *The Causes, Ways, and Means of Understanding the Mind of God as Revealed in His Word, with Assurance Therein*, ed. William H. Goold, Works of John Owen (Philadelphia: Leighton, 1862), 4:125.

[22] *CD* I/1:198.

[23] In addition, Barth rules out the possibility of cooperation between God's determining of humanity and humanity's determining of itself. All such theories of fabrication, initiation, or even of

there can be no synthesis of the two determinations—no competition, no rivalry, and no attempts "to understand them in their co-existence."[24] The task of understanding a person's determination by the Word of God is understanding its utter preeminence over a person's determination of himself or herself.

Barth suggests that error enters into these theories when we attempt to understand the experience of the Word of God from the perspective of a spectator rather than from inside the event itself.[25] In such instances, the narration of the experience is articulated from an anthropocentric point of view rather than a theocentric point of view. In turn, the grace of God in giving the experience is then misconstrued as the freedom of the human person to initiate, fabricate, or cooperate in the experience (or worse, the event is atheistically psychologized and dismissed as psychosis). Instead, Barth insists that we come closest to understanding the right theocentric view by observing this person "who stands in the event of real knowledge of the Word of God" as they are presented to us in Holy Scripture.[26] Only in this way will the human being understand that it is not the cooperation of God's grace with humanity's freedom but entirely God's grace and freedom over against humanity's reprobation and captivity.

The difficulty at this point for Barth's position is that he wants to maintain the self-determination of humanity but somehow "non-competitively." He states, "If God is seriously involved in the experience of the Word of God, then man is just as seriously involved too."[27] Barth recognized that the attempt at total dissolution of the human person and its role in self-determination can only culminate in an absolute turning in on the self—there is nowhere else for the self to go. Barth's conclusion is that, rather than ignoring

---

cooperation in experiencing the Word of God must be rejected for Barth because all such theories set up in humanity a position of rivalry with God, which allows humanity's determination of itself to be in conflict with the determination of the Word of God when it comes in its full power of grace and truth. Instead, "if man lets himself be told by the Word of God that he has a Lord, that he is the creature of this Lord, that he is a lost sinner blessed by him, that he awaits eternal redemption and is thus a stranger in this sphere of time, this specific content of the Word experienced by him will flatly prohibit him ascribing the possibility of this experience to himself" (*CD* I/1:199).

[24] *CD* I/1:200.
[25] This was Barth's observation of the Nicodemus pericope (*Erklärung*, 211).
[26] *CD* I/1:200.
[27] *CD* I/1:200.

self-determination, "our very self-determination needs this determination by God in order to be experience of His Word."[28]

And so this sets up Barth's task of interpreting how knowledge of God's Word becomes possible for humanity. This is explored under the concept of experience because, as we have acknowledged throughout this project, knowledge of God is far more than cognitive—it is determinative of being. It is salvific, redemptive, and ethical. Therefore, articulating the event of illumination in human experience as God's determination of the human person involves far more than affirming accurate thoughts *about* God in the mind of a human being. It is the attempt to work out how it is that there is always the ongoing determination of human beings by themselves as well as the intervening determination of human beings by God in the experience of God's Word.

ACKNOWLEDGMENT

Barth has contributed extensively to our understanding of illumination. He now clarifies in what ways it is appropriate to talk about the human experience of the Word of God. Barth's initial and comprehensive response is encapsulated in a single term: *Anerkennung,* or "acknowledgment."[29] Acknowledgment is also a "middle voice" phenomenon: the event of acknowledgment "happens *and* I am its subject."[30] The following nine theses articulate Barth's defense of the fittingness of the term acknowledgment for capturing what takes place in the human experience of the Word of God. Consequently this defense also explains what is entailed in the human experience of the event of illumination. In each case the execution of this acknowledgment is not a work of the Word alone but a work of the Word in the power of the Spirit.

---

[28]*CD* I/1:200.

[29]"The reality of the Word of God in all its three forms is grounded only in itself. So, too, the knowledge of it by men can consist only in its acknowledgment, and this acknowledgment can become real only through itself and can become intelligible only in terms of itself" (*CD* I/1:187). Barth later writes in the section on the Word of God and experience, "I am aware of no word relatively so appropriate as this one to the nature of the Word of God whose determinative operation is our present concern. And in relation to what we know or think we know of man, this word is precise enough to say the specific thing that needs to be said about him here and yet also general enough to say this specific thing with the comprehensiveness with which it must be said here" (*CD* I/1:206).

[30]Vanhoozer, "Discourse on Matter," 20.

First, acknowledgment entails the concept of knowledge. Because God's Word is first and foremost speech and therefore communication between persons of intellectual and rational faculties, there is an undeniable intellectual component to the experience of God's Word. This certainly does not grasp the experience in its entirety, but this component also cannot be ignored.[31]

Second, acknowledgment is the affirmation of a fact by one person to another. It is accepting as true what has been shared between two people. This is in distinction from a fact of nature. Barth writes, "one does not acknowledge a landslip or a rainbow or the like." "Acknowledge" has a certain confessional nature to it that conveys a *relational* component. In human confrontation with the Word of God, this acknowledgment happens in the relation of human as person to the person of God.

Third, acknowledgment connotes a certain amount of control by the agent of communication. There is control in the sense that the human as creature does not determine what knowledge is conveyed, nor does one determine the kind of relationship that is established in the experience. He or she only approves and accepts this Word and its truth as convicted by the Holy Spirit.

Fourth, acknowledgment of God's Word entails recognition of God's presence. God's Word comes to humanity in church proclamation, in the text of Holy Scripture, and in revelation—the incarnation. "Experience of God's Word, then, must at least be also experience of his presence, and because this presence does not rest on man's act of recollection but on God's making himself present in the life of man, it is acknowledgment of his presence."[32]

Fifth, acknowledgment entails the approval of God's power and supremacy. This approval arises, however, not out of concession to the Word of God as an equal but out of obedient submission and recognition of lordship. In the experience of the Word of God there is an acknowledgment of the need to be drawn into conformity with this Word, an acknowledgment in the conscience and will as well as the intellect and emotions.

Sixth, acknowledgment also means decision. God's Word comes to humanity in freedom and choice. It comes in the freedom of God's good pleasure and never under constraint or obligation to humanity. The decision

---

[31]*CD* I/1, 205.
[32]*CD* I/1:206.

aspect of acknowledgment, then, is that God's decision concerning humanity frees human beings to decide for faith; it frees them for the decision to uphold that freedom or to destroy that freedom in disobedience.[33]

Seventh, acknowledgment is respect for the mystery of the way this Word comes to us. As Barth lays out in section five of *Church Dogmatics*, the Word does not come to us immediately but as mediated. It is mediated through the created form of human flesh in Jesus Christ, human language in Holy Scripture, and human proclamation in preaching. Therefore, this unveiling entails veiling—its concealment. As a result, humanity's experience of the Word of God consists in the mystery of this veiled unveiling. In Augustine's language, in the cover of the flesh the light of the world is uncovered.[34]

Eighth, as a result of this mystery with which the Word comes to humanity, acknowledgment is necessarily a movement and willingness on the person's part to be led. Due to the one-sidedness of the Word of God, it comes to humanity, encounters humanity, not in unity or cooperation but in authority. Therefore, in acknowledgment the person moves from one experience of God's unveiling to another. In the movement of understanding and experiencing God's veiling in his unveiling and his unveiling in his veiling, one "acknowledges the mystery of the Word of God and he has Christian experience."[35]

Ninth and finally, acknowledgment means submission to authority. In the recognition of this authority, one's center of determination moves from the self to the person acknowledged—in this case, God. One's self-determination, then, is moved outside of the self and its basis is now found in God's determination. God determines our existence through the experience of the Word of God in the power of the Holy Spirit. This aspect of the experience of the Word of God—the submission to authority and decentralizing of determination—is a gift of the Holy Spirit. Through this work of the Holy Spirit, the Word of God is appropriated to our lives, or better yet our lives

---

[33]*CD* I/1:206. See also the discussions of "decision" and "freedom" in chaps. 6 and 7 (respectively) above.

[34]"'The light that created the sun' covered itself with a created body, veiled itself under the 'cloud of the flesh,' less to hide than to soften its too bright splendor that weak human eyes cannot bear." Marie Comeau, *Saint Augustin: Exégète du Quatrième Évangile*, 2nd ed. (Paris: Gabriel Beauchesne, 1930), 307.

[35]*CD* I/1:207.

are appropriated and conformed to the Word of God. As a result, Barth's final statement concerning acknowledgment as the comprehensive term for grasping the experience of the Word of God is that it is an attitude. Consequently, as an attitude "acknowledgment" is thus also an aspect of humanity's self-determination. However, even this cannot be separated from the more real and foundational determination by the Word of God because in the work of the Holy Spirit the Word has acted on humanity.

The event of illumination in human experience is the experience of finding oneself in acknowledgment of the truth and mystery and lordship of the Word of God and the acknowledgment that one has been determined by this encounter with the Word of God in the power of the Spirit. This captures what can be said of the Samaritan woman's encounter with the Word at the well, as well as that of the man born blind. It clarifies what was not acknowledged in Nicodemus's encounter with the Word and the way Nicodemus himself was in some way determined by the encounter, even if it was a determination for disobedience and ignorance.[36]

A more holistic vision understands Christian experience as the "rational, experiential, converting, sanctifying and life-changing knowledge of God in and through the incarnate Word by the Spirit."[37] Therefore, in light of all that has been said, Barth's most accurate and effective articulation of his position comes through the employment of Eduard Böhl's analogy of the rainbow.

> It is only an appearance that the rainbow stands on the earth, in reality it arches over the earth; true, it stoops down to the earth, yet it does not stand on our earth, but is only perceived from it. So it is with divine truth; this needs no human support, as the rainbow does not need the earth. True, it shines on man and he receives it; yet it is not dependent on man. It withdraws and man remains in darkness; it returns and man walks in light. But man is not its assistant; he cannot produce the light; similarly he cannot store it.[38]

The experience of the Word of God is a miracle that encounters humanity, which humanity participates in but only as the recipient and the "acted upon,"

---

[36]Barth literally states that Nicodemus failed to *acknowledge* the lifting up in which the Son of God is revealed. "Was gilt nun? Daß er zu *Jesus* gekommen oder daß er des *Nachts* zu Jesus gekommen ist? Hat er den zu Erhöhenden erkannt oder nicht erkannt?" (*Erklärung*, 222).

[37]Thomas A. Noble, "Scripture and Experience," in *A Pathway into the Holy Scripture*, ed. P. E. Satterthwaite and D. F. Wright (Grand Rapids: Eerdmans, 1994), 294-95.

[38]*CD* I/1:223. Eduard Böhl, *Dogmatik: Darstellung der Christlichen Glaubenslehre auf Reformirt-Kirchlicher Grundlage* (Amsterdam: Von Scheffer, 1887), 25.

never as the agent of action. Again, *participate* is a middle-voice verb that has to do with the location of the action more so than the agent of action.[39] The miracle affirms that the true knowledge of God is a possibility—a possibility in faith realized by God's coming to humanity in grace. The psychological location of experience and revelation is not given and the pursuit of this location much like the search for the foot of a rainbow, is done in vain. It is not dependent on humanity: "It shines on him and he receives it . . . but man is not its assistant; he cannot produce [it and] . . . he cannot store it."[40]

CONCLUSION

As this project draws to a close, we maintain that the human experience of the event of illumination, either in the encounter with the Word of God in Scripture or in proclamation, is finding oneself acknowledging and recognizing the lordship of this Word and living a life of faith and obedience in light of that acknowledgment. As an event and as a way of being animated by the power of the Holy Spirit, it is eventually beyond conceptual articulation and rational expression. It may not be the theological *basis* of doctrinal construction, but it is an event of undeniable determination of one's theological existence and it bears tremendously on one's fortitude for *doctrinal* performance. It is a mystery that is eventually beyond sight as its origins recede further back into the brilliance of the divine light, upon which humanity cannot look (and live).

Nevertheless, as the divine light of the Father shines through the illumining Son and completes its illumination in us by the Holy Spirit, humanity is reborn by the will of God, knowledge is received in this event of revelation, and we begin to love and do the truth in the light. In the triune economy of divine light, humanity is invited into and enveloped in light as it basks in the light of divine life. In this triune economy, illumination is humanity's participation in the Son's knowledge of the Father by the power of the Holy Spirit. It is a knowledge that humanity possesses as it participates in it, but humanity is not only informed by it but transformed and conformed to it as illumination has its full effect. This was an aspect of the divine mission in the world. As the true light comes into the world, the

---

[39]Vanhoozer, "Discourse on Matter," 20.
[40]*CD* I/1:223.

revelation of the Word of God would be applied with particularity to men and women, and they would experience the Word of God as it encountered them, healed them, and liberated them from darkness, transferring them to the kingdom of light. In Jesus' flesh humanity beheld the radiance of the Father's glory—the shining of light on humanity, rescuing them from blindness. Through the Spirit's illumination humanity then receives the possibility in rebirth to conceive knowledge of him.

Finally, John's Gospel narrates the light of the world coming into the world. This movement of God in the world mirrors the particularity of God's movement toward specific men and women. God disperses the darkness in the world by dispersing the darkness in human hearts and minds. The repetition of the divine life in us by the power of the Holy Spirit captures this way of God shining his light on us, and thus in us, with exceptional clarity. This has profound pastoral implications—most notably, it impacts how we think about evangelism and social justice. The work of ministry is the repetition of the divine life in us by the power of the Holy Spirit to disperse the darkness of human hearts and minds and to bring light to the dark corners of the world in which we find ourselves. To participate in this lighting of the world is to participate in a mission of the divine light in the world. In this way, God draws men and women into his economy of the divine light in the world and births them anew to conceive knowledge of God that could not previously be fathomed. To conceive knowledge of God is to be subjects in an event that happens to us. To conceive this knowledge of God is to acknowledge a birth that can only come from above.

Bibliography

Ables, Travis E. *Incarnational Realism: Trinity and the Spirit in Augustine and Barth*. T&T Clark Studies in Systematic Theology 21. New York: T&T Clark, 2013.

Allen, Diogenes. *Philosophy for Understanding Theology*. Atlanta: John Knox, 1985.

Anatolios, Khaled. *Retrieving Nicaea: The Development and Meaning of Trinitarian Doctrine*. Grand Rapids: Baker Academic, 2011.

Andrews, James. "Why Theological Hermeneutics Needs Rhetoric: Augustine's *De Doctrina Christiana*." *International Journal of Systematic Theology* 12, no. 2 (2010): 184-200.

Annice, M. "Historical Sketch of the Theory of Participation." *The New Scholasticism* 26 (1952): 49-79.

Aquinas, Thomas. *Commentary on John*. Translated by Fabian R. Larcher. 2 vols. Lander, WY: Aquinas Institute, 2013.

———. *Disputed Questions on Spiritual Creatures (De spiritualibis creaturis)*. Translated by Mary C. Fitzpatrick and John J. Wellmuth. Milwaukee: Marquette University Press, 1949.

———. *Summa Theologica, Prima Pars*. Translated by Fathers of the English Dominican Province. First American Edition. New York: Benziger Brothers, 1947.

Arndt, William F., Walter Bauer, and Frederick W. Danker, eds. *A Greek-English Lexicon of the New Testament and Other Early Christian Literature*. 3rd ed. Chicago: University of Chicago Press, 2000.

Augustine. *De Trinitate*. Edited by John E. Rotelle. Translated by Edmund Hill. Works of Saint Augustine 5. New York: New City Press, 1991.

———. *The City of God Against the Pagans*. Edited by R. W. Dyson. Cambridge Texts in the History of Political Thought. New York: Cambridge University Press, 1998.

———. *The Confessions*. Translated by Maria Boulding. New York: Vintage Books, 1997.

———. *Homilies on the Gospel of John*. Edited by Philip Schaff. Nicene and Post-Nicene Fathers 7. Peabody, MA: Hendrickson, 1994.

———. *On Grace and Free Will*. Edited by Philip Schaff. Nicene and Post-Nicene Fathers 5. New York: Cosimo, 2007.

———. *Sermons 184-229*. Translated by Edmund Hill, O.P. Brooklyn: New City Press, 1993.

———. *Tractates on the Gospel of John 1-10*. Translated by John Rettig. Fathers of the Church 78. Washington, DC: Catholic University of America Press, 1988.

———. *Tractates on the Gospel of John 11-27*. Translated by John Rettig. Fathers of the Church 79. Washington, DC: Catholic University of America Press, 1988.

———. *Tractates on the Gospel of John 28-54*. Translated by John Rettig. Fathers of the Church 88. Washington, DC: Catholic University of America Press, 1993.

Averbeck, Richard E. "God, People and the Bible: The Relationship Between Illumination and Biblical Scholarship." In *Who's Afraid of the Holy Spirit?*, edited by Daniel B. Wallace and M. James Sawyer. Dallas: Biblical Studies Press, 2005.

Barrett, C. K. *The Gospel According to St. John: An Introduction with Commentary and Notes on the Greek Text*. 2nd ed. Philadelphia: Westminster, 1978.

Barth, Karl. *Christmas*. Edinburgh: Oliver and Boyd, 1959.

———. *Church Dogmatics*. Edited by Geoffrey William Bromiley and Thomas F. Torrance. 14 vols. New York: T&T Clark, 2004.

———. *Erklärung des Johannes-Evangeliums (Kapitel 1-8): Vorlesung Münster Wintersemester 1925/1926, Wiederholt in Bonn, Sommersemester 1933*. Karl Barth Gesamtausgabe 2/9. Zürich: Theologischer Verlag Zürich, 1976.

———. *Homiletics*. Translated by Geoffrey W. Bromiley and Donald E. Daniels. Louisville, KY: Westminster John Knox, 1991.

———. *The Epistle to the Romans*. Translated by Edwyn Clement Hoskyns. London: Oxford University Press, 1933.

———. *The Göttingen Dogmatics: Instruction in the Christian Religion*. Edited by Hannelotte Reiffen. Translated by Geoffrey W. Bromiley. 2 vols. Grand Rapids: Eerdmans, 1991.

———. *The Word of God and the Word of Man*. Translated by Douglas Horton. New York: Harper & Row, 1957.

———. *Unterricht in Der Christlichen Religion*. Zürich: Theologischer Verlag Zürich, 1990.

———. *Witness to the Word: A Commentary on John 1*. Translated by Geoffrey W. Bromiley. Eugene, OR: Wipf & Stock, 1986.

Bavinck, Herman. *Reformed Dogmatics*, vol. 2: *God and Creation*. Edited by John Bolt. Translated by John Vriend. Grand Rapids: Baker Academic, 2003.

Beare, Francis. "Spirit of Life and Truth: The Doctrine of the Holy Spirit in the Fourth Gospel." *Toronto Journal of Theology* 3, no. 1 (1987): 110-25.

Beasley-Murray, George Raymond. *John*. 2nd. ed. Word Biblical Commentary. Nashville, TN: Thomas Nelson, 1999.

Bengel, Johann Albrecht. *Gnomon Novi Testamenti: In Quo Ex Nativa Verborum vi Simplicitas, Profunditas, Concinnitas, Salubritas Sensuum Coelestium Indicatur*. 2nd ed. Tübingen, 1860.

Billings, J. Todd. *Calvin, Participation, and the Gift: The Activity of Believers in Union with Christ*. New York: Oxford University Press, 2007.

———. *Union with Christ: Reframing Theology and Ministry for the Church*. Grand Rapids: Baker Academic, 2011.

———. *The Word of God for the People of God: An Entryway to the Theological Interpretation of Scripture*. Grand Rapids: Eerdmans, 2010.

Böhl, Eduard. *Dogmatik: Darstellung Der Christlichen Glaubenslehre Auf Reformirt-Kirchlicher Grundlage*. Amsterdam: Von Scheffer, 1887.

Bolich, Gregory. *Karl Barth & Evangelicalism*. Downers Grove, IL: InterVarsity Press, 1980.

Bonner, Gerald. "Augustine's Conception of Deification." *Journal of Theological Studies* 37 (1986): 369-86.

Bright, Pamela. "St. Augustine." In *Christian Theologies of Scripture: A Comparative Introduction*, edited by Justin S. Holcomb, 39-59. New York: NYU Press, 2006.

Brown, Peter. *Augustine of Hippo: A Biography*. London: Faber, 1967.

Brown, Raymond E. *The Gospel According to John*. Anchor Bible Commentary. Garden City, NY: Doubleday, 1966.

———. "The Paraclete in the Fourth Gospel." *New Testament Studies* 13, no. 2 (1967): 113-32.

Burger, Hans. *Being in Christ: A Biblical and Systematic Investigation in a Reformed Perspective*. Eugene, OR: Wipf & Stock, 2009.

Burnett, Richard E. *Karl Barth's Theological Exegesis: The Hermeneutical Principles of the Römerbrief Period*. Wissenschaftliche Untersuchungen Zum Neuen Testament 145. Tübingen: Mohr Siebeck, 2001.

Calvin, John. *Institutes of the Christian Religion*. Edited by John T. McNeill. Translated by Ford Lewis Battles. 1559 ed. Louisville, KY: Westminster John Knox, 1960.

———. *The Gospel According to St. John 1–10*. Translated by T. H. L. Parker. Grand Rapids: Eerdmans, 1979.

———. *The Gospel According to John 11–21 and the First Epistle of John*. Translated by T. H. L. Parker. Calvin's Commentaries. Edinburgh: Oliver and Boyd, 1959.

Campbell, Constantine R. *Paul and Union with Christ: An Exegetical and Theological Study*. Grand Rapids: Zondervan, 2012.

Campbell, Constantine R., Michael J. Thate, and Kevin J. Vanhoozer, eds. *"In Christ" in Paul: Explorations in Paul's Theology of Union and Participation*. Tübingen: Mohr Siebeck, 2014.

Cassidy, Eoin. "Per Christum Hominem ad Christum Deum: Augustine's Homilies on John's Gospel." In *Studies in Patristic Christology*, edited by Thomas Finan and Vincent Twomey, 122-43. Dublin: Four Courts, 1998.

Comeau, Marie. *Saint Augustin: Exégète du Quatrième Évangile*. 2nd ed. Paris: Gabriel Beauchesne, 1930.

Crump, D. "Re-Examining the Johannine Trinity: Perichoresis or Deification?" *Scottish Journal of Theology* 59, no. 4 (2006): 395-412.

Culpepper, R. Alan. *The Gospel and Letters of John*. Nashville, TN: Abingdon, 1998.

Dana, Harvey Eugene, and Julius R. Mantey. *A Manual Grammar of the Greek New Testament*. New York: Macmillan, 1957.

Davies, Oliver. *A Theology of Compassion: Metaphysics of Difference and the Renewal of Tradition*. London: SCM Press, 2001.

Demarest, Bruce A. *The Cross and Salvation: The Doctrine of Salvation*. Foundations of Evangelical Theology. Wheaton, IL: Crossway, 1997.

Dodaro, Robert. "Light in the Thought of St. Augustine." In *Light from Light: Scientists and Theologians in Dialogue*, edited by Gerald O'Collins and Mary Ann Meyers. Grand Rapids: Eerdmans, 2012.

Dodd, C. H. *The Interpretation of the Fourth Gospel*. New York: Cambridge University Press, 1970.

Doyle, George Wright. "St. Augustine's 'Tractates on the Gospel of John' Compared with the Rhetorical Theory Of 'de Doctrina Christiana.'" PhD diss., University of North Carolina at Chapel Hill, 1975.

Fairbairn, Donald. *Life in the Trinity: An Introduction to Theology with the Help of the Church Fathers*. Downers Grove, IL: IVP Academic, 2009.

———. "Patristic Exegesis and Theology: The Cart and the Horse." *Westminster Theological Journal* 69 (2007): 1-19.

Farrar, Frederic. W. *History of Interpretation*. Bampton Lectures 1885. Grand Rapids: Baker, 1961.

Feuillet, A. "The Christ Image of God According to St. Paul (2 Cor. 4:4)." *Bible Today* 1 (1965): 1409-14.

Fiddes, Paul S. *Participating in God: A Pastoral Doctrine of the Trinity*. Louisville, KY: Westminster John Knox, 2000.

Ford, David. *Barth and God's Story: Biblical Narrative and The Theological Method of Karl Barth in the Church Dogmatics.* Eugene, OR: Wipf & Stock, 1985.

Foulkes, Francis. *The Letter of Paul to the Ephesians: An Introduction and Commentary.* Vol. 10. Tyndale New Testament Commentaries. Downers Grove, IL: InterVarsity Press, 1989.

Fowl, Stephen E. *Engaging Scripture: A Model for Theological Interpretation.* Challenges in Contemporary Theology. Malden, MA: Blackwell, 1998.

Gilson, Étienne. *Introduction à l'étude de Saint Augustin.* Études de Philosophie Médiévale 11. Paris: J. Vrin, 1949.

———. *The Christian Philosophy of Saint Augustine.* Translated by Lawrence E. M. Lynch. New York: Random House, 1960.

Gorman, Michael J. *Becoming the Gospel: Paul, Participation, and Mission.* Grand Rapids: Eerdmans, 2015.

Gourgues, Michael. "The Superimposition of Symbolic Time and Real Time in the Gospel of John: The Symbolism of Light as Time Marker." *Proceedings of the Irish Biblical Association* 31 (2008): 54-65.

Grudem, Wayne A. *Systematic Theology: An Introduction to Biblical Doctrine.* Grand Rapids: Zondervan, 2000.

Hall, Christopher A. *Reading Scripture with the Church Fathers.* Downers Grove, IL: InterVarsity Press, 1998.

Harnack, Adolf von. *History of Dogma.* 7 vols. New York: Dover, 1961.

Harris, Murray J. *Jesus as God: The New Testament Use of Theos in Reference to Jesus.* Grand Rapids: Baker, 1992.

———. *The Second Epistle to the Corinthians: A Commentary on the Greek Text.* New International Greek Testament Commentary. Grand Rapids: Eerdmans, 2005.

Hays, Richard B. "Reading the Bible with Eyes of Faith: The Practice of Theological Exegesis." *Journal of Theological Interpretation* 1, no. 1 (2007): 5-21.

Hirschberger, Johannes. *Geschichte Der Philosophie.* Vol. 1. Freiburg: Herder, 1949.

Hodge, Charles. "The Witness of the Holy Spirit to the Bible." *Princeton Theological Review* 11, no. 1 (1913): 41-84.

Hole, Dwight. "The Relation of Illumination to Emotion." master's thesis, Western Conservative Baptist Seminary, 1976.

Hotchkiss, Valerie R., and Jaroslav Pelikan. *Creeds & Confessions of Faith in the Christian Tradition.* Vol. 1. New Haven, CT: Yale University Press, 2003.

Hunsinger, George. *How to Read Karl Barth: The Shape of His Theology.* New York: Oxford University Press, 1991.

Ingle, Jeff. "A Historical and Scriptural Survey of the Doctrine of Illumination with Application to Hermeneutics." ThM thesis, Grace Theological Seminary, 1987.

Jeanrond, Werner G. "Karl Barth's Hermeneutics." In *Reckoning with Barth: Essays in Commemoration of the Centenary of Karl Barth's Birth,* edited by Nigel Biggar. London: Mowbray, 1988.

Johnson, Keith E. "Augustine's 'Trinitarian' Reading of John 5: A Model for the Theological Interpretation of Scripture?" *Journal of the Evangelical Theological Society* 52, no. 4 (2009): 799-810.

Johnson, Keith L. "Karl Barth's Reading of Paul's Union with Christ." In *"In Christ" in Paul: Explorations in Paul's Theology of Union and Participation,* edited by Constantine R. Campbell, Michael J. Thate, and Kevin J. Vanhoozer, 453-74. Tübingen: Mohr Siebeck, 2014.

Kannengiesser, Charles. "A Key for the Future of Patristics: The 'Senses' of Scripture." In *Dominico Eloquio-In Lordly Eloquence: Essays on Patristic Exegesis in Honor of Robert Louis Wilken*, edited by Paul M. Blowers, Angela Russell Christman, and David G. Hunter, 90-106. Grand Rapids: Eerdmans, 2002.

———. "Augustine of Hippo." In *Dictionary of Major Biblical Interpreters*, edited by Donald K. McKim, 133-40. Downers Grove, IL: IVP Academic, 2007.

Keener, Craig S. *The Gospel of John: A Commentary*. Peabody, MA: Hendrickson, 2003.

Kelly, J. N. D. *Early Christian Doctrines*. New York: Harper & Row, 1959.

Kevane, Eugene. "Augustine's *De Doctrina Christiana* in World-Historical Perspective." In *Collectanea Augustiniana*, edited by B. Bruning, M. Lamberigts, and J. Van Houtem. Leuven: Leuven University Press, 1993.

Köstenberger, Andreas J. *A Theology of John's Gospel and Letters*. Grand Rapids: Zondervan, 2009.

Krötke, Wolf. "The Humanity of the Human Person in Karl Barth's Anthropology." In *The Cambridge Companion to Karl Barth*, edited by John Webster, translated by Philip G. Ziegler, 159-76. New York: Cambridge University Press, 2000.

Lawless, George. "The Man Born Blind: Augustine's Tractate 44 on John 9." *Augustinian Studies* 27, no. 2 (1996): 61-79.

Levering, Matthew. *Participatory Biblical Exegesis: A Theology of Biblical Interpretation*. Reading the Scriptures. Notre Dame: University of Notre Dame Press, 2008.

Lewis, C. S. "They Asked for a Paper." In *Is This Poetry?* London: Geoffrey Bless, 1962.

Lightfoot, John. *Horæ Hebraicæ et Talmudicæ; Hebrew and Talmudical Exercitations upon the Gospels, the Acts, Some Chapters of St. Paul's Epistle to the Romans, and the First Epistle to the Corinthians*. Vol. 3. Oxford, 1859.

Lindbeck, George A. *The Nature of Doctrine: Religion and Theology in a Postliberal Age*. Louisville, KY: Westminster John Knox Press, 1984.

Markus, Robert A. "Signs, Communication, and Communities in Augustine's 'On Christian Doctrine.'" In *De Doctrina Christiana: A Classic of Western Culture*, edited by Duane Arnold and Pamela Bright. Notre Dame, IN: Notre Dame University Press, 1995.

McCall, Thomas H. "Relational Trinity: Creedal Perspective." In *Two Views on the Doctrine of the Trinity*, edited by Jason S. Sexton and Stanley N. Gundry, 113-37. Grand Rapids: Zondervan, 2014.

McCormack, Bruce. "Historical Criticism and Dogmatic Interest in Karl Barth's Theological Exegesis of the New Testament." In *Biblical Hermeneutics in Historical Perspective*, edited by Mark S. Burrows and Paul Rorem. Grand Rapids: Eerdmans, 1991.

———. *Orthodox and Modern: Studies in the Theology of Karl Barth*. Grand Rapids: Baker Academic, 2008.

———. "The Significance of Karl Barth's Theological Exegesis of Philippians." In *Epistle to the Philippians*, 40th Anniversary Edition. Louisville, KY: Westminster John Knox, 2002.

McKim, Donald K., ed. *How Karl Barth Changed My Mind*. Grand Rapids: Eerdmans, 1986.

Meconi, David Vincent. "St. Augustine's Early Theory of Participation." *Augustinian Studies* 27, no. 2 (1996): 79-96.

Michielin, Maico. "Augustine's Interpretation of John's Prologue." *Theology Today* 67, no. 3 (October 2010): 299-307.

Migliore, Daniel L. "Participatio Christi: The Central Theme of Barth's Doctrine of Sanctification." *Zeitschrift Für Dialektische Theologie* 18 (2002): 286-307.

Morris, Leon. *New Testament Theology*. Grand Rapids: Zondervan, 1986.

Muller, Richard A. *Post-Reformation Reformed Dogmatics*. Vol. 2: *Holy Scripture: The Cognitive Foundation of Theology*. 2nd edition. Grand Rapids: Baker Academic, 2003.

Nash, Ronald H. *The Light of the Mind: St. Augustine's Theory of Knowledge*. Lexington: University Press of Kentucky, 1969.

Neder, Adam. *Participation in Christ: An Entry into Karl Barth's Church Dogmatics*. Louisville, KY: Westminster John Knox, 2009.

Noble, Thomas A. "Scripture and Experience." In *A Pathway into the Holy Scripture*, edited by P. E. Satterthwaite and D. F. Wright, 277-96. Grand Rapids: Eerdmans, 1994.

Norris, John M. "Augustine and Sign in Tractatus in Iohannis Euangelium." In *Augustine: Biblical Exegete*, edited by Joseph C. Schnaubelt and Frederick Van Fleteren, 215-31. New York: Peter Lang, 2001.

———. "The Theological Structure of Augustine's Exegesis in the 'Tractatus in Euangelium Ioannis.'" In *Augustine: Presbyter Factus Sum*, edited by Joseph T. Lienhard, Earl C. Muller, and Roland J. Teske, 385-94. Collectanea Augustiniana. New York: Peter Lang, 1993.

Overbeck, Franz. *Das Johannesevangelium: Studien Zur Kritik Seiner Erforschung*. Tübingen: J. C. B. Mohr, 1911.

Owen, John. *Pneumatologia*. Grand Rapids: Sovereign Grace, 1971.

———. *The Causes, Ways, and Means of Understanding the Mind of God as Revealed in His Word, with Assurance Therein*. Edited by William H. Goold. Works of John Owen 4. Philadelphia: Leighton, 1862.

Packer, J. I. "Regeneration." In *Evangelical Dictionary of Theology*, edited by Walter A. Elwell. Grand Rapids: Baker Academic, 2001.

Pegueroles, Juan. "Participación y Conocimiento de Dios en la Predicación de San Agustín." *Espíritu* 27 (1979): 5-26.

Perkins, Pheme. *The Letter to the Ephesians*. Edited by Leander E. Keck. The New Interpreter's Bible. Nashville, TN: Abingdon, 2000.

Plotinus. *The Enneads*. Translated by Stephen Mackenna. 3rd ed. London: Faber and Faber, 1962.

Plummer, Alfred. *A Critical and Exegetical Commentary on the Second Epistle of St. Paul to the Corinthians*. International Critical Commentary. New York: Scribner, 1915.

Porsch, Felix. *Pneuma und Wort: Ein Exegetischer Beitrag zur Pneumatologie des Johannesevangeliums*. Frankfurt am Main: J. Knecht, 1974.

Portalié, E. "Saint Augustin." In *Dictionnaire de Théologie Catholique*. Paris: Letouzey, 1951.

Presbyterian Church (USA). *Book of Common Worship*. Louisville, KY: Westminster John Knox, 1993.

Rahner, Karl. *The Trinity*. Translated by Joseph Donceel. New York: Crossroad, 1997.

Ramm, Bernard L. *The Witness of the Spirit: An Essay on the Contemporary Relevance of the Internal Witness of the Holy Spirit*. Grand Rapids: Eerdmans, 1960.

Reno, Russell R. *Genesis*. Brazos Theological Commentary on the Bible. Grand Rapids: Brazos, 2010.

Rettig, John. "Introduction." In *Tractates on the Gospel of John 1-10*. The Fathers of the Church 78. Washington, DC: Catholic University of America Press, 1988.

Rogers, Eugene, Jr. "The Eclipse of the Spirit in Karl Barth." In *Conversing with Barth*, edited by Mike Higton and John C. McDowell. Burlington, VT: Ashgate, 2004.

Sarisky, Darren. "Augustine and Participation: Some Reflections on His Exegesis of Romans." In *"In Christ" in Paul: Explorations in Paul's Theology of Union and Participation*, edited by Constantine R. Campbell, Michael J. Thate, and Kevin J. Vanhoozer, 357-73. Tübingen: Mohr Siebeck, 2014.

Schlier, Heinrich. "Zum Begriff des Geistes Nach dem Johannesevangelium." In *Besinnung Auf das Neue Testament*, 264-71. Aufsätze und Vorträge II. Freiburg: Herder, 1964.

Schuetzinger, Caroline Eva. *The German Controversy on Saint Augustine's Illumination Theory*. New York: Pageant, 1960.

Schumacher, Lydia. *Divine Illumination: The History and Future of Augustine's Theory of Knowledge*. Challenges in Contemporary Theology. Malden, MA: Wiley-Blackwell, 2011.

Seaman, Michael. "The Indispensability of the Holy Spirit for Biblical Interpretation: A Proposal for the Concept of Transformative Illumination." PhD diss., Southeastern Baptist Theological Seminary, 2010.

Smith, D. Moody. *John*. Abingdon New Testament Commentaries. Nashville, TN: Abingdon, 1999.

———. *The Theology of the Gospel of John*. New Testament Theology. New York: Cambridge University Press, 1995.

Somers, Herman. "Image de Dieu et Illumination Divine." In *Augustinus Magister*. Paris: Études Augustiniennes, 1954.

Soulen, Richard N. *Sacred Scripture: A Short History of Interpretation*. Louisville, KY: Westminster John Knox, 2009.

Stevens, George Barker. *The Johannine Theology: Study of the Doctrinal Contents of the Gospel and Epistles of the Apostle John*. New York: Charles Scribner's Sons, 1895.

Teske, Roland J. "The Image and Likeness of God in St. Augustine's 'De Genesi Ad Litteram Liber Imperfectus.'" *Augustinianum* 30 (1990): 441-51.

Thayer, Joseph Henry, et al. *A Greek-English Lexicon to the New Testament*. Boston: Hastings, 1896.

Thiselton, Anthony C. *The First Epistle to the Corinthians: A Commentary on the Greek Text*. New International Greek Testament Commentary. Grand Rapids: Eerdmans, 2000.

Torrance, Alan. "The Trinity." In *The Cambridge Companion to Karl Barth*, edited by John Webster. New York: Cambridge University Press, 2000.

Torrance, Thomas F. *The Christian Doctrine of God*. Edinburgh: T&T Clark, 1996.

Trapé, Agostino. *Patrology*. Edited by Angelo Di Berardino. Vol. 4. Westminster: Christian Classics, 1986.

Treier, Daniel J. *Introducing Theological Interpretation of Scripture: Recovering a Christian Practice*. Grand Rapids: Baker Academic, 2008.

Valentine, Simon Ross. "The Johannine Prologue—A Microcosm of the Gospel." *The Evangelical Quarterly* 68, no. 3 (1996): 291-304.

Van Fleteren, Frederick. "Principles of Augustine's Hermeneutic: An Overview." In *Augustine: Biblical Exegete*, edited by Joseph C. Schnaubelt and Frederick Van Fleteren. New York: Peter Lang, 2001.

Vanhoozer, Kevin J., ed. *Dictionary for Theological Interpretation of the Bible*. Grand Rapids: Baker Academic, 2005.

———. "Discourse on Matter: Hermeneutics and the 'Miracle' of Understanding." *International Journal of Systematic Theology* 7, no. 1 (2005): 5-37.

———. *First Theology: God, Scripture and Hermeneutics*. Downers Grove, IL: InterVarsity Press, 2002.

———. "From 'Blessed in Christ' to 'Being in Christ': The State of Union and the Place of Participation in Paul's Discourse, New Testament Exegesis, and Systematic Theology Today." In *"In Christ" in Paul: Explorations in Paul's Theology of Union and Participation*, edited by Constantine R. Campbell, Michael J. Thate, and Kevin J. Vanhoozer, 3-33. Tübingen: Mohr Siebeck, 2014.

———. *Is There a Meaning in This Text?: The Bible, the Reader, and the Morality of Literary Knowledge*. 10th anniversary ed. Grand Rapids: Zondervan, 2009.

——. *Remythologizing Theology: Divine Action, Passion, and Authorship*. Cambridge Studies in Christian Doctrine. New York: Cambridge University Press, 2010.

——. *The Drama of Doctrine: A Canonical-Linguistic Approach to Christian Theology*. Louisville, KY: Westminster John Knox, 2005.

——. "The Spirit of Light After the Age of Enlightenment: Reforming/Renewing Pneumatic Hermeneutics via the Economy of Illumination." In *Spirit of God: Christian Renewal in the Community of Faith*, edited by Jeffrey W. Barbeau and Beth Felker Jones, 149-67. Downers Grove, IL: IVP Academic, 2015.

——, ed. *Theological Interpretation of the New Testament: A Book-by-Book Survey*. Grand Rapids: Baker Academic, 2008.

Vanhoozer, Kevin J., and Daniel J. Treier. *Theology and the Mirror of Scripture: A Mere Evangelical Account*. Downers Grove, IL: IVP Academic, 2015.

Wallace, Daniel B. *Greek Grammar Beyond the Basics: An Exegetical Syntax of the New Testament*. Grand Rapids: Zondervan, 1996.

Walls, Andrew F. *The Missionary Movement in Christian History: Studies in Transmission of Faith*. New York: T&T Clark, 1996.

Watson, Francis. *Text, Church and World: Biblical Interpretation in Theological Perspective*. Grand Rapids: Eerdmans, 1994.

Webster, J. B. *God Without Measure: Working Papers in Christian Theology*. Vol. 1. London: T&T Clark, 2015.

——. *The Domain of the Word: Scripture and Theological Reason*. New York: T&T Clark, 2012.

Webster, John. *Barth's Ethics of Reconciliation*. New York: Cambridge University Press, 1995.

——. "Illumination." *Journal of Reformed Theology* 5, no. 3 (2011): 325-40.

——. "'In the Shadow of Biblical Work': Barth and Bonhoeffer on Reading the Bible." *Toronto Journal of Theology* 17, no. 1 (2001): 75-91.

——. "Witness to the Word: Karl Barth's Lectures on the Gospel of John." In *The Domain of the Word*. New York: T&T Clark, 2012.

Wilburn, Michael L. "A Review of Four Views of Illumination: Cognitive, Inspirational, Spiritual Transformational, and Communal Conservative." ThM thesis, Southeastern Baptist Theological Seminary, 2011.

Willems, R., ed. *Sancti Aurelii Augustini In Iohannis Evangelium Tractatus*. Corpus Christianorum Latina 36. Turnhout: Brepols, 1954.

Williams, Thomas. "Biblical Interpretation." In *The Cambridge Companion to Augustine*, edited by Eleonore Stump and Norman Kretzmann, 59-70. New York: Cambridge University Press, 2001.

Wilson-Kastner, Patricia. "Grace as Participation in the Divine Life in the Theology of Augustine of Hippo." *Augustinian Studies* 7 (1976): 135-52.

Wright, William M. *Rhetoric and Theology: Figural Reading of John 9*. Beihefte zur Zeitschrift für die Neutestamentliche Wissenschaft und die Kunde der Älteren Kirche. New York: Walter de Gruyter, 2009.

Zuber, Kevin D. "What Is Illumination?: A Study in Evangelical Theology Seeking a Biblically Grounded Definition of the Illuminating Work of the Holy Spirit." PhD diss., Trinity Evangelical Divinity School, 1996.

Author Index

Subject Index

Scripture Index

THE STUDIES IN CHRISTIAN DOCTRINE
AND SCRIPTURE SERIES

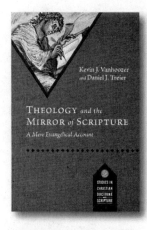

Kevin J. Vanhoozer
and Daniel J. Treier

THEOLOGY and the
MIRROR of SCRIPTURE

A Mere Evangelical Account

STUDIES IN
CHRISTIAN
DOCTRINE
AND
SCRIPTURE

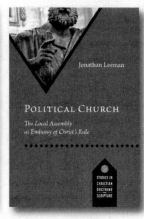

Jonathan Leeman

POLITICAL CHURCH

*The Local Assembly
as Embassy of Christ's Rule*

STUDIES IN
CHRISTIAN
DOCTRINE
AND
SCRIPTURE

Jonathan Hoglund

CALLED BY TRIUNE GRACE

Divine Rhetoric and the Effectual Call

SERIES EDITORS:
DANIEL J. TREIER and KEVIN J. VANHOOZER

STUDIES IN
CHRISTIAN
DOCTRINE
AND
SCRIPTURE

Christopher R. J. Holmes

THE LORD IS GOOD

Seeking the God of the Psalter

STUDIES IN
CHRISTIAN
DOCTRINE
AND
SCRIPTURE

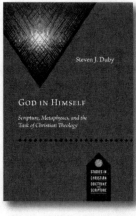

Steven J. Duby

GOD IN HIMSELF

*Scripture, Metaphysics, and the
Task of Christian Theology*

STUDIES IN
CHRISTIAN
DOCTRINE
AND
SCRIPTURE

Ike Miller

SEEING BY THE LIGHT

*Illumination in Augustine's and Barth's
Readings of John*

STUDIES IN
CHRISTIAN
DOCTRINE
AND
SCRIPTURE